Both Sides of the Table

Both Sides of the Table

Photography Portfolio Reviews Do's & Dont's

Debe Arlook & Eric T. Kunsman

RIT Press

Rochester, New York

Published and distributed by:
RIT Press
90 Lomb Memorial Drive
Rochester, New York 14623
https://press.rit.edu

Printed in the United States of America
ISBN 978-1-956313-20-8 (paperback)
ISBN 978-1-956313-21-5 (ebook)

Library of Congress Cataloging-in-Publication Data
Names: Arlook, Debe, editor. | Kunsman, Eric T., 1975–, editor.
Title: Both sides of the table : photography portfolio reviews do's and
    don'ts / Debe Arlook, Eric T. Kunsman.
Description: Rochester, New York : RIT Press, [2024] | Includes index.
Identifiers: LCCN 2024033154 | ISBN 9781956313208 (paperback) | ISBN
    9781956313215 (pdf)
Subjects: LCSH: Photographic criticism. | Photographers—Interviews. |
    LCGFT: Interviews.
Classification: LCC TR187 .B67 2024 | DDC 770.75—dc23/eng/20240725
LC record available at https://lccn.loc.gov/2024033154

We gather on the traditional territory of the Onöndowa'ga': or "the people of the Great Hill." In English, they are known as Seneca people, "the keeper of the western door." They are one of the six nations that make up the sovereign Haudenosaunee Confederacy.

We honor the land on which RIT was built and recognize the unique relationship that the Indigenous stewards have with this land. That relationship is the core of their traditions, cultures, and histories. We recognize the history of genocide, colonization, and assimilation of Indigenous people that took place on this land. Mindful of these histories, we work towards understanding, acknowledging, and ultimately reconciliation.

Cover design: Marnie Soom
Graphic design: Eric T. Kunsman

CONTENTS

Foreword. VII

Introduction. XI

PART I. REVIEWEES

Alanna Airitam 3

Granville Carroll 15

Jo Ann Chaus 25

Adam Chin 31

Matthew Finely 41

Liliana Guzman 49

Jessica Hays 59

Diana Nicholette Jeon 65

David Johnson. 73

Hillary Johnson 87

Ville Kansanen 97

Rania Matar. 103

Marcy Palmer 111

Lydia Panas 117

Lou Peralta 125

Sara Silks 135

Heather Evans Smith 143

Rashod Taylor 149

JP Terlizzi 155

Melanie Walker. 167

André Ramos-Woodard 173

Jonas Yip. 181

PART II. PORTFOLIO REVIEW ORGANIZERS

Scott B. Davis 191

Samantha Johnston. 197

Laura Moya 203

Laura Wzorek Pressley 211
Juliette Wolf-Robin 217

PART III. REVIEWERS

Timothy Campos 229
Debra Klomp Ching. 235
Alyssa Coppelman 241
Alex Decosta 251
Anne Kelly 261
Michael Kirchoff 267
Pradip Malde. 275
Bayley Mizelle 283
Ibarionex Perello. 291
Mary Anne Redding 297
J. Sybylla Smith. 307
Susan Spiritus 317
Gordon Stettinius. 323
Dana Stirling and Yoav Friedlander. 331
Douglas Stockdale 339
Barbara Tannenbaum 351
Jane Yeomans. 359

EPILOGUE

Q & A with Debe Arlook and Eric T. Kunsman. 365
Acknowledgments 375
Colophon 377

FOREWORD

Paula Tognarelli

In my predecessor's tenure as well as my own, as former executive directors and curators of a photography museum north of Boston, we were focused only on photography. International portfolio reviews for photography gave us the opportunity to meet photographers, photography curators, and photography specialists from across the global stage. Most of our exhibitors were discovered during portfolio reviews. Most of the relationships we formed with other leaders in photography institutions were also forged at reviews. Photography portfolio reviews, in general, give photographers the opportunity to meet with curators they may never have access to in person, as well as the potential to meet other photographers from just down the road or from all seven continents.

Photographer-to-photographer introductions, I believe, are one of the greatest benefits that take shape at portfolio reviews. Personally, I have observed the support that photographers give to one another despite long-distance barriers. As to the representatives of photographic institutions, each has opportunities to meet with local constituents, but it is the international portfolio-review circuit that helps grow an institution's reach beyond the local photographic arena. As a former leader of a photographic institution, I found that the relationships made with other leaders in photography at these reviews were an opportunity to move away from feelings of isolation through the sharing of ideas and experiences. In all the careers in my life, it has been the idea of "co-opetition" that resulted in the greatest growth and the number of successes achieved.

My personal focus in photography has been to support emerging photographers. Many will tell you that the institution where I worked was their first exhibition venue. It has been my pleasure to watch photographers grow in their careers. Often, I would look to photography media sources and find once-emerging photographers, now at their prime, in major venues across the globe. I'm not saying that the institution where I worked brought them to success, but I do take pride in that we recognized photography talent early in their careers and that we had been at it for a very long time.

I am still involved in meetings with photographers to view portfolios, but not at portfolio reviews as I have no venue to offer for exhibitions, and the bulk of my life now is lived with an abandon of responsibilities. Exploring an artist's work is such a gift bestowed by any author, whether they be a photographer or other visual artist, writer, performer, et cetera. That is why it is so important that reviewers, given this opportunity, show respect and give a review that discusses improvements to be made, as well as the successes seen. A reviewer should never close a portfolio or walk away from the review table because there is no interest in the work, nor should they be late for reviews, nor engage in any distractions like taking phone calls. (I've seen all happen over the course of my review experience.) Additionally, I find that venues that provide advanced training for both reviewers and reviewees run very well and without many glitches.

Photography portfolio reviews are expensive. Photographers pay large amounts of money to participate. Examples of costs include the entrance fees to the reviews, hotel rooms and plane fares, meals, and some transportation. The time it takes to prepare for a review should be considered in addition to the assessment of all material expenses needed for a review. Photographers deserve our best.

Portfolio reviewers do not get paid for their review services, despite what people think. They receive reimbursement for flights that reviewers pay in advance. Reviewers' hotel rooms are covered by the venue. What is never taken into consideration is the additional costs reviewers and photographers pay to come to the reviews. Babysitters, pet-sitters, transport to and from the airports, parking, and postage (or additional luggage charges) to bring home overmatter received at the reviews are all out of pocket.

At portfolio-review sessions, reviewers give full attention to their daily sixteen prescheduled reviewees. Some reviewers may schedule more reviews in their free time. Other reviewers may adhere only to their original scheduled review slots and add no more reviews into their daily allotment. The review days are long and arduous for both sides of the table, as the day's events do not end after the official review times end. I have had photographers upset with me for saying "no" to an additional review after I had already done twenty on that day. The good news here is that there usually will be a portfolio walk, where all reviewers and the public gather to access photographers' work and meet the photographers face-to-face.

Contrast a reviewer's experience at reviews with trying to research for exhibition candidates during an average workday back at one's home base. I found the research to be impossible unless I did it in the wee hours of the night and learned quickly that my efforts couldn't be sustained.

There has never been a book produced that is just about photography portfolio reviews. Essays have been written on the subject. For years, there has been talk and jokes have been made over the reviewer lunch table that there should be a book made. This book, *Both Sides of the Table: Photography Portfolio Reviews Dos and Don'ts*, organized by Debe Arlook and Eric T. Kunsman and printed by RIT Press, is a much-needed guide that reveals preferences, perspectives, and experiences from portfolio-review organizers, veteran reviewers, and photographers. The book—coupled with preflight training offered by review hosts; a preview list of all portfolio reviewee participants, accompanied by a listing of the photographers' website addresses and one representative image of their work shown in review; and portfolio reviewer bios—should give reviewees and reviewers alike the lay of any portfolio-review event.

I offer up one more suggestion that I have always wanted at the reviews because it seems I never brought enough business cards. With permission, of course, from each reviewer, with the right to opt out, I always found it a helpful gesture on the part of the host organization when they supplied reviewer contact information to all reviewers in a PDF document.

In fellowship, everyone can flourish.

—Paula Tognarelli, December 2023

INTRODUCTION

After many years of attending reviews in person and many hours talking about the review process, we all were hit with the pandemic in 2020. In 2021, online portfolio reviews became the new way to hold reviews, and everything changed.

After the quarantine and two years into the pandemic, we could finally gather in person for portfolio reviews, albeit masked and cautious. Organizers, reviewers, and reviewees (photographers) were eager, excited, and grateful—as well as apprehensive—to connect and reconnect with friends and colleagues and show prints in person.

In the spring of 2022, during Photolucida in Portland, Oregon, a gaggle of reviewees (newbies and seasoned) toasted and dined while decompressing through communal experiences of our reviews. A variation of the same process of questions and answers was voiced above the din. To support each other, we exchanged our individual before, during, and after review practices and discussed what we had learned from preparatory portfolio-review seminars offered by various organizations, reviewers, and photographers. We realized there was so much to learn from those experiences. We wanted to make a book that unmasks the secrets from both sides of the table—as reviewee or reviewer— and that will prepare and guide attendees for online and in-person portfolio reviews. A few organizations offer advice, mentorship, workshops, and presentations before their events. However, there is no book dedicated solely to this subject.

As the editors of this book, we each made a list of seasoned reviewers and photographers whom we admire and respect and who have a mixture of experiences. To narrow down our selection of reviewers and reviewees, we went through a process of ranking participants, similar to selecting reviewers for portfolio reviews. Individually, we ranked our lists and reconvened to discuss and provide our opinions. We concluded with a comprehensive and diverse selection of contributors, focusing on age, gender, race, nationality, and genre of the photographic process. With the extensive breadth of knowledge each individual brought to the table, making the final selections was a challenge. Ultimately, we focused on ensuring the book had the broadest portrayal of expertise available across the board and was a fair representation inclusive of all those in contemporary photography.

At the same time, we hunkered down and wrote two broad sets of questions specific to reviewers and reviewees. Again, we ranked the questions and narrowed them down to what we felt was essential. Initially, we envisioned writing two sets of 22 questions for 22 reviewers and 22 reviewees, referencing F/22. Further into our process, we realized there was much to learn from the organizers' perspective, so we included a third category. On these pages, you'll read responses from five organizers, seventeen reviewers, and twenty-two reviewees: twenty-two questions for organizers, twenty-five for reviewers, and twenty-five for reviewees. Ultimately, the breadth of questions stems from those we consistently hear from individuals we've mentored in preparation for attending portfolio reviews, whether first-time or seasoned reviewee. We often find ourselves expressing that each person needs to find the correct approach for their reviews, and these questions and answers will help one learn from others' mistakes and form one's game plan.

Much has been said and written about reviews in seminars, workshops, blogs, and essays; this book serves as a collection of shared knowledge among a diverse group with a broad range of experiences and backgrounds—stories from both sides of the table. Contributors include photographers, photo editors, curators, museum and gallery directors, portfolio organization directors, educators, and photography consultants. Each shares views, thoughts, and advice based on personal experience. Our reviewees (photographers) include award-winning artists in various stages of their careers, and our reviewers are no strangers to the world of portfolio reviews—they are often the most sought-after reviewers.

This book is the first dedicated solely to the ins and outs of photography portfolio reviews. With our combined experience of fifteen years in attending portfolio reviews on both sides of the table, we recognized the information gap from our own encounters and those of our colleagues. We intend to fill that gap with a diverse and full range of experiences on both sides of the table to serve our colleagues and those new to the game.

One of the many reasons we created this book is to help both reviewers and reviewees understand the emotional dynamics involved in this process. We hope you will learn from these colleagues and the one sitting across from you or on the screen during portfolio reviews.

—Debe Arlook and Eric T. Kunsman

Reviewees
(Photographers)

Alanna Airitam

Alanna Airitam

Tucson, Arizona

My name is Alanna. I'm a midcareer artist living and working in Tucson, Arizona. Photography is my primary medium, but I often create photo-based objects incorporating other materials such as varnish, resin, and metals into my work. I use both film and digital medium–format photography in and out of studio. My work often takes on a painterly feel as I create portraits and still life images that explore themes of hidden histories, truth, representation, and complicated power structures while referencing art history and our cultural history as Americans. In my quest to understand the subjective nature of truth, I allow my practice to be my guide. Through my practice, I've learned I'm a part of this process, but I am not in control of the process. This gives me the freedom to explore these themes with whatever tools and materials best tell the story. I'm constantly learning new ways to hear and work with this creative energy by simply allowing it to show up when and how it needs to. I know it all sounds a bit esoteric and woo-woo, but that's just the way it works for me. I'm obsessed with the way stories shape our existence and the way we understand truth. This obsession with understanding truth is what intrigues me about photography. With a photo, I can see the past. A photo is proof that the person, place, or thing I am looking at existed—even after it is gone.

1. What led you to attend your first portfolio-review event, and what stood out about the one you chose?

Before attending my first portfolio review, I wasn't clear on the benefits of attending a review. I was under the impression it was for artists who wanted to receive feedback on their work. I had already finished my first body of work and was showing and selling it. It seemed counterproductive to spend money and time on a review to get feedback on work I wasn't going to change. But in 2020, when the pandemic hit, I was looking for ways to get my work out and connect with curators across the country. Mary Virginia Swanson suggested I check out the Photoville/Annenberg Space for Photography Reviews because I was specifically interested in meeting Dr. Rhea Combs from the Smithsonian's National Museum of African American History and Culture, who was listed as a reviewer. I was led to attend my first review out of a desire to connect with curators during the pandemic, and I chose that specific review because of the reviewers and the institutions they represented.

2. Please list, in order of importance, why you attend portfolio-review events.

- Connect and build relationships with other art professionals.
- Discover opportunities for placement of the work.
- Test-drive—to have a better understanding of how others view the work—share ideas, and receive feedback.
- Gain insight on what curators are currently looking for.
- Practice speaking about the work. I would (most likely) be showing new work at a portfolio review, and this gives me an opportunity to speak about it to someone outside of my studio. This helps me understand the work in a different way.
- See how my work fits in to the larger, overall cultural conversations being created by other artists.

3. How do you go about choosing which photography portfolio-review events you want to attend and which reviewers you want to meet?

To decide on which photography review event to attend, I first ask myself some questions to determine what I want out of a review. Some questions I ask are:

- Does it benefit me to attend a review right now?
- Is the work ready to share?
- Why do I want to attend a review now?

If I answer yes to the first two questions above and have a valid answer to the last, then I ask myself:

- What do I want this work to do?
- Where do I want it to live?
- How do I want it to function?
- Who would benefit from seeing this work?

Once I have answers to these questions and I feel I'm ready to show a new body of work, the next thing I do is look at the list of reviewers for upcoming review events. If there are curators, gallerists, museum directors, photo editors, et cetera, who I feel could understand my work and who it would resonate with, who have shown work with similar narratives in the past, who have expressed interest in showing work like this, or who have an audience I believe would connect with this work, I put that review event on the list of ones to attend.

My decision to attend a review event mostly comes down to (first) cost: Can I swing the cost of a review at the time? Does it make financial sense?; and (second) list of reviewers: Are reviewers I would like to meet with scheduled at any of the reviews?; and (third) reputation of the reviews/organization: Does the organization have a good reputation of being organized, equitable/accessible, successful? What do other reviewers and reviewees have to say about the organization?

4. What is your average cost per year to attend portfolio-review events, including event registration fees, travel, print production, and leave-behinds? Do you have a budget for self-promotion? If you're not using this amount for attending portfolio-review events, what do you think would be an effective, comparable use of funds in promoting your work in a different way?

Let's break this down: Let's say the average cost of a review is $500, then you add in travel to the event, hotel, food, and other travel expenses; printing your portfolio pieces; and producing leave-behinds. This equals more money than I usually have lying around, or even budgeted, for a review. I am a working artist. That means I don't have a second income to help pad the income I make from my art practice. This is usually a huge stretch for me, which is why I opt for online reviews to mitigate some of the cost. I use my PDF as a leave-behind and can follow up with other promotional materials later if the reviewer would like some. And the money saved from not having to travel? I can put that into creating those promotional materials that would go to key people who would actually want, keep, and use them.

5. What are the standout pros and cons of virtual reviews versus in-person portfolio-review events?

Virtual Reviews Pros
Cost-effective. I like the focused concentration and privacy in the individual review session; the "lobby," or waiting room, is usually a great place to see everyone who is attending; not having to travel means I can continue attending to my practice and personal responsibilities; the cost savings can (and most likely will) go back into my practice. The thing I like best about virtual reviews is the ability to give a quick studio visit. I can show finished work I wouldn't, due to scale or weight, normally be able to bring to an in-person review. I can also give a quick tour of the studio so reviewers have a good sense of how and where I work. It adds a unique perspective that you can't have during an in-person review.

Virtual Reviews Cons
Missing out on in-person, face-to-face connections; being able to show real, printed/finished work

In-Person Reviews Pros
There's nothing better than face-to-face communication. Being able to show actual prints, making new connections with other photographers, attending other events connected to the review, visiting another city, and being able to explore other arts organizations around the host city.

In-Person Reviews Cons
Cost, inability to share finished work that cannot be brought to the reviews due to size or weight.

6. For virtual reviews, please share your process for making a PDF version of your portfolio.

I start on the first page with my "brand identity," meaning I have a typeface for my name that I use on any printed materials. I also include my website, my email address, my phone number, the date, the name of the project, and the name and logo for the review organization. All of this information allows the reviewer to immediately know who I am, what project I am sharing, and where we met—if they bring up the PDF in the future or if they share it with a colleague. On the inner pages, I have the images from the project (one per page), which take up the full page. Underneath each image, I include the name of the image, the project name, and the date it was created. The last page is similar to the front page with a "Thank You."

7. How many photographs do you typically include in each project and why? How many projects do you typically show at a portfolio review and why?

I try to share eight to ten photos from each project. I feel this gives reviewers a decent sense of the overall project; it's enough to get an idea of the narrative and the consistency of the photos in the short time frame we have together. Considering my personal goals for the review session will help me determine how many projects to share. For example, I may be moving my practice in a different direction and may need to share both past work and present work to give the reviewer an idea of evolution. Maybe I'm working on more than one project at a time and I'll be meeting with some reviewers who would be interested in one project and other reviewers who would be interested in another. That doesn't mean I have to go through both projects during each meeting, but I would include them both. I let my goals for the review guide what and how I share.

Alanna Airitam

8. How do you make your prints or presentation materials? Do you do anything special to your portfolio to enhance the narrative of your project?

Sometimes my photographs are finished in a way that turns them into objects. The scale and weight of some of my work makes it unrealistic to bring to a portfolio review, but I want the reviewers to be able to understand what the finished pieces look like and how they function. For in-person reviews, making smaller prints to bring to a review makes better sense. I may not be able to finish them with materials such as metal or resin, but for work that has been varnished (for example), I will go ahead and varnish the smaller prints so the reviewers can have a better understanding of the work. For virtual reviews, I keep finished pieces next to me that I can pick up and show on camera so they can see the finished work beyond the photos in the PDF.

9. What is your opinion about attending reviews with a body of work in progress versus a completed project?

I don't believe it's always necessary to show up with a completed body of work. Again, I allow my goals for attending a review to guide me on what to bring and how to prepare. I attended a review session when I was embarking upon a new project that was very different from my past work. My goal going into that review was to talk with curators about my approach to the new work (which did not exist at the time). I showed previous work and presented the concept for the new work and asked them to help me discover how to make the leap from what was to what would be. I enjoyed involving the curators in the beginning of a new project. From the feedback and advice I received, I believe they enjoyed getting to have some input into my new work. It was helpful for me to hear what they had to say, and they had a bit of investment in this new work. That experience taught me that there are no hard rules for these things. What's important is to really have an understanding of why you are attending, why you chose to meet with your selected reviewers (what are you asking of them?), and what you want to get out of it—and to have the confidence and understanding of your own work to be able to articulate what it is you are asking of your reviewers. If you know this, you'll have a better direction for knowing what to show and what not to show.

10. What are your thoughts about leave-behinds? If you use them, please describe yours.

I have yet to attend an in-person review, but I would make leave-behinds that are personal to each reviewer. For example, a leave-behind for a curator of a university museum could look and function differently from a leave-behind for a gallery. Again, I don't believe in a one-size-fits-all approach to these things. Each and every opportunity to meet with someone will be unique. Every reviewer has their own needs. I research them before requesting them to make sure our needs somewhat align or overlap, and a leave-behind should effectively remind them of our conversation and where our work overlaps long after the reviews are over.

11. Do you make time to see the work of other artists? If so, have you noticed where you are in the spectrum of work, experience, and education? How did it make you feel?

It's always inspiring to see what others are working on, and I love cheering on my friends and peers. A huge part of what I enjoy about being a photographer is having such an incredible community of like-minded folks to be in conversation with. But I am also watchful of any mental comparisons I might be making. I don't believe in comparing my practice to someone else's. We are all on our own separate journeys. What works for me might not work for you and vice versa. Comparison is a creative killer, and I do my absolute best to stay away from that. If I find myself starting to go there, I stop looking at other photographers' work completely. Art is not a competition.

12. After looking at the work of your fellow reviewees, did you seek out any connections or collaborations, or were you simply inspired by their work? If yes, how did you approach the person?

There have been many connections made with other artists in reviews. Most often it's people who I am following on social media and who I finally get to interact with outside of those platforms. There have been a couple of occasions when I've been approached for possible collaboration. Oftentimes, I am simply inspired by their work and feel excited to have made a new connection. And who knows what the future holds!

13. Has there been any auxiliary programming (lectures, workshops, photobook fair, portfolio walk, et cetera) at a portfolio-review event that was exceptionally memorable for you personally?

I'm not saying this because I'm currently on the board, but I really love the programming Medium Photo offers. The keynote speaker is always someone at the top in our field. There is also an emphasis on cross-border pollination of photography. You can go across the border to do studio visits and gallery/museum tours in Mexico. To be able to see what photographers are having conversations about across the border provides a unique and interesting perspective to photography and how we are connected. I promise, this isn't a shameless plug. I just think Medium is doing that brilliantly.

Alanna Airitam

14. Please share your most memorable portfolio-review experience (either positive or negative).

I've been lucky to have only positive experiences. The most memorable portfolio-review experience was the connections I made during the virtual Click Reviews in 2020. I presented the idea of a new project to several curators. I didn't have any work to show for that new project, but I went into the reviews with the goal of making connections during COVID and to get advice about making a leap from studio-based work to a project that would have me in the field, working in ways I had not previously worked and on a project that was much more personal than my prior work. I was surprised by the positive response I received from many of the reviewers—considering I had nothing but older work to show and a new idea to share. Several of these connections turned to relationships that have grown over the past few years and led to museum exhibitions, editorial work for magazines, and personal investment of time to help me realize the new project. The 2020 Click Reviews resulted in a very unexpected and positive impact on my career through relationships and opportunities that are still unfolding several years later.

15. What is your favorite and least favorite part of portfolio-review events?

My favorite part is building relationships. I truly enjoy getting to meet so many interesting people. My least favorite part of portfolio reviews is the limited time in each session. It never seems like enough time.

16. What do you think is the ideal length of time for a review session—twenty, twenty-five, or thirty minutes?

Thirty minutes would be a perfect amount of time. Twenty minutes never seems to be enough time.

17. What are some positive outcomes you've experienced from attending portfolio-review events?

One of my most recent positive outcomes was being a part of the exhibition "Called to the Camera: Black American Studio Photographers," which was at the New Orleans Museum of Art and curated by Brian Piper. Brian and I met during the 2020 Click Reviews and connected over our love for the history of Black American studio photographers. When Brian had the opportunity to put this exhibition together, he remembered my work and reached out. Being a part of this historically important and beautifully curated exhibition and to have worked alongside some of my heroes has been an overwhelmingly positive experience and has helped me better understand the work I am doing.

18. Have you met with a reviewer who was not a good fit for your work? If so, were you able to work around it and/or did you learn from the experience?

Absolutely! Not every reviewer is a good match, but there's always something to learn. The way I look at it is this: I paid to be a part of this review, and I can't afford to throw anything away, so I'm going to get whatever I can out of this experience. Even if I'm not clicking with a reviewer, or we realize there's just not a lot for us to explore, I find the gold. There's always gold in there somewhere. Whether it's a bit of advice or I get to practice my presentation, there's always been a positive takeaway.

19. Has a reviewer been disinterested in your work and clearly finished before the session was complete? If so, how did you handle the situation?

Oh, wow! Does this happen? I guess this must happen sometimes. I'm relieved to say this has never happened to me. However, I had an experience once where someone looking at my work was really triggered and got really upset with me to the point of calling me names ... a "bottom feeder and waste of time," in fact (no, I'm not joking; this really happened). On another occasion, when I was presenting my work, someone else told me that I should focus on "all lives matter." In both of those instances, I remember the heat rising in me. I thought I would snap and say something equally unprofessional, but instead I decided to hear what they had to say ... not take it in, but to hear it. I wanted to dissect it later and see what was in there for me to discover—either about myself, my work, or the situation. In both of those cases, I learned a lot. But most importantly, I used those experiences as fuel for my own success. I knew they were wrong, and I was happy to let them eat their words and choke on them while I remained composed, professional, and unbothered by their insecurities and ignorance. I guess I'm sharing this to show that this is how I deal with situations that are unprofessional and challenging. So, if this were to happen to me, I think I would handle it very similarly. I would look for whatever useful takeaway I could and leave the rest.

20. What are your thoughts about public portfolio walk-throughs, and have you ever made a sale this way? Do you have any pointers for new reviewees about the walk-throughs?

I have not participated in a public portfolio walk-through, but I enjoy attending them and think it's a great way to share your work with a broader audience. I

Alanna Airitam

imagine the public who would attend a portfolio walk-through would be very interested in photography, and having the opportunity to look at portfolios up close and talk with the artist about the work is a great way to connect collectors with artists. I hope these events have led to successful connections between artists and collectors.

21. How do you handle connecting—away from the review table—with a reviewer during an event?

I try to stay in contact with reviewers authentically and organically. I say hello and am cordial and professional when I see reviewers outside of the context of reviewing. I respect their space and right to have a break, so I don't lead with conversation about my work. If they bring it up, great. If they don't bring it up, great—but I don't bring up my work for discussion. I keep conversation professional and friendly.

22. Have you ever gotten to the point with your work when you don't feel the need to attend portfolio reviews? If so, why?

I think there is a point in an artist's career where the work is accessible enough to be seen and the relationships have been built, so they are on the radar and don't necessarily need portfolio reviews to establish those relationships. For me, I primarily go into reviews to meet other professionals I'd like to work with. It is a way for me to make those relationships that are nurtured and developed and authentic. If or when there is a time for us to work together, it'll happen, but I don't push for things. That's the number one lesson of my entire practice. Plant the seeds, water and nurture, and be open for the possibilities of what growth looks like. This is where I currently am in my thoughts around reviews and my own practice. I let the work guide me. I won't attend a review simply because I made new work. Sometimes it doesn't require that. Sometimes it's already on the radar. Sometimes I want/need advice or feedback on something specific. I let the needs of the work dictate whether I attend a review.

23. Please comment on relationships that have developed from attending portfolio-review events.

The relationships I make and maintain are based on mutual respect. I don't believe in hierarchies, gatekeepers, or superiority. I meet everyone on an equal playing field, understanding we all have our individual roles to play and paths to journey down. Whether I'm meeting a fellow artist (emerging or established), a museum executive, a gallery director, a curator, or whomever, I am meeting them all respectfully as equals. I am very fortunate and grateful for the relationships

I've built. I have some truly brilliant people in my corner whose voices I value tremendously.

24. What is the biggest "no-no" for individuals attending portfolio-review events?

The biggest "no-no" to me is not being prepared and not knowing exactly what you want out of the review. There is a very short amount of time to get your point across, and you don't want to spend it floundering—looking for information or not knowing why you chose to speak with this reviewer. Reviews are not cheap, and many times you only have that one opportunity to make a good impression. You'd better make the most of it by being prepared and professional.

25. What one piece of advice would you pass on to first-time reviewees?

Don't go into a portfolio review waiting for someone to tell you that your work is good or bad. Why would you pay all that money to get someone's opinion of your work? You can get opinions all day for free. If you don't believe me, post something on Instagram and wait five minutes.

Your work is your work. Your practice is your practice. No one knows your practice better than you.

Be specific with your ask. You have a very short and finite amount of time to make an impression and get whatever you can out of these very busy people. Squeeze as much out as possible. That will require you to understand your work and what you are trying to say with it. That will require you to be able to honestly defend the parts you believe in while remaining open to helpful feedback and constructive criticism.

I've met quite a few emerging artists who were attending a review for the first time without a clear goal as to why they were attending and what questions they were hoping to get answered.

Ask yourself these questions:
- Why is this a good time for me to attend a portfolio review?
- What questions do I need answers to? What insight can I use to reach my goals?
- Which professionals do I feel aligned with for this work? Are any of them listed as reviewers at upcoming reviews? (Choose your portfolio reviews based on the number of reviewers you'll be able to connect with who may have interest in work like yours.)
- Do I believe in this work?
- Where can I receive a critical eye to make it better?

Alanna Airitam

- Is the work ready to show?
- Which institutions would benefit from showing it?
- Are any of those professionals listed as reviewers?
- Do I have the money/time to attend an in-person review?
- What about a virtual review?
- My overall advice is: Show up with belief in your journey and confidence in yourself and your work.

Granville Carroll

Granville Carroll

Tucson, Arizona

C

I am a photographic visual artist currently based in Arizona. My photographic career started in 2012 when I took my first photography class. Since then, I have received my BFA (2018) and my MFA (2020) in photography. As a fairly recent MFA graduate, I would define myself as an emerging artist. My photographic mission is to represent reality in a more imaginative and speculative perspective. I do this through Afrofuturism, using technology like Photoshop and other digital tools to create a new vision of the future and attempt to understand our cosmological origins. As a child, I was always intrigued by the idea of magic, mysticism, and otherworldly or supernatural expanse. This interest has formed itself into an artistic practice prompting me to question our reality—past, present, and future conditions—as well as who we are individually and collectively. I grew up with a transient lifestyle. I find that this has played a huge part in how I see the world and, therefore, how I create art. The impermanence of reality and the constant shifts that occur are themes that are embedded in the core of my artistic practice.

1. What led you to attend your first portfolio-review event, and what stood out about the one you chose?

I attended my first portfolio-review event in graduate school during a photography conference. This one stood out to me due to its accessibility and the range of people available to connect with. Even if I was unable to land a review with a particular person, I could still connect with them at the overall conference, which was nice. The reviews were also geared toward professionals and students (both BFA and MFA), which made it feel a lot less intimidating than if it were just a professional review. Since this was my first review, I did not know what to expect or which questions to ask. Knowing that the reviewer was expecting a student with work in progress allowed me to ease into the experience and move through it fluidly. I felt like I did not have to perform, but rather just share my work and connect on a humanistic level.

2. Please list, in order of importance, why you attend portfolio-review events.

- Connect with people.
- Obvious answer: share work (new, old, in progress).
- Get feedback on what is working or not working for new projects.
- Networking, specifically for exhibition opportunities, interviews, features, et cetera.

3. How do you go about choosing which photography portfolio-review events you want to attend and which reviewers you want to meet?

Honestly, all the reviews I have attended have either been at photo conferences or I have been invited to participate. I rarely have researched reviews to attend—simply because the cost to attend is prohibitive. I have been blessed to receive scholarships to attend some reviews, have had institutions assist in paying for my attendance at photo conferences, and/or have participated in free reviews. When selecting my reviewers, I look for people who are open to various forms of photography. I do not work in a traditional manner, so it is important that I speak with reviewers who have an open mind about what photography can be and who look toward the future evolution of the medium. In addition, I also want to speak with people who are different from me. This allows me to be presented with new ideas outside of my own thought process or belief system. There is a bit of research that is necessary when selecting the reviewers. Aside from reading the provided bios, I also Google them for additional information. If they are an artist, I look at the work they make and how that connects to me and my ideas. If they do not create, I look to see which artists they have supported and how they talk about photography and the various genres that stem from the medium. Overall, it is a fine balance between finding people who will champion your work and those who will challenge you to push further. I love a good challenge, and I love honesty, so I also look for these aspects in my reviewers.

4. What is your average cost per year to attend portfolio-review events, including event registration fees, travel, print production, and leave-behinds? Do you have a budget for self-promotion? If not using this amount for attending portfolio-review events, what do you think would be an effective, comparable use of funds in promoting your work in a different way?

I currently do not have a budget set aside for yearly portfolio reviews. My self-promotion is usually done on social media. This is easy and free, which is great. Most people are on social media in some way, so it can also be a great way to connect and share the work. Another way to promote one's work is via newsletters, which can be an inexpensive way to share monthly or quarterly updates with your audience. Having a website is also a good way to promote your work. I have a news section on my site where I share updates on my practice.

Granville Carroll

5. What are the standout pros and cons of virtual reviews versus in-person portfolio-review events?

Virtual Review Pros
- Cost of attendance. Much cheaper since you do not have to worry about travel expenses, printing fees, et cetera.
- Comfortability. Being in a familiar space may help some with the anxiety of sharing work in person.
- More control of the pace at which the work is shown.

In-Person Review Pros
- Can connect with more people during downtime or at other events like lectures, workshops, et cetera.
- Opportunities to connect outside the event at dinner/a bar.
- You can show the true physical object, like a matte print, art object, et cetera.

Virtual Review Cons
- Fewer opportunities to connect with other reviewees or reviewers.
- Some reviewers may not want to participate in an online review format.
- Can be hard to show more physical works.

In-Person Cons
- Cost of attendance can be prohibitive.
- Shared review space can be loud.
- Lighting may not always be the best. Consider this when printing work (brightness and color temp of light).

6. For virtual reviews, please share your process for making a PDF version of your portfolio.

I use a combination of Adobe Lightroom and Acrobat to create my PDFs. Lightroom is used to efficiently export multiple images, and Acrobat is used to create the PDF. I start by selecting the ten to twenty images in my Lightroom catalog. I organize and sequence them in a specific collection and then export. My export settings are straightforward. I begin by creating a new folder for my screen-resolution images (something like EventName_72 Jpegs). Then I rename the images so that they stay in the sequence created. The renaming sequence will look something like this: Carroll_Granville_01 *or* ImageTitle_01. I then set the resolution to 72 ppi, since they will not be printed, and the quality to 100. File format as jpeg, and then it is time to export. After this, I move to Acrobat and select Create PDF>select Multiple Files>select Combine Files>click Next> click Add Files>select files from 72 Jpegs folder> verify the sequence is correct> then click Combine> then Save As.

It is important that you note that these are exported for viewing on digital devices only. Whenever I create screen-resolution images, I am sure to note this in the folder name or file name in some way. This acts as a quick reminder that these are not print files, due to the low resolution. I prefer to make my PDF in Acrobat versus Lightroom, simply for the way Acrobat handles the PDF creation process. To me it is more straightforward and efficient. Additionally, there are no borders with the image page (think full bleed when printing). I like how this looks, and it mimics the way I would usually show the work in exhibition form. I also add in a cover page that I design in Photoshop or InDesign, along with a contact page with name, email, website, et cetera. This is also added to the PDF via the Acrobat method mentioned above. I save the cover page and contact page as a jpeg file and include it with my images in the final PDF.

7. How many photographs do you typically include in each project and why? How many projects do you typically show at a portfolio review and why?

I typically include up to twenty images per project and will bring two to three projects with me. I feel that twenty images can effectively show the overall concept of the project. It also allows for the reviewer to quickly go through and spend a bit of time with each image or with images that they find interesting. I am careful to not inundate the reviewer with too much, as I do not want to overwhelm them. Also, I consider the amount of time I have to present the work (on average, my reviews have been twenty minutes). I bring additional projects with me in case the reviewer is not interested in the first project I show. Having a little variety can help the conversation flow and, hopefully, engage your reviewer in other ways.

8. How do you make your prints or presentation materials? Do you do anything special to your portfolio to enhance the narrative of your project?

I do not do anything special for presentation. I really want the focus to be on the images themselves. My images are usually very intricate in design (photo composites), so I think having a simple display allows the viewer to sink into the work as I intend. When preparing my portfolio, I make smaller-scale versions for easier transport. I make sure to print on good-quality photo paper that matches the aesthetics I am going for. I want to represent that quality and intention go into the work—even for portfolio prints. When working with color images, I usually print on luster-type paper, and when printing monochrome images, I usually print on matte paper. There are conceptual and aesthetic reasons for why certain paper choices are made per project. Often, I will talk about why I chose the specific paper for that project and how it aids in the understanding and experience of the work.

Granville Carroll

9. What is your opinion about attending reviews with a body of work in progress versus a completed project?

This really depends on the reviewer and the overall idea behind the portfolio-review event. I have shown both completed projects and works in progress in the same review, and I have fared well. Though I have seen that some reviewers prefer to see completed projects versus works in progress or vice versa. Reviews that I have attended have provided this information in the reviewer bio, which is helpful. If this information is unavailable, then it is necessary to ask yourself what you need from the review. Some people just want another pair of eyes to help them formulate new ideas or see if the project is moving in the right direction. Others seek exhibition opportunities, interviews, book publications, et cetera, and these usually require a completed (or nearly completed) project for a reviewer to offer these opportunities. In short, it is important to identify where you are at in your creative project and if the reviewer is open to seeing a range of development in projects.

For students, it is usually safe to assume that a reviewer is okay with seeing work in progress. If the review event is for students, they realize that projects will be at all stages of development. It is still good to verify this, but in my experience, I have found I did not need a complete project for student reviews.

10. What are your thoughts about leave-behinds? If you use them, please describe yours.

My leave-behinds are usually just business cards, though this can feel a little too formal and impersonal compared to more creative leave-behinds I have seen from other artists. My goal for future reviews is to create something a bit more meaningful that can act as a thank-you for the reviewer's time and as a contact card to keep connected. Some form of a leave-behind is important so that it makes an impact with the reviewer, whether that is a business card or something more creative.

11. Do you make time to see the work of other artists? If so, have you noticed where you are in the spectrum of work, experience, and education? How did it make you feel?

I do my best to look at the work of other artists at the overall event. My experiences and education are usually in line with others. However, I have found that the way I think about photography and how I create can be quite different. I knew early on in my photographic career that I wanted to work in a nontraditional manner. This inevitably brings about some fear of nonacceptance and being further othered by the community. But in my experience, most people are receptive to my approach to photography. They are intrigued or curious about my process. So, it helps to create conversation and introduce people to consider other methods and possibilities of the photographic medium.

12. After looking at the work of your fellow reviewees, did you seek out any connections or collaborations, or were you simply inspired by their work? If so, how did you approach the person?

I usually don't seek out collaborations. Mostly because I work as a self-portrait artist, and my process is very internal and meditative. My landscape images are taken on meditative walks that are usually done alone. Additionally, the ideas I present in my work are a bit unorthodox in some ways, so it can be hard to find folks who are working or thinking in a similar capacity as I am. I do seek connections, though. I love connecting with people, especially those who are different from me so that I can learn more about their world, experiences, and perspectives. It helps me grow and evolve as an artist and a human. Looking at other artist's work is always inspiring and influential.

13. Has there been any auxiliary programming (lectures, workshops, photobook fair, portfolio walk, et cetera) at a portfolio-review event that was exceptionally memorable for you personally?

Yes, there have been. The lectures are some of my favorites—I can learn more about an artist and their personal relationship to their work. I love portfolio walks as a way to engage with artists and their work. Having some downtime to see and experience other avenues of ideation, conceptualization, and experimentation is one the highlights of auxiliary programs at reviews.

14. Please share your most memorable portfolio-review experience (either positive or negative).

My most memorable review experience was recent. I brought two projects with me: a completed book project and a project I started in summer 2022. I was the last reviewee for the day. We talked about the in-progress work first. We then moved on to my book project, and they were so completely enthralled by it. They sat there and looked at the entire book in almost complete silence. It was such an amazing experience to see someone engage with the work with such genuine authenticity. Though few words were said, the silence said everything. Their full awareness and engagement gave me the encouragement that the project was successful in reaching and pulling people into the world I had created for the project. We went well past the review time, and when they finished, we continued to talk. They were interested in my work, but they were also interested in me as a person. They invited a friend over and introduced us, and we all had a great conversation about future goals and dreams. I am forever grateful and thankful for this experience. In that moment I truly felt seen and heard. This experience was unique, which is why it stands out to me. On average, my positive reviews have ended on time with the potential to connect further (via email, social media, et cetera)—a more traditional and formal response.

15. What is your favorite and least favorite part of portfolio-review events?

My favorite part is just sharing and connecting over art. My least favorite is having to answer to the question, "What can I do for you?" I usually do not like going into reviews with the expectation that I will get something or to ask for something, though sometimes that is the assumption. At the end of the day, I simply look to connect with people on a deeper level—without the expectation that we must exchange more than our time and energy in that moment. I look for the balance between knowing what to ask for and being genuine in my approach to connect and share work.

16. What do you think is the ideal length of time for a review session—twenty, twenty-five, or thirty minutes?

I believe the ideal time is thirty minutes for a review session. This provides ample time to share the work and ideas and allow the reviewer to quickly digest the work, then converse over it. Twenty minutes can feel rushed at times, though any time shared is always appreciated.

17. What are some positive outcomes you've experienced from attending portfolio-review events?

I have been blessed to receive wonderful outcomes from reviews. I have been offered exhibitions, artist interviews and features, artist talks, and even curatorial experiences. Reviewers have shared my name and work with their colleagues or others in the industry, who have then provided me with other opportunities.

18. Have you met with a reviewer who was not a good fit for your work? If so, were you able to work around it and/or did you learn from the experience?

I have met with a reviewer who was not a good fit for me. They did not understand the work. Thankfully this was a short review, and we were able to work through the misunderstanding in a positive manner. In this scenario, the work just wasn't for that person, which I quickly understood, and I pivoted the conversation to encompass other ideas beyond the work.

19. Has a reviewer been disinterested in your work and clearly finished before the session was complete? If so, how did you handle the situation?

Thankfully, I have never experienced someone who did not complete the session. There have been those who struggle to understand my work or even see my composites as photography, but we usually work through it quickly. It at least makes for an interesting conversation when I must defend the work as photographic. But no, never has someone finished before the session was complete.

20. What are your thoughts about public portfolio walk-throughs, and have you ever made a sale this way? Do you have any pointers for new reviewees about the walk-throughs?

I love public portfolio walk-throughs. I have only done these a few times, but they are great ways to casually connect with a lot of people and share your work. I have never made sales this way though.

For new reviewees, I recommend having business cards or some takeaways for walk-throughs. Many people want to stay connected, so this can be a quick way to provide that information. Make sure to have work you do not mind people potentially handling or interacting with. My experience has shown me that people want to pick up the work and look at it closely. So, take this into consideration when making prints and bringing certain images to the table. Also, be prepared to talk a lot about your work, process, ideas, et cetera. Having a quick elevator pitch ready will be helpful when critics, reviewers, curators, et cetera, come and approach your table.

21. How do you handle connecting—away from the review table—with a reviewer during an event?

This is the most difficult part of the review process for me. I can be shy when it comes to connecting with a reviewer after the event has ended. Oftentimes the reviewer will provide an email address and advise that you send them a follow-up. This can make it easier to connect. I will usually send an email with the subject as the review event name or something of the sort. I have received responses from some reviewers, and others I have not. This can be discouraging at times when the response is nonexistent, but I just move through and continue working on my practice. I will also connect on social media via Instagram if this is okay with the reviewer. Some reviewers find me on Facebook and add me there. I find it easier to send the follow-up email and then connect on social media so they can stay up to date with my new work, which allows for another level of engagement.

22. Have you ever gotten to the point with your work when you don't feel the need to attend portfolio reviews? If so, why?

I am currently at the point where I don't feel the need to attend reviews often. I do find them helpful, but I find it more helpful to share the work with friends and colleagues who are familiar with me and my work. Mostly, I want feedback on developing projects, and reviews aren't always the best place for this.

23. Please comment on relationships that have developed from attending portfolio-review events.

These relationships have been fruitful. I've met many wonderful people, both reviewees and reviewers, who I would never have met if I never attended these events.

24. What is the biggest "no-no" for individuals attending portfolio-review events?

Do not go into reviews with a transactional mindset. It is understood that reviewees are looking for opportunities, but it can come across as negative if it feels like a transaction. I wait for the reviewer to ask me if there is anything I am looking for in terms of opportunities. I go in with the mindset that they know what they are looking for and that if they have something for me, then it will be stated at that time or later. Do not go into a review expecting that people owe you something.

25. What one piece of advice would you pass on to first-time reviewees?

Be genuine and authentic in your reviews. Present your work as you intend it to be experienced. This goes a long way. People can tell when the work is presented as genuine versus it trying to mirror the ideas or values of the reviewer to try to get opportunities. It is important to be confident in the work. The merit of your work is not conditional on it being featured or shown in some way. If you believe in what you do, then it opens the door for others to do the same.

Jo Ann Chaus

Jo Ann Chaus
Edgewater, New Jersey

For me, I engage with the world by and through making images. I make images that connect the past with the present I carry within, honoring those who came before me, and that show what it feels like to be in this skin. I have a strong need to understand the incongruities around and within me and do so with props, the still life, and gestures and expressions—posing questions and finding answers through the images. I have a great appreciation for beauty in the light, in the natural and in the human-made worlds. I follow the light and put things in it, including myself, conjuring unconscious memories—mine or inherited ones. There are metaphors and relationships between all living things and in assemblages of objects; I create a kind of narrative, conscious or unconscious, in each image.

I am a midcareer artist, having practiced for a solid ten years. I have published one book, in 2016, and am in edit mode for another—each one a seven-year project.

1. What led you to attend your first portfolio-review event, and what stood out about the one you chose?

I was at a point where portfolio reviews seemed to be the next step. I was quite green, but I made a few important connections.

2. Please list, in order of importance, why you attend portfolio-review events.

The result of attending portfolio reviews is about developing, broadening, and deepening relationships with other artists; the opportunity to meet and re-meet the gatekeepers/reviewers; the opportunity to socialize on a personal level with artists and reviewers—to talk about your work and what others are doing, where others are going, what opportunities you learn about, what opportunities may present themselves in the new relationships, what you can learn about your own work through all the conversations

3. How do you go about choosing which photography portfolio-review events you want to attend and which reviewers you want to meet?

Much of it is word of mouth from friends, or if I see in the reviewers' bios one who may be able to help me advance my career, and my work would be a good fit for them/their institution. I usually consult with a mentor (one who knows my work) for advice on who to meet with. Some are for conversations to get an outside opinion on my work/edit, some are for potential exhibits/opportunities, and some are for advice on where to go with the work or who else should see it.

4. What is your average cost per year to attend portfolio-review events, including event registration fees, travel, print production, and leave-behinds? Do you have a budget for self-promotion? If you're not using this amount for attending portfolio-review events, what do you think would be an effective, comparable use of funds in promoting your work in a different way?

I do not have a budget; each event can run $3,500+/-. Perhaps hiring a publicist would be effective at this point—to get the work in front of the right eyes. I suppose I/the artist should know what my goal is with my work while presenting at a portfolio review: being in a conversation on social issues, seeking to have work acquired by an institution, having gallery representation, having opportunities for solo/group shows, as well as the opportunity to meet collectors, sell prints and sell books, do artist talks for those reasons, and to talk about the issues embedded in the work. We artists have and can express keen insights on key subjects (those that matter to them) and bring that into a larger public view through the images

5. What are the standout pros and cons of virtual reviews versus in-person portfolio-review events?

I feel in-person is just a better and more memorable life experience—sharing your work online is good as a follow-up; it is less formal and harder to connect online in twenty minutes. But the online version, with a strong PDF and a focused presentation, could be effective. I found that online reviewers were interested in seeing more of my work (through Lightroom). I feel the online reviews are less personal, or perhaps less memorable, unless the reviewer has a strong connection/reaction to your work; it's harder to read body language and feel the emotion/tone.

6. For virtual reviews, please share your process for making a PDF version of your portfolio.

I have not been successful in producing a strong PDF—I am a photographer, not a graphic designer. It should be a professional package, though, and include a bio, an artist statement, a project statement, installation views, exhibition proposals, and the work, all ready to send to the reviewer.

7. How many photographs do you typically include in each project and why? How many projects do you typically show at a portfolio review and why?

I use twenty-five images because I have large bodies of work that can be configured many ways. I carry two in case the first one doesn't hit the mark with the reviewer or they want to see more.

Jo Ann Chaus

8. How do you make your prints or presentation materials? Do you do anything special to your portfolio to enhance the narrative of your project?

I print my work on 13/19 paper in a leather-bound portfolio box. I have not "enhanced" my box in support of my project, but I have heard it is a great idea.

9. What is your opinion about attending reviews with a body of work in progress versus a completed project?

Both have benefits. A completed body is ready to go; a work in progress, without a very clear understanding by the artist of what the work is about, may be harder to talk about. As long as the artist can realize every review is just a conversation to help them gain insights into their process and work, a review of a work in progress can be helpful.

10. What are your thoughts about leave-behinds? If you use them, please describe yours.

I generally print a collection of 5 × 7 cards with assorted images on one side and my info on the other, letting the reviewer choose their favorite. I feel it's easier for them to put in a file to reference later.

11. Do you make time to see the work of other artists? If so, have you noticed where you are in the spectrum of work, experience, and education? How did it make you feel?

I am always amazed at the breadth of work I see at portfolio walks and the ways it is displayed. I feel I may fall short in having only my prints and leave-behind cards for the portfolio walk. Lacking a formal degree in photography sometimes makes me feel less adequate, but I have been at it long enough and have had enough eyes on the work to feel confident about it. At this point, I know many of the artists and am familiar with their work, but I learn about others at the art walk. If the venue has a place to sit and convene with other artists, it is more conducive to sharing and looking at others' work.

12. After looking at the work of your fellow reviewees, did you seek out any connections or collaborations, or were you simply inspired by their work? If so, how did you approach the person?

I have never sought collaboration, but I have heard about doing so—as in, putting together possible group exhibition proposals. The prospect is daunting; for example, finding a venue available and interested in your work. It is something I am just now beginning to investigate.

13. Has there been any auxiliary programming (lectures, workshops, photobook fair, portfolio walk, et cetera) at a portfolio-review event that was exceptionally memorable for you personally?

At one portfolio walk, I did receive an invitation to show my work at a Blue Sky group exhibit.

14. Please share your most memorable portfolio-review experience (either positive or negative).

Perhaps my answer to the previous question (13). Aside from that, it is really fun and inspiring hanging out with so many dedicated artists for days.

15. What is your favorite and least favorite part of portfolio-review events?

I do like speaking with the reviewers and hanging out with the other reviewees in a casual setting—in between reviews, at meals, and after dinner.

16. What do you think is the ideal length of time for a review session— twenty, twenty-five, or thirty minutes?

Maybe twenty minutes is adequate, considering how many reviewees the reviewers have to see. I suppose if the reviewer is interested in continuing the conversation, that can be arranged.

17. What are some positive outcomes you've experienced from attending portfolio-review events?

- The invitation mentioned above (question 13) re: Blue Sky.
- My work was written about by Jonathan Blaustien in his blog.
- Invited to be interviewed in *Analog Forever* when my new book is published
- Unbeknownst to me I was invited to participate in Cortona On the Move Photo Festival based on the portfolio walk.

Jo Ann Chaus

18. Have you met with a reviewer who was not a good fit for your work? If so, were you able to work around it and/or did you learn from the experience?

I have had reviewers who were not a good fit, and the time we spent was on other things. That, of course, is beyond disappointing, considering the time, energy, and expense of being at this event.

19. Has a reviewer been disinterested in your work and clearly finished before the session was complete? If so, how did you handle the situation?

At a very early review event, a reviewer told me he didn't like the work at all, which, in retrospect, he could have handled in another way. If I had been more seasoned, I could have engaged him to explain why, to get some feedback. Everyone is not going to like everything.

At the same review event, another reviewer spent the twenty minutes talking about "his" opinions that my work had stimulated in him. Again, had I been more seasoned, I would have turned the opportunity around to have a deeper conversation about it after the reviews.

20. What are your thoughts about public portfolio walk-throughs, and have you ever made a sale this way? Do you have any pointers for new reviewees about the walk-throughs?

I enjoy sharing the work at the public walk-throughs, but I have never made a sale. I do not have any advice—maybe I need advice!

21. How do you handle connecting with a reviewer during an event, away from the review table?

I am friendly and respectful. How I feel our meeting went dictates how I would handle the "away-from-the-table" encounter. I would not speak about the review in particular. Not sure if it's another opportunity to "push" the work, but I feel it's after hours, and we are all just people with a common interest; best to talk about nonpersonal things/ideas.

22. Have you ever gotten to the point with your work when you don't feel the need to attend portfolio reviews? If so, why?

I feel the reviews are always good networking events and a great opportunity to organize and hone my portfolio and talking points, but as I've had few tangible results, I feel less driven than before.

23. Please comment on relationships that have developed from attending portfolio-review events.

So many friends as reviewee and reviewers, absolutely invaluable conversations throughout the year.

24. What is the biggest "no-no" for individuals attending portfolio-review events?

Not believing in your work. Before my first portfolio review, I was told: "Remember, it is a privilege for them to see your work." I think it's common to be unsure about what you're showing, as in many cases the work is personal and you as the artist can feel exposed, naked, and vulnerable. But be brave, and share the work, and realize the person on the other side of the table is a person like you in this field, generally with great generosity.

25. What one piece of advice would you pass on to first-time reviewees?

Practice what you want to present and say; be very familiar with your work and "own it" (that is, be confident about it).

Jo Ann Chaus

Adam Chin
San Francisco, California

I am a fine-art photographer who spent a career as a computer graphics artist for TV and film. I was one of the original employees of Pacific Data Images, a pioneering computer graphics studio that later became part of Dreamworks Animation. I did computer graphics lighting on the *Shrek, Madagascar*, How to *Train Your Dragon*, and *Kung Fu Panda* series of animated feature films.

In my practice, I use machine learning neural networks trained on databases of real photography to create images. By augmenting traditional photography with neural networks, I am exploring the concept of how much information is contained in a given photograph.

I approach photography from the metaphoric "atomic" level; that is, the pixel level. I study the information contained in a pixel. The question I'm asking is, "What does a pixel know?" And, in aggregate, "What does a photograph know?" And, finally, on a conceptual level, I'm asking, "What is a photograph?"—as defined by the information in its pixels.

1. What led you to attend your first portfolio-review event, and what stood out about the one you chose?

I chose my first portfolio-review event for mostly practical reasons. It was local; I didn't have to travel. The second reason I chose the event was because I had a friend, a fellow photographer, who was also attending for the first time. I was very fortunate to have a "review buddy" to go through this process with. We traded ideas on how to prepare for the event and talked during and after the review. I was very fortunate to have this fellow traveler; obviously, not everyone will.

Would I have gone by myself without the "review buddy"? Probably yes, because I felt I was ready. I had built up a body of work and had four series of photos that were ready for feedback.

2. Please list, in order of importance, why you attend portfolio-review events.

Photography is not my original field, and when I first started going to portfolio-review events, I quickly saw that I was a "newbie." This was a whole new field, profession, industry, calling, I knew nothing about. So, I decided to simply watch and learn. The reviewers were skilled and had seen much, much more photography than I had and could articulate their thoughts about what they were seeing much better than I could.

I felt like I was witnessing a photographic ecosystem that was entirely new to me. At the portfolio-review events, I saw museum curators, arts-organization curators, writers, journalists, educators, gallerists, book publishers, and artists. My reason for attending the reviews was to see how and where I fit into this ecosystem. It was like trying on clothes to see which "fit." Over time, I was able to see where my work had a better fit—was it more applicable to galleries or museums? Would a book publisher be interested in my material, or would a journalist?

I still see the photographic field this way, as an interconnected ecosystem, and I am a part of it.

3. How do you go about choosing which photography portfolio-review events you want to attend and which reviewers you want to meet?

At my first portfolio-review event I was asked to choose my preference from a large slate of reviewers. Due to scheduling constraints, I would not be able to meet them all, but maybe only half of the available reviewers. My initial instinct was that I wanted to meet people from the most prestigious institutions. The fantasy, of course, is that they would love me and my work and that they somehow had the power to change the course of my life. I think this is a normal human reaction.

The truth of the matter is this: It doesn't matter which reviewers you get. They are all different and human, like you. They have as much power to change your life as you have yourself. And what you get out of the experience is mostly intangible, and the intangible is the most important part.

And here's the thing: All of the reviewers know each other. They are part of a community. They talk among themselves. So, if you make a good impression on one reviewer, all of the other reviewers will hear about you, including the ones you don't meet in person. So, in the end, I did not have to worry that I wasn't meeting my most-desired reviewers.

Lately, I have been choosing portfolio-review events on the basis of geographic exposure. Most of these are Zoom reviews. I do it to show my work in other markets and to see if there is a receptive audience in other places—basically, anywhere outside of my local area. Part of this is to learn how photographic tastes differ in each place. Photography is global, so I thought I might as well learn what's valued in other places.

Adam Chin

4. What is your average cost per year to attend portfolio-review events, including event registration fees, travel, print production, and leave-behinds? Do you have a budget for self-promotion? If you're not using this amount for attending portfolio-review events, what do you think would be an effective, comparable use of funds in promoting your work in a different way?

I do not have a budget for portfolio-review events, but obviously money is important. I don't attend more than one portfolio-review event a year, and I look for different geographic locations each time.

The other thing I spend a lot of money on is competition submission fees. I have to balance this spending with portfolio-review costs. Competition submission fees can add up very quickly; there are a lot of competitions to enter, and some are quite expensive. Over time, I learned that not all competitions were appropriate for my work—I spent a lot of money on competitions that I had no chance of getting into. I learned how to avoid those competitions. I also figured out that some competitions have hundreds of people applying and that the odds of getting in are quite low. So, I learned how to avoid those as well.

5. What are the standout pros and cons of virtual reviews versus in-person portfolio-review events?

From my experience, the in-person portfolio review is much, much more likely to create a lasting relationship with a reviewer than a virtual review. The virtual review does not create a relationship; after a Zoom review, the two of you walk away, retreat to your own homes, and that's it. In many respects, you haven't really met. The in-person review is an actual meeting between two people. This is real. We are much more likely to contact each other again afterward. Or say "hello" when we run into them in person again.

So, does the virtual review have any value? For me, it's a way to learn about the photographic market in some other part of the world.

6. For virtual reviews, please share your process for making a PDF version of your portfolio.

For virtual reviews, I usually prepare a Google Slides presentation. As alternatives, Apple Keynote and Microsoft PowerPoint are equally good. Google Slides requires an internet connection because the presentation is in the cloud. If you don't have an internet connection, you can download the presentation and run it locally, but not everything works in Google Slides when running locally. So, if I'm giving a talk in person and I don't have a Wi-Fi connection, I'll use Apple Keynote or Microsoft PowerPoint and run the presentation locally from a laptop.

The most important thing to do is rehearse your startup procedure, so that when called upon in Zoom, you can "share screen" immediately and have your presentation ready to go. This takes practice. I'm not kidding. To rehearse, go into Zoom and start a meeting with just yourself, and then practice your startup procedure over and over again.

If you don't rehearse, there is a good chance you'll screw up in the actual review and lose valuable time. I often attend online roundtable critiques, where I watch six online presentations over a two-hour period. Invariably, half the people have trouble starting their presentation each time.

7. How many photographs do you typically include in each project and why? How many projects do you typically show at a portfolio review and why?

I tend to show too much. Each of my series usually has ten photographs, and I have shown up to four series in a twenty-minute review. That's a bit much. I can do it if I have prepared a coherent through-line (that is, a story) that connects the four series. If one series naturally leads to another series, then I can get through all of this material.

It does help to rehearse. With this many images, it's important to be able to get through the presentation in under fifteen minutes, so that the reviewer has time to give a thoughtful response.

If the reviewer isn't seeing my material well and isn't "getting it," I will cut my presentation short and not show all of the series. In this case, I kind of know it's a lost cause, and forcing more material on the reviewer isn't going to help the situation.

8. How do you make your prints or presentation materials? Do you do anything special to your portfolio to enhance the narrative of your project?

I don't do anything special. I did buy nice portfolio cases, which are sturdy enough to survive being hand-carried all day and carried through airports and plane travel.

I show darkroom-made gelatin silver prints. I do not put them in any protective covering because I want the reviewer to be able to see them clearly. The prints do get beat up due to all the handling. Usually at the end of the review, you're in a rush to put all the prints back into your case. This is when you're most likely to mishandle them. I just have to accept the fact that the set of prints I bring to an in-person review may get beaten up.

Adam Chin

9. What is your opinion about attending reviews with a body of work in progress versus a completed project?

I tend to bring a series only after it is well developed or is actually finished. And in many cases, the "well-developed" series might be one that I've been working on for ten years and is one that may never finish.

I think this is a personal choice about when to bring a series to a review. Everyone is different. Maybe the criterion should be: "When do I need help? When do I feel like I've hit a wall with what I'm doing and I could use some advice about how to move forward?"

I have been to many critiques where photographers bring work that is in a much-less-developed state than I ever would. There is absolutely nothing wrong with doing this. For myself, I'm probably too scared to bring a truly underdeveloped idea to a review.

10. What are your thoughts about leave-behinds? If you use them, please describe yours.

Ilford makes a 4" × 6" RC paper that is the size of a postcard. I will go into the darkroom, print my favorite image on the postcard, and make a copy for each reviewer. And then I'll write my contact info on the back. This is my "leave-behind." Obviously it's a lot of work, but I think it's really worth it. Handing the reviewer an actual print feels a lot more special and memorable. And I was thrilled to see afterward that a couple of reviewers posted pictures of my leave-behind on their Instagram story! I think that's significant.

This darkroom-printed leave-behind was not my idea. It was an idea I got from a fellow photographer.

11. Do you make time to see the work of other artists? If so, have you noticed where you are in the spectrum of work, experience, and education? How did it make you feel?

Absolutely. During the course of a portfolio-review event, it is difficult to spend quality time with other artists' work. But I regularly attend roundtable critiques of other artists' work, both in person and on Zoom. This is an invaluable experience because, through this, I get a very good overview of the art that is being created in my community. I often marvel at the quality of the reviewers and at how they are able to identify value and articulate their thoughts. I learn how to see through the reviewers.

Here is what happens when I attend a critique of someone else's work: My mind drifts, and I get ideas for my own work. This is not stealing; this is actual

C

inspiration. Seeing someone else's work frees my mind to see my own work in another light. Getting inspired is one of the main reasons I attend critiques.

Obviously, there is a selfish aspect to what I just said. It shouldn't be just about me getting inspired. Seeing other artists' work and meeting and inspiring other artists creates community. That's the reason to see other artists' work. One of the things I get out of attending reviews, particularly in person, is that it's not just about me. I get to see myself as part of a much larger ecosystem/community.

12. After looking at the work of your fellow reviewees, did you seek out any connections or collaborations, or were you simply inspired by their work? If so, how did you approach the person?

I haven't done this. However, I recently received feedback from a reviewer who thought I should seek out collaborations with other artists. I thought this was a very perceptive comment. I think the reviewer sensed there was power and potential in my work that could be used to fuel another artist's work.

So, the question is: How do you know when your work and another artist's work contain the potential for the other? I don't know the answer to this, but it is clearly one more thing on the checklist you have in your mind when you view another artist's work.

13. Has there been any auxiliary programming (lectures, workshops, photobook fair, portfolio walk, et cetera) at a portfolio-review event that was exceptionally memorable for you personally?

I don't have much experience or any strong opinions about attending auxiliary programming.

14. Please share your most memorable portfolio-review experience (either positive or negative).

A year ago, I had a very bad negative review. It was a virtual review, and the reviewer decided they hated my work and were determined to let me know it. For the first fifteen minutes, they railed against my work, telling me everything that was wrong about it. The reviewer was mean-spirited and borderline abusive. I just sat there and listened. I was shocked.

In general, I am very uncomfortable with conflict; arguing is difficult for me. At the end, I finally tried to argue back just to defend myself. But the reviewer argued me down again, and we finished the last minute of the review in stoney silence, staring at each other.

Adam Chin

A year later, I still wake up in the middle of the night thinking about this review. The experience was truly traumatic. Was there a grain of truth to what the reviewer said? Yes. Did the reviewer overlook very important aspects of my work? Absolutely. Was this review helpful in any way? Absolutely not; I was really hurt by this experience. It was damaging to me.

What advice can I offer from this? For people going into the review process, please be aware that you can get your feelings hurt. I just happened to run into a mean person, but that possibility always exists, and it's not fun. Nonetheless, the benefits of the portfolio-review process far outweigh this negative.

To the reviewers reading this, please be kind. Reviewees are in an extremely vulnerable position. Your words have much more power than you realize.

15. What is your favorite and least favorite part of portfolio-review events?

My favorite part of portfolio-review events is meeting the community of reviewers and getting the feeling of being a part of a community.

16. What do you think is the ideal length of time for a review session—twenty, twenty-five, or thirty minutes?

Twenty minutes is more than sufficient for a review. With most reviews, I find that the reviewer and I would love to talk for another twenty minutes. That feeling is the best possible ending for a review. To finish with the desire to meet again and to continue the conversation forms the basis of a more lasting relationship.

If there was nothing left to say after twenty minutes, why would you ever want to meet again?

17. What are some positive outcomes you've experienced from attending portfolio-review events?

To be honest, I've had terrific outcomes from attending portfolio reviews. I had my first solo exhibition from a gallerist who had been a reviewer. And I've also had an online magazine profile written by a reviewer. I've been fortunate. That being said, you should not enter this process thinking any of those things will happen. You should expect nothing but be open to whatever happens.

And here is the good thing about this process: The reviewers are here to look for you! Gallerists need artwork to show. It's hard to find good artwork to exhibit, and that's why they are here. The same goes for journalists and writers. They need to find subjects and stories to write about. Book publishers are looking for content to publish. So, the need for a successful encounter is mutual. You actually shouldn't be surprised if good things come out of your review!

18. Have you met with a reviewer who was not a good fit for your work? If so, were you able to work around it and/or did you learn from the experience?

I'm going to rephrase this another way: Sometimes I have met reviewers who are younger and who have not given many reviews before. In this situation, I feel like I am engaged in helping the reviewer gain experience. I feel like I'm training the reviewer. And I find nothing wrong with this. We all have to start somewhere. Usually this occurs when the young reviewer doesn't necessarily like my work but is not skilled enough to articulate it well, and it starts getting awkward.

When I find myself in this situation, I just try to help them along. I don't argue with anything, and I search for rapport, to keep the conversation going.

19. Has a reviewer been disinterested in your work and clearly finished before the session was complete? If so, how did you handle the situation?

I did have a review where the reviewer was not that interested in my work and did not regard it that highly. So, after a while, I cut my presentation short, and I started asking the reviewer about their business. I used it as an opportunity to learn more about the field of photography. Basically, I became the interviewer. I could tell this reviewer liked to talk. So, I just let them talk and thought, "Well, maybe I'll learn something."

20. What are your thoughts about public portfolio walk-throughs, and have you ever made a sale this way? Do you have any pointers for new reviewees about the walk-throughs?

I have not done anything like this.

21. How do you handle connecting—away from the review table—with a reviewer during an event?

This situation obviously happens very often, particularly at lunchtime, where you might end up sitting at a table with a reviewer. You should maintain your professionalism and be respectful. If you're nice, this is a great opportunity to learn more about the field of photography.

I once ended up at a lunch table with a reviewer who had not been wild about my work. But through this lunch encounter, I was able to grow our relationship by not talking about my work. It turns out both of us liked obscure old movies from a certain era. And by talking about our favorite movies from that era, we learned about each other, and this humanized our relationship. I would like to believe that this lunchtime conversation helped grow their opinion of me—and, possibly, of my work.

22. Have you ever gotten to the point with your work when you don't feel the need to attend portfolio reviews? If so, why?

Yes. I use the portfolio reviews to show new work and to learn about my new work. When I make a new series, it might take a year or two to really learn what it is that I have made. Through things like portfolio reviews, I learn what the work is all about.

But after that period is done, and after I've gotten a good understanding of what I've made, I do not continue to bring it to reviews. I will wait until I have made new work before I return. This may take a year or two or three before I return to a review, but to me, that's okay.

23. Please comment on relationships that have developed from attending portfolio-review events.

The relationships that I have made through these events are hugely important. I have met gallery owners, photography curators from major museums, curators from important photography organizations, and writers. And they know me now. They are now "friends" on Instagram, and they follow what I'm doing, and I follow what they are doing. And when I had my first solo exhibition, a few of them came to the show! I don't think any of this happens without the portfolio reviews.

And by following these people on Instagram after meeting them in person, some of these people have become real friends. That's huge.

24. What is the biggest "no-no" for individuals attending portfolio-review events?

I don't really have a list of "no-no's," but I would simply reiterate that the reviewers have seen much more photography than you have, and through their eyes, you can get a pretty good idea of where your work fits in the grand scheme of things.

Some people write follow-up thank-you notes (emails) to all of their reviewers in the days after a review. I haven't done this, but I think it's a good idea and plan to do it in the future.

25. What one piece of advice would you pass on to first-time reviewees?

Bring a small notebook and take notes about your reviews. Every time you have a break, make sure you sit down and write down the comments the reviewer said. If you don't do this, you will forget and lose their valuable insights. This is what you're paying for. In the evening, go back to your room, check your notebook, and write up a full set of notes for yourself about what was said.

Matthew Finley

Matthew Finley
Los Angeles, California

I use a variety of photography processes to communicate my life's experience and form emotional connections to viewers.

Growing up queer in a religious family, I experienced feelings of loneliness and separation from the world around me and a fear of being singled out; yet, at the same time I desired to see and truly be seen by others. Now, as an adult with social anxiety, I see the studio as a safe space where I can be vulnerable and express my true self who wants a dialogue with an audience. Creating and exhibiting my work is a way to forge relationships with viewers outside of traditional social pressures. My photography tells autobiographical stories that convey an emotional honesty of experience. I address issues such as my coming-out story, my intimate relationships, and the healing power of nature.

My images are conduits to expose my personal and closely held emotions, which would otherwise go unexpressed, and to start a dialogue around reflection, recognition, and universal emotions.

My work has shown in solo and group shows in multiple galleries across the United States. Most recently, my work was on the walls of the esteemed Fahey/Klein Gallery in Los Angeles alongside the likes of Herb Ritts and Herbert List. Other works have circled the globe as part of the FOTOFILMIC 17, a traveling exhibition. I have pieces in the permanent collections of the Museum of Contemporary Photography at Columbia College (Chicago), The Museum of Art and History (Lancaster, California), and the Center for Fine Art Photography (Fort Collins, Colorado). My images have also appeared in publications including *Oxford American, SHOTS Magazine*, and *Plates to Pixels*, where I won the Juror Award in The Visual Armistice 10th Annual Juried Showcase.

1. What led you to attend your first portfolio-review event, and what stood out about the one you chose?

In 2015, I had been studying photography for a few years, and after making a couple digital fine-art photo series, I began working in wet-plate collodion and created a series of tintypes. I applied to Review Santa Fe with that work and got in. Looking back now, I wish I could have a do-over. While I'm still very proud of the work, at the time I didn't know how to transport the tintype plates safely to show them, so I took prints. It worked out fine, but showing the plates would have made a greater impact. I also didn't realize at the time how challenging it is to get into that review. In hindsight, it might have been better to make those mistakes at smaller events.

2. Please list, in order of importance, why you attend portfolio-review events.

- To get my work in front of people I feel are important and knowledgeable in the photo community.
- To get feedback on my work.
- To start a relationship with those people or show new work to people I have met before and reconnect with them.
- To meet and catch up with other photographers from all over the country (and the world).

3. How do you go about choosing which photography portfolio-review events you want to attend and which reviewers you want to meet?

There are a number of criteria to consider.

Cost: Oftentimes, the online reviews are more cost-effective. If the project I want to show comes across better in person (alternative process or something more tactile), I may prioritize one of those over an online review.

Audience: I investigate whether there are enough reviewers with the types of organizations or backgrounds I want to target for the body of work I'll show. How many of them have I reviewed with before? Reading about the reviewers is a big factor. While I may not get all of the reviewers I want, I usually get most of them, so it's important to align your work with those who might respond to it. Coming back to cost again, in the end I ask, Will it all be worth it? Travel, lodging, et cetera. I wish I could attend several reviews every year, but that is just not affordable, so I have to try to make an educated guess as to which ones will have the most impact.

4. What is your average cost per year to attend portfolio-review events, including event registration fees, travel, print production, and leave-behinds? Do you have a budget for self-promotion? If not using this amount for attending portfolio-review events, what do you think would be an effective, comparable use of funds in promoting your work in a different way?

Oh no, math! Don't make me do math. LOL. It's a little hard to say with the world-changing event that was the pandemic. Before that, I would say I did one in-person review a year. Since we've returned to a kind of normal, I've done a couple online and one in person recently. I don't have a set budget for self-promotion. Like a lot of artists, I have to get better at that. Other than my website and an occasional review, I don't do a lot of regular self-promotion. Reviews are one of the best ways to know people are seeing your work. You could use that money to hire someone to handle your social-network promotion, but will the people who run galleries, or curate museums actually see the work? Maybe not. It depends on

Matthew Finley

your main goal. If you already have a large audience and a way to sell your own work, then maybe spending the money on marketing is the way to go. Many of us don't have that audience yet, so galleries, museums, and other venues can help grow it.

5. What are the standout pros and cons of virtual reviews versus in-person portfolio-review events?

As I mentioned, online reviews usually cost less (you don't have the expenses of travel, hotel, meals, transportation, leave-behinds, et cetera). They can be great. You still get to meet the reviewer, show them the work, chat a bit, get feedback, and now you have a connection. Where online reviews fall short is when your work benefits from being touched, like with some alternative processes or books or prints with surface texture or embellishment that catches the light. Most of that is missed in the online experience. Another potential drawback: If you're like me who doesn't have a naturally "big" personality, we might not make as much of an impression over a screen as we would in person. With the reviewer meeting ten to fifteen people a day, that could be a factor to keep in mind.

6. For virtual reviews, please share your process for making a PDF version of your portfolio.

Google Slides is easy to use. It is pretty simple to put one together, and you can export it as a PDF if you need to send it.

7. How many photographs do you typically include in each project and why? How many projects do you typically show at a portfolio review and why?

I try to keep it to twenty to twenty-five images, a short project statement, a grid of all the images together, and contact info. I have two bodies of work ready to show, and I prioritize the first one. I may say, "I have two bodies of work to share, if we have time for both." If we spend the whole time on the first one, that's okay because that means they responded to it and had lots to say. If they don't really respond to it, you know you have the second one, and you can move on. Even if they don't, you will have filled the time and done what you could. It's those dead silences with nothing left to say that can be the most painful. (It happens.)

8. How do you make your prints or presentation materials? Do you do anything special to your portfolio to enhance the narrative of your project?

Once I realized how to transport my tintypes and ambrotypes, people responded well to seeing the originals in person. More recently, I was showing a book-project "dummy" in person because I felt it was more powerful for reviewers to turn the pages and see the breadth of the project versus scanned pages online. I have seen a number of creative presentations with prints, like that of one photographer who used a vintage suitcase to display her images (which had vintage motifs). It's great if it fits with your project. Making a good impression and being memorable (in addition to great work) is the whole point of a review.

9. What is your opinion about attending reviews with a body of work in progress versus a completed project?

It's great. It's important to tell them upfront, "This is a work in progress; I'd really like to get your thoughts on . . . (sequencing, clarity of concept, where I might go from here)." Whatever would be most helpful for you. Reviewers often like questions or a little direction as to what it is you want out of your session. Same with a completed body of work, asking something like, "Do you have any thoughts or suggestions on what organizations might respond to this work?" They may say they don't, but then again, you don't know until you ask.

10. What are your thoughts about "leave-behinds?" If you use them, please describe yours.

I do use them. Again, I have seen some beautiful ones. For me, it starts with budget. What can I afford to make? Then I consider, of those possibilities, does one fit better with the themes of my work? It's also good to remember that many times the reviewers are flying in, so they have to be able to pack the leave-behinds easily; otherwise, they might really leave them behind, and you don't want that! In the past, I have done sets of five moo.com postcards in a little reuseable fabric pouch, a very small accordion book, and small 3" × 5" custom prints in a small box, among other things.

11. Do you make time to see the work of other artists? If so, have you noticed where you are in the spectrum of work, experience, and education? How did it make you feel?

Oh yes, that is one of the highlights of going to reviews—seeing the variety of work people bring. Often, I don't have the time to see it all, but I try. I find that

Matthew Finley

there is great variety not only in the work, but also in the participants. Usually, it runs from first-timers to seasoned veterans and everything in between. It can vary from review to review, but generally there's a great mix. It may be more challenging for the reviewers when someone is new to photography and reviewing, but everyone has to start somewhere. You can learn by seeing how the more seasoned people present their work. It can spark ideas for next time.

12. After looking at the work of your fellow reviewees, did you seek out any connections or collaborations, or were you simply inspired by their work? If so, how did you approach the person?

I haven't created any photographic collaborations to this point, but I have made friends and acquaintances, which has led to crit-group invitations, and those have been a great support system.

13. Has there been any auxiliary programming (lectures, workshops, photobook fair, portfolio walk, et cetera) at a portfolio-review event that was exceptionally memorable for you personally?

When I did Photolucida a few years ago, they had a wonderful thing called the "Roving Reviewer Room," where a reviewer who wanted to see more people in a less-formal setting would sit at a table and have a sign-up sheet. You could put your name down, and it was a great way to get another review in between your regularly scheduled ones. And you knew those reviewers were eager to see more work: it was a supportive environment.

14. Please share your most memorable portfolio-review experience (either positive or negative).

The first time I reviewed with a local museum curator, they mentioned that they program their shows two years out. I made a point to review with them another two to three times over the next two years, and during that second year, they invited me to be a part of a photo-based show. They told me that besides the work, my persistence kept me on their radar when the time came to set who should be in the show. As far as what you might call a negative review, I have only had a couple in all these years. One was due to being paired with a reviewer who was so opposite my work. They worked for a tech magazine, and my work was queer bodies with an alternative process. You couldn't get more opposite, so we just chatted about the weather for twenty minutes! The other was a personality conflict. He seemed to be of the opinion he was there to teach me what I was doing wrong. It just shut me down, and I counted the minutes until it was over.

So, bad reviews happen, but in my experience they're rare. Most reviewers are coming from a place of support and encouragement. Usually, you come away with useful information, if only names of other photographers working in your similar area whom you should be familiar with and might learn from.

15. What is your favorite and least favorite part of portfolio-review events?

My favorite part is getting the work out there. It leaves me with a sense of accomplishment to know people I respect are seeing it, seeing me, and generally responding positively. If something more comes of it, great. My least favorite parts are cost (I would love to see them more accessible so that lower-income people could have the same opportunity) and the anxiety of those first few minutes walking into the room and sitting down. Sharing your work with a stranger is a vulnerable moment. To lay it all out there. I will say that it has gotten easier having done it for a while, but I still feel it.

16. What do you think is the ideal length of time for a review session—twenty, twenty-five, or thirty minutes?

It would almost always be good to have more time. With the adrenaline and energy in the room, the time flies. I have mostly done ones that are twenty minutes, but I imagine thirty minutes would be great.

17. What are some positive outcomes you've experienced from attending portfolio-review events?

I sold a piece to a museum in Chicago because of a review. I have had some online features directly from reviews. And meeting so many people in the community who I admire and respect, and who now know me and my work, means a lot.

18. Have you met with a reviewer who was not a good fit for your work? If so, were you able to work around it and/or did you learn from the experience?

Of course, there are always reviewers who, for one reason or another, don't fit. Maybe they like the work but it's not for their gallery or organization. I will try to ask something to the effect of, "Can you think of any organizations that might respond well to the work?" It can be disappointing, but I try not to take it personally and remind myself that this relationship is just beginning, and in the future, maybe they will be somewhere that aligns better with my work.

Matthew Finley

19. Has a reviewer been disinterested in your work and clearly finished before the session was complete? If so, how did you handle the situation?

I would say that in the past, I would try to make small talk, ask them questions about themselves, et cetera. As I've gotten a little more used to the process, I am not above saying, "Well, thank you so much for your feedback and time. It looks like we are done a little early; I will give you a little more time to grab a coffee in between. Take care," before grabbing my things and leaving. If I feel it's over and they seem to, too, there's no point sitting there in silence.

20. What are your thoughts about public portfolio walk-throughs, and have you ever made a sale this way? Do you have any pointers for new reviewees about the walk-throughs?

They can be stressful and exhausting, but they are also a great way to get your work seen. They also help you get your "elevator pitch" honed. As people come up and ask what the work is about, you only have a couple of minutes of their attention. You learn as the night progresses, through repetition, how to deliver a quick synopsis of the work. I almost wish the event was before the reviews, so that your most efficient version was practiced for the reviewers. Try to make your presentation interactive. Instead of leaving a stack of prints out for them to thumb through, you turn the prints as you talk about the work. It can be tiring, but it will engage them more, and it will allow you the experience of talking about your work.

21. How do you handle connecting—away from the review table—with a reviewer during an event?

It's tough. I'm pretty shy, and so I will say hello and attempt to make small talk, but I never want to seem to intrude on their personal time, so I won't stay long. I admire those folks who can talk to anyone with ease. If I am not reviewing with them, and it seems appropriate, I may say, "I didn't get you this time around, unfortunately; can I at least give you my card?" They may or may not look at my website, but at least I tried.

22. Have you ever gotten to the point with your work when you don't feel the need to attend portfolio reviews? If so, why?

Not yet. Maybe if you were well known, with a big gallery pounding the pavement for you. Or if your sales and collector base were solid enough that you had no interest in galleries, museums, or online venues, then perhaps it would be something to ignore. It depends on your goals.

23. Please comment on relationships that have developed from attending portfolio-review events.

I have made new friends with people from all over the country and have been able to follow their careers via social media. I have also had the opportunity to review with certain people more than once, who have given me helpful feedback on my work and whom I know are rooting for me, which is a good feeling.

24. What is the biggest "no-no" for individuals attending portfolio-review events?

Being unprepared, coming in with way too many images, not knowing what your work is about, et cetera. You want to come across as thoughtful, professional, and open to what they have to say. If you come across as if you didn't put any time and thought into your presentation, they won't want to put in any effort, either.

25. What one piece of advice would you pass on to first-time reviewees?

Try to go in with no expectations. You'll hear stories about so-and-so who got a big solo show from a review yesterday, or whatever, and that can be discouraging if you don't get those tangible, immediate results. I have learned to focus on finding joy and accomplishment in sharing the work. We may not have a ton of opportunities to share the work with someone who really knows a lot about photography throughout the year, and it takes a lot to do a portfolio review—a lot of time and money. So, it's an accomplishment to get there. Keep that in mind, try to be proud of that along with your work, and try not to focus on what you may or may not get out of the reviews. The seeds you plant at that review may take years to bloom. Just keep at it.

Matthew Finley

Liliana Guzman
Bloomington, Indiana

G

My name is Liliana Guzmán, and I am a Colombian American photographer and painter currently residing in Bloomington, Indiana. My artwork entwines topics of the body, memory, sexuality, and the hidden landscapes of the self. I was born in Baltimore, Maryland, and raised in Indiana, completing my BA at Earlham College with a double concentration in photography and French and francophone studies and my MFA at the Eskenazi School of Art, Architecture + Design at Indiana University Bloomington.

In my practice, I use a wide range of techniques and mediums from film photography and alternative processes to digital photography, collage, painting, and drawing. My current research and ongoing project, titled "Next to Myself," combines painting and photography to reflect upon the layers and formation of the self—inspired by my bicultural upbringing. I am fascinated with touch and gesture and make artwork to express touch not only as a formative and intimate experience, but as one that establishes both internal and external connections within ourselves and those around us.

I consider myself an emerging artist, and I am grateful to have ventured into the world of solo exhibitions. "Next to Myself" was included in the 2021 Lenscratch Student Prize: 26 to Watch and was exhibited for the first time at the Amalie Rothschild Gallery in Baltimore in May 2022. Since then, I have been honored to receive the Blue Sky Solo Show Award through Photolucida's Critical Mass and my second solo exhibition at Blue Sky Gallery in Portland, Oregon, in April 2023. Most recently, "Next to Myself" traveled to Candela Gallery in Richmond, Virginia, where I debuted a new piece to the series and look forward to continuing to share and grow this project.

1. What led you to attend your first portfolio-review event, and what stood out about the one you chose?

I first became aware of portfolio reviews as a graduate student. Coming from a small liberal arts college, I didn't have the exposure to the world of portfolio reviews as I did once I started my graduate program. It was here where I learned about the various portfolio-review opportunities and heard about how beneficial the experience is in the journey of a working artist.

When I chose my first portfolio review, I was most interested in the organization of the event itself. While some portfolio reviews are one or two days, this particular review was a weeklong venture that focused not only on the reviews, but also on meeting and lodging with a small community of artists. This was a juried portfolio review, so I knew that if I was selected, I would be able to meet and really spend time with both the reviewers and the reviewees.

2. Please list, in order of importance, why you attend portfolio-review events.

- Community—Creating new connections and learning more about what projects, visions, and topics my peers in the art world are exploring and expressing.
- Exposure—Getting my artwork out there! Making art is to share it, and portfolio reviews allow for new and fresh eyes to look at the artwork.
- Feedback—Part of being a working artist is to be open to new critiques and to listen to how others react to the artwork.
- Professional Practice—Portfolio reviews allow me to make and keep deadlines. They also help me revisit projects and keep my artist statements and CVs up to date.

3. How do you go about choosing which photography portfolio-review events you want to attend and which reviewers you want to meet?

Determining which review might be beneficial sometimes depends on my current project's creative stage. If, for example, I have a fairly solid project that I'm interested in making into a book, I would look specifically at portfolio reviews and reviewers who are in publishing or who have published photography books. If I have a few projects that I would like to share and receive feedback on, then I would opt for perhaps a variety of reviewers, including those I am both familiar and unfamiliar with, so that I can be sure to get new perspectives on the artwork.

4. What is your average cost per year to attend portfolio-review events, including event registration fees, travel, print production, and leave-behinds? Do you have a budget for self-promotion? If not using this amount for attending portfolio-review events, what do you think would be an effective, comparable use of funds in promoting your work in a different way?

I love this question because as an emerging artist, this is something that I am learning and wish I had paid more attention to sooner! Portfolio reviews can be very pricey. In my experience, travel and accommodations are the biggest expense, ranging anywhere from $1,000 to $3,000, including the plane ticket to and from, renting a car, and finding a place to stay, not to mention food—that's a lot, I know! However, I think it is important to think about these costs as an investment in your practice.

There have been moments where I had to choose not to attend a portfolio review, and while this is always a little bit heartbreaking, I ended up using the money that I saved on making new pieces, framing, and having travel expenses for exhibitions! If you are unable to attend portfolio reviews, using these funds to apply to online exhibitions or even exhibition proposals is another great way to promote your work. Financial balance between making artwork and self-promotion is tricky, but very important.

Liliana Guzman

5. What are the standout pros and cons of virtual reviews versus in-person portfolio-review events?

The first standout pro of a virtual portfolio review would be the opportunity to receive feedback! Even though it is ideal to be face-to-face with your reviewer, a virtual review is great for making new connections and sharing your work with someone whom you otherwise may not get a chance to speak with. The biggest con of a virtual review would be that artwork translates so differently over a computer screen than in person. I work with painting and photography, so to demonstrate colors, marks, and other details of my artwork, meeting in person is ideal. However, I have also found virtual portfolio reviews to be a wonderful alternative that can still help you gain critical feedback and get new eyes on your art. Plus, virtual reviews are much more affordable, not having travel expenses.

G

6. For virtual reviews, please share your process for making a PDF version of your portfolio.

I start with designing a very simple slideshow that focuses on photographs of the artwork. I like to include detailed images of particular pieces and exhibition documentation so that the reviewer can get a sense of scale. I do not want to overwhelm the reviewer, so if I am sharing a particular project, I use about ten to fifteen of the strongest images. I'll also include works in progress, as well as an artist statement and the title, medium, year, and size of each artwork that was shown in the PDF. Having contact information, such as your email, website, and social media, is another important part of my virtual portfolio that I am always sure to include.

7. How many photographs do you typically include in each project and why? How many projects do you typically show at a portfolio review and why?

When I have a project that I feel is "exhibition ready"—that is, the images that are the most cohesive and final—I like to limit this selection to between ten and twenty photographs. I choose the strongest pieces to focus on first and foremost in the review. If there is a project that is more in the "in-progress stage," I think it is appropriate to collect and share about twenty pieces, regardless of whether you feel that they are the final images.

The number of projects I share during portfolio reviews sometimes depends on the reviewer. If they are interested and feel compelled to focus on one project, then I will generally allow the reviewer to focus just on one project, and I will, perhaps, share a different project at the next review. If it is important for me to share one or two projects, then I will state at the beginning of the review that I have one or two projects that I would appreciate feedback on. Sometimes there may only be time for the reviewer to focus on one project, and other times, a reviewer will want to lay out photographs from multiple projects on the table and give insight that way. I think it is important to go into each review with the mindset of being flexible while also stating some of your goals for the review.

8. How do you make your prints or presentation materials? Do you do anything special to your portfolio to enhance the narrative of your project?

When I am focusing on one project, I like to make each print as beautiful and true to an exhibition-ready print as possible. For example, my final pieces use a very specific type of thick photographic paper. This is the same paper that I use for my portfolio review. Because I use painting and photography, I also would ideally include pieces that are painted on rather than just art prints of the original. However, because of the size of original pieces, this is sometimes hard to travel with, so it's important to keep that in mind when preparing for a review if you deal with larger print sizes. I like to keep my prints 11" × 14", which is not so small that details of the original artwork are lost, nor too large to fit in a suitcase when traveling. The goal is to give the reviewer an insight into how the artwork could look if it were gallery ready.

However, for more in-progress projects, I will use cheaper materials that are still going to look polished and clean. When I am sharing multiple projects, I always keep my main project, or the project that I am interested in exhibiting in a gallery, at the top of the photograph pile. Then I will place examples of other projects that I may be working on and would like to share, depending on what direction the review takes.

9. What is your opinion about attending reviews with a body of work in progress versus a completed project?

I approach portfolio reviews with these reflection questions in mind: How can I most benefit from this opportunity? What is my goal? If one of my main goals is to think about the next steps on a project that I feel is mostly completed, then I think the best thing to do is focus on that one particular project and get as many new eyes on it as possible. I have had successful portfolio reviews that have focused on one project and that I felt benefited me as far as what pieces had the strongest reaction, where in the project can I make improvements, and even what galleries or communities this artwork might most fit in with. Sharing one project at a portfolio review is definitely a great way to approach the event if you are thinking about how to get your project even more out into the world.

Alternatively, sharing a project or multiple projects that are in progress can be beneficial if you are really looking for a variety of input that might help you make some decisions on how to really push your project to a higher level.

Liliana Guzman

10. What are your thoughts about "leave-behinds"? If you use them, please describe yours.

I think "leave-behinds" can be a great tool to have at portfolio reviews. For me, I like to have two types of leave-behinds. The first is a postcard-sized art print with my contact information on the back, along with website, social media, email, and title and dimensions of the image used. The second is a business card that is smaller but has the same contact information on the back. I like having two sizes at my disposal, in case a reviewer prefers something smaller over a postcard. Using online printing companies, such as Moo, has been great because they are high quality and fairly affordable for larger batches.

What I really love about having postcards and business cards is that these are excellent ways to keep in contact with all of the artists and new friends you meet at portfolio reviews! Even if I do not give a lot of business cards or postcards to my reviewers, I definitely give many to the new friends and connections I make at the event. Plus, it's a wonderful thing to trade with other artists.

11. Do you make time to see the work of other artists? If so, have you noticed where you are in the spectrum of work, experience, and education? How did it make you feel?

While meeting with the reviewers is a big and important part of portfolio reviews, taking time to connect with your peers in the photo community is a really wonderful way to see what other artists are passionate about. I always make time to see what other artists are making and doing, asking questions and learning more about what inspires others to make artwork. What I have learned is that the art community is full of individuals who come from various educational and work backgrounds. While a little bit cheesy, meeting with other artists does remind me that each person is on their own journey, and that's what makes everyone's point of view, project, and expression so unique. I have met amazing artists who have gotten an MFA and others who haven't, and some artists who approach photography more technically while others are more experimental. In the end, I always appreciate the inclusion and openness that exists in the art and photo community.

12. After looking at the work of your fellow reviewees, did you seek out any connections or collaborations, or were you simply inspired by their work? If so, how did you approach the person?

The best thing about looking at the artwork of fellow reviewees is that the art is the perfect conversation starter. I try to ask questions or point out a specific photograph that caught my attention and why. This always opens the door for a

G

longer conversation and deeper connection! Sometimes portfolio reviews can be a bit chaotic, so if I am really interested in a possible collaboration or speaking with a particular artist again, I'll either arrange to meet with them again before the event is over or ask for one of their "leave-behinds" and follow up with them after the review. I think keeping in contact is also key, because after the rush and excitement of the review, you now have a new circle of friends and artists you can reach out to and connect with long after the review is over.

13. Has there been any auxiliary programming (lectures, workshops, photobook fair, portfolio walk, et cetera) at a portfolio reviews event that was exceptionally memorable for you personally?

Even when I may feel tired or overwhelmed at times during portfolio-review events, I remind myself to take advantage of being in the same place as so many artists! It is key for me to make an effort to attend lectures and, especially, portfolio walks, which, for me personally, is the best time to meet new people and make connections. Portfolio shares are very memorable for me since it's an optimal time to hear what my peers have to say about my work and to learn more about theirs!

14. Please share your most memorable portfolio-review experience (either positive or negative).

While I've had some wonderful experiences, my most memorable ones are the reviews with artists that I look up to and am inspired by. For me, making artwork can be fairly solitary work, so being face-to-face with an established artist and hearing firsthand their point of view on my artwork is an incredible feeling and never fails to give me the encouragement to keep moving and making. One of my favorite reviews was with an artist I admire, and it was really special to hear them point out which pieces struck them. Having the sense of belonging to a community of creatives is the memorable experience that carries me on to and through each project.

15. What is your favorite and least favorite part of portfolio-review events?

My favorite part of a portfolio review is hearing the feedback of so many different voices. This never fails to help me find threads in my artwork and offer some reflection and clarity on where to go next.

Easily, my least favorite part of the portfolio-review events are the financial expenses! The money put in to entering, attending, and traveling to portfolio events causes a lot of stress and financial burden, especially for an emerging artist like me.

Liliana Guzman

16. What do you think is the ideal length of time for a review session— twenty, twenty-five, or thirty minutes?

Depending on how well the conversation with the reviewer is going, thirty minutes definitely allows enough time to introduce yourself and the artwork, listen to feedback, and ask any questions you may have. Especially if you are with a reviewer that you particularly admire, having enough time can feel rewarding and worth the preparation and effort that you put into meeting with them.

17. What are some positive outcomes you've experienced from attending portfolio-review events?

Having finished my graduate studies, it has been a very difficult transition from constantly meeting deadlines, attending critiques, and receiving feedback to suddenly being on your own in the art world—especially during a pandemic. The most positive outcome from portfolio-review events is the reminder that even though making artwork can be solitary, there is a big community of artists, publishers, curators, and professors who are excited to meet you and see your artwork! The sense of encouragement and drive that I feel after meeting with so many artists is a very special and lasting feeling.

18. Have you met with a reviewer who was not a good fit for your work? If so, were you able to work around it and/or did you learn from the experience?

I have met with reviewers who weren't able to provide the feedback I had been looking for; however, that didn't mean that the review was a waste. Instead, the conversation about art-making in general was really helpful. I think it's important to remember that you can always take something away from a portfolio review. If the conversation around your artwork is not very fruitful, there are things you can ask about professional practices that can hopefully make the meeting worthwhile.

19. Has a reviewer been disinterested in your work and clearly finished before the session was complete? If so, how did you handle the situation?

This goes hand in hand with finding ways to reroute the conversation in a way that can be more productive. While I have never had a reviewer who was disinterested, there have been reviewers who did not know exactly how to react to my artwork and who have even said they are not sure how to provide feedback. In these situations, I would instead ask them questions about publishing or exhibitions or ask for advice on resources that have been helpful to them in the past.

20. What are your thoughts about public portfolio walk-throughs, and have you ever made a sale this way? Do you have any pointers for new reviewees about the walk-throughs?

Unfortunately, I have not yet attended a public portfolio walk-through, but I am no stranger to tabling art events in my own community. Though that's a little bit different, it was still a way to connect with my local arts community and make connections to local galleries and artists. While I have made sales during public tabling events, I would say it is much harder, for me personally, to calculate the benefit of effort versus outcome, since the success of sales at public events is more unpredictable.

21. How do you handle connecting—away from the review table—with a reviewer during an event?

There have been instances where I was not scheduled to meet with a reviewer whom I was really excited about meeting. In those cases, I made a point to try to approach them during social events and introduce myself. Even though it can feel awkward or intimidating, I always remind myself that they are there to meet artists! Once I introduce myself, I'll ask if they have the time or would be interested in seeing some of my work, and more likely than not, they agree.

22. Have you ever gotten to the point with your work when you don't feel the need to attend portfolio reviews? If so, why?

Even with projects that in my mind are "exhibition ready," I always want to stay open to feedback and critique. Continuing to share and receive feedback is an integral part of my art practice, especially after graduate school. Though a project may be done in my mind, portfolio reviews can help me decide what the next steps could be, such as making an art book, what gallery might be a good fit for this artwork, and how I can further transform and level the project in general. Additionally, making connections is rewarding, and a portfolio review is an excellent place to do just that.

23. Please comment on relationships that have developed from attending portfolio-review events.

I have left portfolio reviews with a new and bigger circle of creative friends whom I still keep in contact with a year later! I have shared new work with them, asked for advice, and received creative opportunities that have all been helpful and rewarding. For example, I was hesitant to apply for a particular art call, so I reached

Liliana Guzman

out to a friend I had met at a review. They encouraged me to apply and described their experience with this particular art call, and that was very helpful. It's this type of community that can arise from making new friends at reviews! Additionally, I have traded art prints, had virtual studio visits, and even talked about collaboration with new friends and relationships made from portfolio-review events.

24. What is the biggest "no-no" for individuals attending portfolio-review events?

The worst thing you could do is let a bad review or bad experience get in the way of enjoying the event. It can be overwhelming to share your artwork and be surrounded by a lot of people who may seem a little nonstop at times, but in my experiences, I have pushed myself to talk with others, attend social events, and really try to make an effort to soak up all of the opportunities for connection.

25. What one piece of advice would you pass on to first-time reviewees?

Keep an open mind and have fun! This is a special time to get new eyes on your project, so focus on what you feel is important to get out of the portfolio review, and always be open to receiving the variety of feedback, critique, and reactions that will undoubtedly come your way. Even if you had a review or interaction with your artwork that didn't go your way, chances are others have had that same experience. You are not alone; your fellow reviewees are in this boat with you. Remind yourself that you have a singular vision and voice to share, and this community is ultimately excited to interact with what you have to give! Keep moving forward and making connections.

G

Jessica Hays

Jessica Hays

Bozeman, Montana

I am a conceptual photographer, alternative-process printmaker, and artist based in Montana and Chicago. My intimate work draws on personal experience to communicate ubiquitous human experiences, tackling topics like mental health, landscape change, and loss. Grounded in the American West, I am interested in relationships between people, places, and experiences of being deeply connected to one's surroundings. My work blurs the lines between the uniquely individual and collective experiences.

Process is an important part of my work, manifesting in a variety of ways including pigment printing, handmade artist books, video, and historic and experimental photo processes. I have lectured on topics of mental health, climate issues, and contemporary photography at conferences, mental-health summits, and as a guest speaker in classrooms. My work is shown nationally and internationally in galleries and museums, published in a variety of magazines and textbooks, and is held in several public and private collections in the United States and Canada. I earned an MFA in photography from Columbia College Chicago, and I earned a BA in film and photography and a BA in environmental studies concurrently at Montana State University. Recently, I have been recognized as a Critical Mass finalist, shortlisted for the BarTur Environmental Award, and named a 2023 Chulitna Artist Fellow. My work aims to explore the interactions between psychology and climate change—investigating how landscapes affect the human psyche, from trauma to restoration. To view more of my work, visit jessicahaysart.com

1. What led you to attend your first portfolio-review event, and what stood out about the one you chose?

I worked as an intern at the Photolucida reviews when I was in college, through a partnership with my undergraduate university. Observing and being in the room, I saw some of the meaningful connections that were made there and met artists who I learned had received opportunities to exhibit their work following the review event. I always thought it would be a good idea to attend some at a later point, especially since I had also had good experiences doing student portfolio reviews at SPE. As a graduate student, I also attended a few reviews—one or two a year—at Filter Photo, which was a great experience. I've attended several reviews at this point, but I applied that first year to both Chico and Photolucida and ended up getting into and attending both. Both were valuable experiences for me—and both very different. I often work in books and was thinking about working toward a published book when I attended Chico, which is the obvious reason to attend one that is so geared toward photobooks. I knew PhotoLucida from when I had been an intern, so applying for their reviews was appealing, and I had met people who had received opportunities.

2. Please list, in order of importance, why you attend portfolio-review events.

- Finding opportunities to exhibit/place/show the work
- Receiving feedback on projects
- Fostering creative community

3. How do you go about choosing which photography portfolio-review events you want to attend and which reviewers you want to meet?

When choosing, I am always thinking about what my priorities are for the review and my work. I think about what reviewers tend to be there (or who will be there, if the list is already published) and what kind of work I'm making, what stage it is in, and what sorts of opportunities I am trying to pursue. I also think about overall cost and whether I think I will be able to find a grant or if I have friends I can stay with in the city that's hosting the review. When picking reviewers, I am most interested in people who I think will have thoughtful feedback about the work (that's almost everyone, in most cases) and what types of work they are looking to see. Ultimately, though, even if someone doesn't necessarily have an opportunity for my work (or the type of work I make), they might know someone else who is more interested in featuring the work in an exhibition. Some of my best reviews have been with people who were not at the top of my lists.

4. What is your average cost per year to attend portfolio-review events, including event registration fees, travel, print production, and leave-behinds? Do you have a budget for self-promotion? If not using this amount for attending portfolio-review events, what do you think would be an effective, comparable use of funds in promoting your work in a different way?

It really depends on the year and the review, as well as the funding and support I am able to secure. In graduate school, I utilized every opportunity for professional-development funding and attended several reviews. Other years, I am usually attending one, and I typically invest around $2,000 to $2,500 in expenses. The registration fee is usually the biggest part of my expenses, as I am a fairly savvy budget traveler. I produce leave-behinds in larger quantities to have for other events, too, like when I give lectures or have studio visits; this makes the cost per unit a little cheaper. My annual budget for self-promotion varies, dependent on where I am in certain projects as well as the availability of funding sources. Some

Jessica Hays

years, there is simply too much going on. I am not sure how else I would spend that portion of my studio budget, except perhaps to hire someone to manage things for me.

5. What are the standout pros and cons of virtual reviews versus in-person portfolio-review events?

The biggest con of online reviews is that there isn't a hangout space between reviews to meet other photographers. I have found a wonderful creative community and friends I keep in touch with whom I met outside the review room or ended up getting lunch with during portfolio reviews. A pro is that I find the review can be a bit less hectic feeling during online reviews. There is never the problem of overly noisy ballrooms or stress about finding the right table. Things are quiet and organized, and you can have as much extra time beforehand as you would like to prepare, have all your files open, et cetera. Another pro is that it is way more affordable and accessible to do reviews online, since you don't have to buy a plane ticket or hotel room.

6. For virtual reviews, please share your process for making a PDF version of your portfolio.

I usually edit a sequence of images similarly to how I would in the box of prints and lay them out in a document with a little bit of white space around them. I think, in hindsight, I may include more text, like titles in the slides, and maximize the opportunity to illustrate what I'm planning on speaking about with pictures of the finished product (that is, installation photos or pictures of the handmade books I create). I always focused on creating a polished presentation, but I typically had additional files open in the background if a reviewer was interested in seeing more.

7. How many photographs do you typically include in each project and why? How many projects do you typically show at a portfolio review and why?

I usually include twenty, which seems like a good amount to give a good idea of the project. An exception would be when I bring a handmade book dummy to a review, in which case there are typically more than twenty images—depending on how "finished" of a dummy it is—ranging up to fifty or sixty. That is a lot for reviewers to take in—perhaps too much in some cases—but I found it useful to express what I envisioned for my project in its book form. At this point, I prefer to bring at least two projects: one that is finished/nearly finished and one or two that are more in progress or in development stages. Sometimes there are reviewers I have met with before, so I can focus on showing them a new project if they are already familiar with the "finished" one, then on showing how that project has developed.

8. How do you make your prints or presentation materials? Do you do anything special to your portfolio to enhance the narrative of your project?

I print my own portfolio prints on an archival-pigment printer. I usually use a black portfolio box, but I have been considering building custom clamshells for my work. For some projects, if I envision them as a book, I will bring a handmade book dummy/maquette as well. I make handmade artist books in addition to the dummies, so I usually craft these very carefully. For prints in the box, I have also been including installation photos for context of the actual size of the work, especially for projects that are very large prints when shown.

9. What is your opinion about attending reviews with a body of work in progress versus a completed project?

There's a place and a reason for both, and I think it really depends on what you are looking to achieve with portfolio reviews. As I mentioned, I often come with two bodies of work, one of which may be more in progress. For that work, I am interested in feedback and thoughts on the work, but with projects that are in their finished stages, or where I have the working methods and process figured out, I am more interested in discussing opportunities. At every review event I've attended, I've met with people who fell more into one category or the other, and I find it helpful to bring both types of projects. I am usually working on multiple things at once, though, at varying levels of intensity, so bringing multiple projects and multiple stages matches my artistic practice. It may be different if you tend to focus entirely on one thing and one thing only.

10. What are your thoughts about "leave-behinds"? If you use them, please describe yours.

I always had at least a business card or postcard for a leave-behind at reviews. Now, I often include a small booklet about one body of work, which includes a project statement and bio as well as contact info. If I give one of those to a reviewer, I also leave a business card; I think having something small that's the exact same size as everything else has value in its likelihood to be kept and referred back to easily. If I have a large exhibition coming up, sometimes I will also leave a show card if they are printed in time.

Jessica Hays

11. Do you make time to see the work of other artists? If so, have you noticed where you are in the spectrum of work, experience, and education? How did it make you feel?

Yes, I love seeing other photographers' work, ranging from seeing a few pieces quickly to sitting down and looking through their entire portfolio. Maintaining and growing a creative community is a big part of attending reviews for me, and that includes looking at other peoples' work, sharing stories, and getting lunch or dinner with fellow attendees. Especially since I spend half of my year in more rural and remote areas, finding friendships and other photographers to connect with has so much value. I am (at the time of this publication) a fairly early-career artist. Some reviews tend to have more emerging/young artists, while at others I notice more of the attendees are well established. Overall, I think it has made me aware of the breadth and depth of work in the world. I feel like I am doing good, important work and that so many others are doing good, important work, too. I also appreciate getting to see artists who have had longer careers and talk with them about the path from A (emerging) to B (established) as an artist and think about the road map their careers might provide.

12. After looking at the work of your fellow reviewees, did you seek out any connections or collaborations, or were you simply inspired by their work? If so, how did you approach the person?

Both! I've kept in touch with many fellow attendees in various ways. Most commonly, I have just had people I can run ideas by or ask about their experience working with X or Y, showing with A or B, publishing with C or D, et cetera. I've also done some follow-up informal review-type meetings where we've updated each other about projects and gotten feedback on new developments. My participation in this book comes from keeping in touch with people I met at reviews and seeing them at several events!

13. Has there been any auxiliary programming (lectures, workshops, photobook fair, portfolio walk, et cetera) at a portfolio-review event that was exceptionally memorable for you personally?

I'm not sure if there's one in particular that really stands out, but overall I find them to be really engaging parts of the review weekends. I have a photobook addiction, so I always love a good book fair, but I have also found portfolio walks to be a great way to connect with many fellow attendees in a short time span. In Houston, there are organized bus shuttles to exhibitions throughout the city, which are always a really great experience as well. Generally speaking, I would want any review event I attend to have some sort of auxiliary programming in addition to the reviews themselves.

14. Please share your most memorable portfolio-review experience (either positive or negative).

At one of my first portfolio-review events, I was barely five minutes into meeting with the reviewer, and they looked up from my book maquette and said, "We are going to talk about this project for the full half-hour until the next person shows up, okay?" I of course said okay, and we had a great conversation about strategies for exhibiting the work, publishers that might be a good fit, and some tweaks to the sequence in the book. I had been feeling a little overwhelmed up to that point, and the review was so positive, while also being incredibly specific in constructive feedback. His enthusiasm went a long way, and it may have been one of the best reviews of the event, even though it wasn't specifically an offer or opportunity. I have kept in touch with him and have had several conversations since, as well.

15. What is your favorite and least favorite part of portfolio-review events?

My favorite part is forging connections with so many people in such a short span of time. I have really made some great friends and professional connections at these events. My least favorite part is dealing with the occasional person who is looking to exert a strange power dynamic or ego-driven interaction.

16. What do you think is the ideal length of time for a review session— twenty, twenty-five, or thirty minutes?

I prefer the twenty-five- and thirty-minute sessions. Twenty is very short and can fly by too fast. One review I attended had twenty-five-minute slots with five-minute breaks in between each review. That was probably my favorite time schedule. There was plenty of time to talk, and even time to run over a little bit without cutting into anyone else's time. It also gave the reviewers a chance to get a glass of water or refill their coffee between reviews without feeling rushed. Some of my reviews at that event ran twenty-eight or thirty minutes when the conversation was really a good fit, and others ended on schedule at twenty-five minutes.

17. What are some positive outcomes you've experienced from attending portfolio-review events?

I have been featured in exhibitions as a result of connections I have made at portfolio-review events and have received really valuable feedback on my book maquette that has made it significantly stronger. I've also received opportunities for publication and connected with someone who has helped me refine the writing and promotional materials surrounding *The Sun Sets Midafternoon*.

Jessica Hays

18. Have you met with a reviewer who was not a good fit for your work? If so, were you able to work around it and/or did you learn from the experience?

Yes. I think it's pretty common; not every reviewer is the perfect fit for your work in terms of the kinds of opportunities they may have to offer or even in their area of expertise, but I have always found things that can be useful. Sometimes it's as simple as acknowledging that their institution may not be a good fit and asking if there may be others they know of that are a good fit, or asking for feedback regarding sequence, edit, or exhibition planning.

19. Has a reviewer been disinterested in your work and clearly finished before the session was complete? If so, how did you handle the situation?

Yes, I had one reviewer who barely glanced at my portfolio before handing out some very generic advice. They did listen intently to what I had to say about the work, but then weren't all that interested in the pictures. We finished eight minutes early, and rather than press it, I said, "Great to meet you" and walked away. My time was better spent talking with other photographers for five minutes than dragging out something that was clearly not going to be useful.

20. What are your thoughts about public portfolio walk-throughs, and have you ever made a sale this way? Do you have any pointers for new reviewees about the walk-throughs?

I think they are a great way to become briefly familiar with many artists' work and take note of ones whose work you may want to revisit, either online or by meeting with them later in the review event. I personally have not yet made a direct sale at one, but I have arranged a print trade and was invited to be a part of a small group exhibition during a walk-through.

21. How do you handle connecting—away from the review table—with a reviewer during an event?

I usually approach them early in the event and ask if they would have any time before or after the scheduled reviews. Or, if there is a walk-through event, I ask them to come by my table; if they seem to be interested, I try to schedule a more in-depth conversation for later. Sometimes it works out and sometimes it doesn't. It is important to strike a balance between expressing why you would like to share your work with them specifically and not being too demanding of their time. As much as attending these review events are marathons for photographers, I think that is true even more so for the reviewers.

22. Have you ever gotten to the point with your work when you don't feel the need to attend portfolio reviews? If so, why?

No. I am an early-career artist right now, and I have attended reviews alongside photographers at all stages of their careers. It seems like reviews are part of putting new projects out into the world, or, at least, a good option to do so at any stage of one's career. There are and will be projects that I don't think I'll feel the need to bring to reviews as a "primary project," but I think there will be value for me in these events for many years to come.

23. Please comment on relationships that have developed from attending portfolio-review events.

Attending these events has been the launching point for many relationships. I keep in touch with several of the artists I have met to talk about work or ask about their experiences working with certain organizations. There are many ongoing professional relationships that began at reviews. For example, someone wrote an essay for an exhibition catalog for me; we met at a review. Some relationships result in something tangible like that fairly quickly, and others seem to take more time. Ultimately, though, I think of these relationships as my friends and colleagues in the art and photography communities. I am always interested in hanging out with people who like great pictures as much as I do.

24. What is the biggest "no-no" for individuals attending portfolio-review events?

Don't be an asshole.

25. What one piece of advice would you pass on to first-time reviewees?

Don't overthink it. Be serious about your work and putting your best foot forward, but don't stress yourself out too much. Experiment with how you introduce the work for your first few reviews, and take note of what leads to a better conversation and what doesn't. Half of it is finding out how to briefly, powerfully, and concisely describe your work so there is enough time left for a conversation.

Jessica Hays

Diana Nicholette Jeon

Honolulu, Hawaii

I bring personal history and experimental processes to my lens-based art, and I often use beauty as a conceit to engage viewers to look deeper at challenging subject matter they might otherwise not consider. I believe media has "mana" (the Hawaiian word loosely translated as "power") and often uses it to underscore the conceptual underpinning of a series. For me, the message always comes before the tools I employ. I'm drawn to art conveying raw emotions; I also expose my inner self via my work. My creations often carry a sense of forlornness and melancholy as they delve into deeply personal aspects of my life. In order to communicate my message effectively, I tackle each project by asking myself, "What do I need to do? What materials should I use? How should I present it?" This approach allows me to transcend the boundaries of specific mediums and integrate various artistic forms. By breaking free from conventional limitations and merging diverse techniques, I strive to create thought-provoking pieces that transcend materials and challenge perceptions.

My work has been exhibited worldwide in solo and group exhibitions; recent venues include the Honolulu Museum of Art; Blue Sky Gallery; Mira Forum; and the Exposure, Capture, and Head On Photo Festivals. Awards include multiple Hawaii State Art Collection Purchase Awards, the Julia Margaret Cameron Award, and the 2020 and 2022 LensCulture B&W Awards. *Gente di Fotografia, Black & White Magazine, SHOTS, Pf Photography Magazine, Don't Take Pictures*, and Lenscratch are among the media outlets where my work has been featured.

I was awarded an MFA in imaging and digital art from UMBC and a BA in studio art from the University of Hawaii at Manoa. I live and work in Honolulu, Hawaii.

1. What led you to attend your first portfolio-review event, and what stood out about the one you chose?

Living in the middle of the Pacific Ocean as I do, I am far removed from the contemporary art centers in the United States. Although I was getting some attention for my work, I knew I needed to do something else to get to the next level of exhibitions. I heard about reviews in an online photo group and started researching them. I spoke with my husband about the cost, and we decided it would be a worthy investment in my career, even if it was a financial stretch for us.

My first one was not a great experience. I was nervous, I didn't know anyone, people were very cliquey, and I kept getting asked why I "brought this work to a *photo* review?" Luckily, a couple of reviewers liked it and became good contacts for me. My first one was so expensive and unproductive that I thought about never doing one again, but people with better experiences than I steered me to some that they thought I might like better. Thankfully so, because I have participated in them productively every year since.

2. Please list, in order of importance, why you attend portfolio-review events.

- Make and maintain professional contacts
- Get feedback on my work(s) in progress
- Find opportunities for completed projects

3. How do you go about choosing which photography portfolio-review events you want to attend and which reviewers you want to meet?

I look at the overall cost I will incur to attend, including travel, meals, fee per review, the scale, whether virtual or in person, and if the current year's reviewers are those whom I am interested in discussing my particular body/bodies of work with. I must balance cost and benefit, as leaving Hawaii is very expensive. Yet even for virtual ones, I still have to decide if it is worth it for where I am with the work, who would see it, and if spending this money now would preclude me from doing something more substantial later. Also, I am shy in groups where I do not know many people, so I also look at whether it is one where I am likely to know other attendees and reviewers and the sort of activities that go along with the review.

For selecting reviewers, I keep an ongoing spreadsheet detailing info about the reviewers. I update that continually and make decisions based on whose feedback would most benefit me at any moment, based on what they say about themselves and the data I have collected vis-à-vis the work I am showing.

4. What is your average cost per year to attend portfolio-review events, including event registration fees, travel, print production, and leave-behinds? Do you have a budget for self-promotion? If not using this amount for attending portfolio-review events, what do you think would be an effective, comparable use of funds in promoting your work in a different way?

Yes, I have a budget for self-promotion. It varies yearly, depending on my net income from the previous year. I'm not comfortable sharing my actual costs. The process is quite expensive, given my remote location, and I justify my choices in this area as a worthy investment in myself and my career. I'm not sure there is a "comparable" use of funds for self-promotion. There are obvious ones, like letters, exhibition proposals, promotional print materials, and brochures, but nothing will ever be as effective as relationships built one-on-one over time.

Diana Nicholette Jeon

5. What are the standout pros and cons of virtual reviews versus in-person portfolio-review events?

The obvious pros of virtual ones are the dedicated, distraction-free time of a Zoom space and the lack of travel expenses. The pros of in-person reviews are the events and the time in the lobby or hallway seeing peers' work, meeting peers I knew from a distance or never met any other way, and the ability to socialize with some of the reviewers at the events associated with the review or festival.

6. For virtual reviews, please share your process for making a PDF version of your portfolio.

My process is the same as any time I have to make a PowerPoint of my work for an event or talk. I begin by looking at the assigned reviewers and the work I want to show them. Then I make a slide deck in Keynote with ten to twenty images per project I want to feature (I generally have different ones for different reviewers, and having multiples is good in case one bombs with someone). Finally, I make it look good, with layout and typography being of concern to me.

From the initial selection of images to the final typography, I pay attention to how what I give someone presents me and if it represents me, my work, and my style well. I aim to use my most evocative images to cause the reviewers to want to continue the conversation after the review event. It's not just images and sequencing, but also document design. Though typography is not intuitive for me, I work it through until the typography is kerned, well chosen, and fitting for the work I am showing. I add the project statements, my contact info, and my bio, and I export it as a PDF.

7. How many photographs do you typically include in each project and why? How many projects do you typically show at a portfolio review and why?

I include ten to twenty photos, depending on the project and what state it is in, vis-à-vis completion, at the time of the review and my reason(s) for including it. Given our short time together, it is challenging to get through the work and discussion if there is more than that and the reviewer is interested. It typically involves one run-through to look at as a whole and then a second for commentary.

8. How do you make your prints or presentation materials? Do you do anything special to your portfolio to enhance the narrative of your project?

In person, I make them look as close to the way they would show on the wall, sans framing, even if they are not the same size as the work I would exhibit. I use the same substrates and inks as if they were on exhibition.

I have seen some creative portfolio packaging from others and even envied it, but I have yet to attempt it myself. Given the logistics of getting mine from Hawaii to wherever, I stick with protective and simple to replace.

9. What is your opinion about attending reviews with a body of work in progress versus a completed project?

Both are valid for different reasons. It depends on the project and what I need to push it forward or get it seen. There is no one-size-fits-all in art.

10. What are your thoughts about "leave-behinds"? If you use them, please describe yours.

Leave-behinds can be essential to differentiating yourself. Sometimes they can be expensive, though, so you might have one type for people with genuine interest and another kind for the lesser-interest situations.

If a project still needs to be completed, mine is simply a postcard or brochure. For completed projects, I leave something that will directly remind the person of the work. For example, I made non-editioned mini-tin versions for my series "Nights as Inexorable as the Sea," a project in Altoids tins. I gave the reviewers a "party goodie bag" with the mini work, my card, and a postcard.

11. Do you make time to see the work of other artists? If so, have you noticed where you are in the spectrum of work, experience, and education? How did it make you feel?

Of course, at the in-person events, I have looked at the work of my peers. That is one of the essential benefits and highlights of in-person reviews versus virtual ones. I don't compare my work to others; grad school is over. Each person has to walk their own path with the talent, ideas, and skills they possess. There will always be work I wish I had made, work I like, work I dislike, and work I think is undercooked. My work will hold those same places in the minds of others. What is most important to me is to focus on my journey, grow, and do my best work.

12. After looking at the work of your fellow reviewees, did you seek out any connections or collaborations, or were you simply inspired by their work? If so, how did you approach the person?

No, I have not sought others I met for any collaborative work. Once, years later, I applied for an exhibition with a person I met at my first review (but our proposal was not selected). However, I have become friends with many people I met at the reviews, and I have several whose opinions I value for feedback while working on projects.

13. Has there been any auxiliary programming (lectures, workshops, photobook fair, portfolio walk, et cetera) at a portfolio-review event that was exceptionally memorable for you personally?

Not more so than the others I attended. I haven't had the luxury of attending one that also offered technical workshops.

14. Please share your most memorable portfolio-review experience (either positive or negative).

That would be my last review on my first day at my first review event ever. The reviewer spent fifteen of the twenty minutes having me answer questions about the work while they looked at the images back and forth. Then they pronounced, "You know, this work is all about 'Look what I can make Photoshop do.'" (The work never entered Photoshop.) They further stated, "If you want to make work about the experience of being a woman in America, then you need to research what that is like." In my mind, I was thinking, "*Are you freaking kidding me? What do you think my entire life experience has been?*" But I thanked them for being authentic in their feedback, then told them I didn't personally agree with it but was glad they felt comfortable sharing it. The next day, I heard from the two people I met during that review event that the same reviewer made them cry.

15. What is your favorite and least favorite part of portfolio-review events?

It's not that black and white for me; I can't say. Every review and situation is different vis à vis the state of my work at any given time.

16. What do you think is the ideal length of time for a review session—twenty, twenty-five, or thirty minutes?

Thirty minutes.

17. What are some positive outcomes you've experienced from attending portfolio-review events?

I've had my work featured in several publications, gotten exhibitions, including two solo exhibitions; made good friends; and made national and international contacts who have supported my work over the past seven years. I have found that the latter often led to additional opportunities later on. I've also had opportunities to teach classes or workshops come from those contacts, though I haven't taken anyone up on those; I feel as though I spent my time teaching earlier in my career and that it takes away time from me making work.

18 & 19. Have you met with a reviewer who was not a good fit for your work? If so, were you able to work around it and/or did you learn from the experience? Has a reviewer been disinterested in your work and clearly finished before the session was complete? If so, how did you handle the situation?

I'm combining this question and the following because I cannot separate them easily and don't want to be repetitive.

More than once, unfortunately. Sometimes the luck of the lottery draw does not pan out in one's favor. At in-person events, I have tried to trade or give my spot away totally, depending on how far away from the reviewer's preferences my work is. Occasionally, the person was interested in my work even though their description of their interests made it sound quite the opposite. I've learned that some people are more interested in hearing their own voice than yours. Some people have set ideas about "how work should be," and when yours does not fit their mold, they will give advice that is utterly out of place with your goals.

I've learned that I can say I disagree with an opinion and why—and still thank them for giving their honest thoughts. I've learned that some people are so self-involved and uninterested in assisting the reviewee, to the point of literally being insulting, that it is best to thank them for their time, end the meeting, and escape out the door because more time will not change the situation. Interestingly, you can overhear stories in a lobby and immediately identify which reviewer another photographer is talking about because they extend their poor behaviors to many, not just to you. We are customers, and the reviewer is supposed to be there to give us assistance of one sort or another. Most reviewers are adept at this and can provide helpful information to reviewees. But sometimes, someone cannot.

20. What are your thoughts about public portfolio walk-throughs, and have you ever made a sale this way? Do you have any pointers for new reviewees about the walk-throughs?

I like the portfolio walks. I have not made a sale, though many people have said they wanted to buy but did not follow through. My advice is to be yourself, answer questions, and be proud of what you bring to the table (pun not intended).

Diana Nicholette Jeon

21. How do you handle connecting—away from the review table—with a reviewer during an event?

I have yet to attempt this. The reviewers need space and downtime, just like we do; hence, I do not ask for reviews from people I was not assigned.

22. Have you ever gotten to the point with your work when you don't feel the need to attend portfolio reviews? If so, why?

No.

23. Please comment on relationships that have developed from these events.

The personal friends and professional connections I have made at these events have been instrumental for me, given my isolated location.

J

24. What is the biggest "no-no" for individuals attending portfolio-review events?

Do not overstay your time slot; you infringe on the time of the following person or the reviewer's free time.

25. What one piece of advice would you pass on to first-time reviewees?

It's impossible advice, but try not to be nervous. It's hard, but after a few outings, you will wonder why you ever were, so start humble—but confident. Remember, not everyone will appreciate your work, but if someone "gets" you and it, you are a winner, in my book.

David Johnson

David Johnson
Conway, South Carolina

My work has settled at the intersection of society, architecture, and the individual. Multiple bodies of work demonstrate ways in which space can affect personality and how individuals impact environments they occupy, even momentarily. Most projects are created in a long-term documentary approach—a visual investigation utilizing multiple image-making strategies. This reveals commonalities of everyday human-made environments. I'm interested in visually articulating questions that allow the viewer to consider the spaces they inhabit or briefly traverse—whether it be an office, an art museum, a campsite, or the human form. The hope is that viewers might become more self-aware.

In 2019, my first book, *Wig Heavier Than a Boot*—a collaborative project with poet Philip Matthews—was published by Kris Graves Projects; the following year, the project was featured at the Fotofest Biennial in Houston. In 2021, the University of Texas Press published my second book, *It Can Be This Way Always: Images from the Kerrville Folk Festival*. My work has been exhibited internationally in venues that include the Contemporary Art Museum in Saint Louis; the National Building Museum in Washington, DC; Rathaus in Stuttgart, Germany; Blue Star Contemporary in San Antonio; and, in the fall of 2023, Griffin Museum of Photography in Winchester, Massachusetts.

I'm an assistant professor of photography at Coastal Carolina University in Conway, South Carolina. My creative practice includes utilizing lens-based mediums, a passion for teaching photography, and curating events from exhibitions to dinner parties. A friend once stated in an article that "David is hungry for culture." It's an accurate sentiment. Exploring, and attempting to learn from, creative achievements—from the museum wall or bound into books to what's on the dinner plate and upon the stage—is the fuel for my life and art.

1. What led you to attend your first portfolio-review event, and what stood out about the one you chose?

Fresh out of graduate school I was hungry for a different kind of feedback and for new audiences, and I was eager to get out of my head to help understand what was on my studio wall. Portfolio reviews seemed to be a place that would offer conversations and assessment. The thing that resonated from that first review was the quickness of a twenty-minute conversation about my work. It was a shock to my newly minted MFA self. I'd been used to hours-long conversations, studio visits, and the critique that graduate school provides. I'm not sure I was ready to be that effective and efficient in explaining my project goals and the images.

2. Please list, in order of importance, why you attend portfolio-review events.

• To connect and build community and lasting relationships.
• To converse deeply about the work and what we are doing—and then laugh some.
• To learn about other photographers and their projects.
• To understand the framework of photography's professional and creative opportunities.

3. How do you go about choosing which photography portfolio-review events you want to attend and which reviewers you want to meet?

I rotate regions or cities, never repeating the same event every year. A new location may provide new reviewers and unique experiences or programming. While considering which review event I'd like to attend, the reviewer list is at the forefront of the decision-making process.

I prefer to find events with a mix of reviewers and organizations I know and others I don't. When selecting reviewers, I try to break it up into thirds: One-third are reviewers I know and have met with before, especially if it's been a few years in between meetings. The next reviewers I look for are those I've not met with, but whose organizations I think are a good fit for my work. The final set of reviewers would be people and organizations I'm unfamiliar with but whose programming or curatorial lens I'm curious about. Oftentimes this third set is the most exciting meeting. Just like Robert Adams said, "There are a lot of surprises in photography. If you are not interested in surprises, you should not be a photographer . . . at your best it teaches you to be open about new experiences." The same goes for portfolio reviews; I try to be open to where the conversations go.

Once I look at the where and who, I'll look at my budget, what I'm hoping for out of the event, and where my projects are; that is, between in progress and gallery ready. These aren't cheap events, so sometimes I'll have to choose between one big-ticket event for one year and then I'll do multiple smaller regional events the next year.

4. What is your average cost per year to attend portfolio-review events, including event registration fees, travel, print production, and leave-behinds? Do you have a budget for self-promotion? If not using this amount for attending portfolio-review events, what do you think would be an effective, comparable use of funds in promoting your work in a different way?

I stay between $4,000 and $6,000 annually for fees, travel, and hotel for reviews and conferences. This also depends on my exhibition costs for the year; I'll spend

David Johnson

less on portfolio reviews if my exhibition prep and shipping costs are higher in any given year.

I print my own working proofs for portfolio reviews (smaller prints) and studio critiques, so the printing budget is tied to my overall studio expenses, not solely portfolio reviews. But considering portfolio reviews and how prints get handled, I'll print the image a bit smaller on the sheet paper. Once the edges and corners show wear, I'll trim each sheet, making a smaller and cleaner border. This helps extend the life of a review print and keep the budget low.

I don't have a budget for physical leave-behinds. Are we still doing them? Haha.

Good business cards can be cheap to make, and, increasingly, I've seen people use digital business cards or QR codes.

5. What are the standout pros and cons of virtual reviews versus in-person portfolio-review events?

I prefer in-person reviews: Connecting and reading the conversation in person is more manageable for me. In-person reviews often provide room for surprises and an organic flow of dialogue. However, you have less control of the environment. Is the room loud? How close to other reviews are you? Is the temperature comfortable for you or the reviewer? Is there something distracting happening behind you that the reviewer is taking note of? This can be hard for someone who is neurodivergent; I have had to practice focusing techniques to stay present during portfolio reviews.

Virtual reviews provide an excellent opportunity to meet with reviewers from all over the world; those connections can be insightful and rewarding. It's lovely to have opportunities to meet new photo-community members from your home, keeping costs low, and it's more equitable for those who cannot travel. I find the virtual reviews are more focused during the conversation. Still, I have often found it more challenging to reconnect with those virtual reviewers after the event. It's also a hard transition point to have a twenty- to twenty-five-minute virtual meeting from my studio and then have to go do studio/house chores before the following virtual review.

For me, the travel helps set the intention for the review event. To do this, I'm going to an in-person review and having this type of conversation repeatedly. In-person review events afford the opportunity to unpack a meeting with another reviewee friend in real time or to open the door to continue the conversation at dinner or in the hallway.

6. For virtual reviews, please share your process for making a PDF version of your portfolio.

- Title page, with an image of the work or book cover, project name, and your name. Note contact information in the header or footer of each page.
- Context page, a short project statement, and other materials to help viewers set the intention for the document. For example, a map if the project is at a specific location, exhibition installation documentation, book spreads, or hyperlinks to videos.
- In the following pages, include fifteen to twenty single images on each page of the PDF, with title and year.
- After the image section, provide biographical info and the artist's statement.
- Follow with specific project information, edition information, previous exhibition sites, and possible programming you can provide; some thumbnail images of the work can help so your viewer doesn't have to scroll back to the image section.

7. How many photographs do you typically include in each project and why? How many projects do you typically show at a portfolio review and why?

I start with ten intro images and have another ten to fifteen images to keep the conversation going if the reviewer shows interest in the project. Over thirty prints total can be overwhelming for me to keep organized and pack up quickly once my time is over. I will likely have another eager artist coming right after me, and I don't pack my prints during their time; it throws the rhythm off for the next review.

I'll have at least two projects available, and sometimes a third, depending on who the reviewer is and what I think their organization would be interested in. Generally, one project is exhibition ready, and the other is in progress.

Having one project at the table seems risky. If the project isn't for the reviewer, your time and conversation might not be as fruitful. A secondary project may help the reviewer understand your creative practice, interests, and visual language. Allowing space for a comparison between a completed project versus an in-progress one can inform the reviewer about your decision-making process and the entirety of your practice. It will enable the reviewer to help see how to conclude the in-progress project.

8. How do you make your prints or presentation materials? Do you do anything special to your portfolio to enhance the narrative of your project?

I print at a home studio with an Epson printer on 11" × 14", 11" × 17", or 16" × 20" museum-quality sheet paper. I'll wrap each body of work into its own folio of glassine paper to protect it and keep it organized. I'll number each print on

David Johnson

the back corner of each sheet. This helps reorder the photos quickly in between review sessions. The order never stays intact during a review; I let the reviewer cycle through the prints as they see fit after I introduce the work.

I include a few prints portraying the image-making process (depending on the importance) and exhibition documentation within the selected portfolio; this can be helpful. The reviewer can envision the final outcomes in their space, and these prints also showcase my abilities to finish a project with professional craft and exhibitions in mind.

I do not do anything special. I prefer to spend the time and resources on making the best prints I can and let that speak to my abilities in the craft. I've seen some artists create very elaborate and beautiful portfolio boxes. These are ideally for reviewers managing a special collection in which you hope to get your work placed. However, most reviewers are not at collecting institutions or may need organizational help to get the entire box. Handmade portfolio boxes can be expensive and heavy. I've witnessed artists struggle to efficiently get the prints in and out of particular containers.

J

9. What is your opinion about attending reviews with a body of work in progress versus a completed project?

I like to have both. Most reviewers respond well to finished bodies of work but may have little to say if it's not a good fit for their organization. In-progress projects open the door for unexpected conversations, feedback, and planting the seed for future opportunities. Having a well-completed project is helpful in seeing that an artist can finish a project, and an in-progress project informs the reviewer of where the artist is headed.

Suppose we are building relationships with the reviewer. In that case, allowing your entire creative self—where the work has been and where the work is going—is ultimately helpful. One note about in-progress projects: make sure it has a strong, thoughtful edit, and have predetermined questions for each reviewer.

10. What are your thoughts about "leave-behinds"? If you use them, please describe yours.

I don't care for leave-behinds; it seems like they create lots of clutter and can get discarded at the end of the review session.

But my most noteworthy leave-behind does not have anything to do with any of my artwork. It's a postcard with a scanned Polaroid with a person giving the middle finger; (most) reviewers have found it funny, and I have given away all these postcards multiple times. Has this postcard led to an exhibition or another opportunity? Probably not. I find much more value in a well-designed and coherent PDF sent as an email later.

11. Do you make time to see the work of other artists? If so, have you noticed where you are in the spectrum of work, experience, and education? How did it make you feel?

The opportunity to view work from other artists is one of the more exciting aspects of the in-person portfolio-review event. The side conversations in the waiting room and the informal portfolio reviews between artists provide additional insights and help unpack what was said during a discussion at the table. Several reviewee-to-reviewee conversations have led to exhibitions, introductions, and other opportunities. I've curated exhibitions with several peer artists I met during portfolio reviews. Not to mention the lifelong friendships that can grow from this shared experience. I've traveled to other cities, countries, and art fairs with other portfolio-review friends; attended their weddings; and traded artwork. I often ask around to see who else is attending which future events.

I enjoy learning the unique paths and ways each artist takes to find photography and then a portfolio-review event. Often, there are a diverse set of life courses—from career visual artists, to academics, to commercial photographers with fine-art projects, to individuals navigating photography as a second or third career, to just people with a passion.

I was much younger than most attendees when I started doing portfolio-review events. Still, I had two art-related degrees and several years of teaching experience. In those first few portfolio-review events, I talked to artists new to the scene but much more my senior. I'd help them navigate the more complicated discussion they had at the table from earlier in the day, provide historical or contemporary context, give some suggestions on print order, or explain why a reviewer may suggest one thing or another; it was a different kind of teaching for me.

Now that I know more artists in the field, these informal conversations are more robust, like extended studio visits with old friends. The table conversation is twenty or twenty-five minutes, but the informal discussions with peer groups gathered in lobbies and hotel rooms can last hours. At some portfolio reviews, I'll bring a new body of work ready for knowledgeable feedback to show a friend and not show it to a reviewer at the table.

12. After looking at the work of your fellow reviewees, did you seek out any connections or collaborations, or were you simply inspired by their work? If so, how did you approach the person?

All the above. If it is inspired work, after review events I'll come home and share with my classes and students what I've learned and which new artists have exciting work. We'll spend an entire day diving into the artist's website and PDF portfolios. Hopefully, my excitement in meeting and sharing these new artists will carry over

David Johnson

to my students—instilling a sense that this practice requires continual research, looking at others' work, and building peer relationships. Students often respond well to this exercise; it makes the art world more accessible for a young person.

As mentioned previously, I've curated exhibitions with artists I've met at portfolio-review events. I've asked artists to present in my classroom and sought out workshops and collaborations. Generally, reaching out via email or social media has worked.

13. Has there been any auxiliary programming (lectures, workshops, photobook fair, portfolio walk, et cetera) at a portfolio-review event that was exceptionally memorable for you personally?

I enjoy these events, and when extra programming is available, it often allows artists to meet other reviewers who are not scheduled to meet them and other artists you have not yet crossed paths with. Many times, these events are away from the host site, so I can stretch my legs, see another part of the city, and play the cards right to get the bus driver to drop me off at a restaurant or bar with newfound friends.

That's the most memorable moment—following an off-site gallery opening with a bus full of hungry reviewers and reviewees. We convinced the bus driver to take us to a restaurant instead of the hotel, and, thankfully, they patiently waited while the entire group ate. This unplanned "hijacking" was not scheduled and probably cost the organization a little extra, but the whole group benefited from the camaraderie of that shared evening; the laughter back to the hotel was riotous.

J

14. Please share your most memorable portfolio-review experience (either positive or negative).

A memorable moment at the table was during my first big portfolio-review event. In my portfolio box are two distinctly different bodies of work in subject, form, and content. I met a reviewer whose initial demeanor was kindhearted, like a doting grandparent. Personal introductions flowed easily, and some intentions were set for our twenty minutes.

I introduced the first project, cycling through a dozen prints. As I prepared to ask my planned questions, the reviewer quickly requested to see the second body of work. After the second introduction, the reviewer starts quietly looking and digging through both sets of prints simultaneously. That was a first for the day. With an increased rhythm, the reviewer started reorganizing both bodies of work together, setting some photographs aside, and instantly building different stacks. Some prints were now upside down, flipped over, and caddywhompus across the table. I witnessed a voracious type of looking, cycling back and forth swiftly between all my prints. I watched this curation of sorts in silence for a few minutes, hoping that some sense of came from it.

Then a rapid succession of questions, insights, and mostly positive comments came: "This is interesting, why did you do this, this here works better than that there, have you thought about . . . . David, these two images are completely different; why?"

"Umm, they're from two different bodies of work and have different intentions. So, I wanted to . . . ."

"Right, okay, on we go."

At the five-minute warning, I looked down. Prints spread across the table and stacked on my portfolio box's top and bottom, and some photos had flown onto the floor behind the reviewer's chair. The reviewer looked up with glasses now perched at the tip of the nose, with arms raised and with multiple prints in both hands. And they loudly declared in a proper accent, "David, you are schizophrenic in your photography, and many of these are wonderful photos."

A bit speechless, I chose to take it as a compliment and said, "Thank you." The reviewer looked down and then acknowledged, "I may have reorganized your portfolio a little bit." We both laughed.

It was an early lesson on embracing whatever happens at the table and on not getting stuck with the order of things—and it was a bit of an affirmation. I'm an artist who makes different bodies of works, concerned with attempting various visual forms and subjects, depending on the concept. I'm okay with that. Some may be vexed by it, and that's okay, too.

15. What is your favorite and least favorite part of portfolio-review events?

My least favorite—ego. I've witnessed artists be nasty to another artist, literally stepping over someone to attempt to talk to or meet a desired curator. I've seen artists complain and berate volunteer staff about things beyond the organization's control. I've watched reviewers disregard reviewees disdainfully because their project isn't quite "there," or they might not be as ready as another artist is. I've watched reviewees demand an unscheduled meeting and respond negatively when the reviewers state they don't have the capacity to meet right then.

These events are intense: money, work, emotion, and time have gone into preparing, and everyone has an agenda and goals. I try to remember that introspection and patience can go a long way while at a portfolio review. Sometimes I'm good at remembering that; other times, I could be better. I take a breath and know I can be more present for my colleagues knowing I have no idea how the previous meeting went or what may be happening for the human across the table from me.

David Johnson

Favorite—the people and relationships. The photography portfolio review is viewed as a unique event in the larger art world. Most of my academic colleagues working in other mediums are impressed and envious that the photography community is accessible between artists and industry professionals. I've developed great friendships and working relationships with many of the individuals, both reviewers and reviewees, I've met. I do not do these events solely for another line on my CV. I do this because I want to be a better photographer and artist. I can build upon my creative self and my photos by having meaningful and lasting conversations about my work; these events put you in front of people who want to have meaningful conversations.

16. What do you think is the ideal length of time for a review session—twenty, twenty-five, or thirty minutes?

I prefer a twenty-five-minute review with a five-minute break in between each meeting. A five-minute break is a huge help; everyone needs space and time to process. I've had some reviews not start well because the reviewers were still clearly processing the prior conversation. Sometimes it's because they were blown away by a great project, but more often, the previous artist was either unprepared or had unrealistic expectations for the conversation. I know this because it was expressed to me by the reviewer or witnessed by me in the final exchange.

Twenty-minute reviews are so quick, and when you land back-to-back reviews, it becomes intense. The "getting to know you" introductions are cut short in favor of the sprint to show and explain the work, hoping that enough time is available for the reviewer's feedback. By the time the conversation gets into the work, the five-minute warning bell rings, and you're packing up prints and trying to trade contact information or work out the next steps.

Thirty-minute reviews drag on. If you can't get to the heart of what's in the box in a few minutes, it's time to rethink your delivery. It could be a flop and a waste of time if the reviewer is not a good match. I've seen more artists walk away, disappointed, from the tables before the five-minute warning during a thirty-minute review than longer reviews; that's not a great look for anyone.

Twenty-five minutes is the sweet spot.

17. What are some positive outcomes you've experienced from attending portfolio-review events?

I tell my students that 90 percent of my CV is because I had an opportunity to get a coffee or drink with someone and that meeting a new colleague whom you are sympatico with is one of the greatest joys in our field. Often, it feels like portfolio reviews are speed dating—a professional speed dating. But these micro-

J

meetings can and have led to tremendous outcomes. Meeting outstanding people is a positive gift a review event can provide.

On the tangible side, I've met future editors, consultants, and curators who have helped me navigate the publication of my work, place my work in exhibitions, and write about my work. Most of these items were years in the making after the initial review. My advice is to keep in touch with those reviewers you feel connected to.

It's rare, but it has happened—getting an exhibition or publication offer at the table. This is a shocking moment, a rush. Be grateful and optimistic, but realistic, and follow up, and ensure it can happen; you never know what's happening within an organization.

18. Have you met with a reviewer who was not a good fit for your work? If so, were you able to work around it and/or did you learn from the experience?

In every review event, I've met reviewers who are not a great fit for various reasons. I take it with a grain of salt and know there is a lesson somewhere and possibly a future conversation down the line. I hope the reviewer will be straightforward, tell me it's not a good fit, and explain further, if they are generous. Before the review goes sideways, or as I sense disinterest building, I bring up three or four questions.

- "If this work is not a good fit with [insert organization name], do you have any suggestions on where this work might fit?"
- "Can you list some examples on where you see the work progressing or who I should be looking at as an influence?"
- "You mentioned being interested in this one photograph; can you elaborate on why it works for you?"
- "I'd like to hear more about the projects you're working on."

The answers to the first three questions can better explain how they perceive my prints and delivery. The last question is for my personal Rolodex; I may have an artist friend who is a better fit for the reviewer's project and therefore I may ask to make the introduction.

19. Has a reviewer been disinterested in your work and clearly finished before the session was complete? If so, how did you handle the situation?

I don't recall leaving the table before the end of a review—because of the follow-up questions I ask. If those do not extend the conversation for the rest of the review time, I ask if they are done or want to provide any further insights. If they are done and have nothing else to say, I thank them for their time and go find a friend to vent to for a minute, then great ready for the following review.

20. What are your thoughts about public portfolio walk-throughs, and have you ever made a sale this way? Do you have any pointers for new reviewees about the walk-throughs?

I have mixed feelings about public portfolio reviews. It's a lot of time and energy following a generally long day of reviews. Still, it provides an excellent opportunity for community engagement with the participating artists. Another positive is the possibility of picking up an additional review. I may not have gotten a reviewer I wanted; if the desired reviewer swings by my table, I'll introduce myself and ask them if they would be willing to meet the next day. I enjoy seeing the work of other artists, and I've often opted to attend portfolio walk-throughs as just an observer.

J

I've had interested collectors make offers or request a discount on prints, but sales are rarely concluded. Selling my photobooks is a better fit for me. Most community members like the price point and enjoy getting a book signing at the table.

Suppose you are new to the public portfolio walk-through; in that case, ensure your name, QR code, or takeaways are visible and available. Do not leave a stack of prints out with no context. Make eye contact, say hello, and ask the person across the table a question. I invite the public to, with some instruction, sort through my prints, or I will continuously rotate through the photos. I suggest you start talking about your work to whomever; people will be more engaged and will begin to gather if you are talking about the work. Once a few people are at the table, they seem more willing to ask questions. Be mindful that your elevator speech should be slightly different and shorter for this audience; you'll sound like a broken record, but it's better than standing there in silence.

Also, dance (a little); it gets the blood flowing, and joy can be contagious. This should be fun.

21. How do you handle connecting—away from the review table—with a reviewer during an event?

If you have met with them, say hello and be kind; they're people too, and they may be just as tired as you. A reintroduction might be needed. Remember, reviewers are often meeting eight, ten, or twelve artists per day.

If you have not met them, ask a friend who knows them for an introduction. Don't walk up and interrupt a conversation already underway. Just be cool, don't sweat it; most reviewers are there to meet people as well.

22. Have you ever gotten to the point with your work when you don't feel the need to attend portfolio reviews? If so, why?

Yes. It depends on where specific projects are and who's reviewing at a particular event. Suppose the project is complete and exhibition ready. In that case, it has a shorter portfolio-review shelf life, plus many reviewers have already seen the work. If I've established relationships with most of the reviewers at an event, I won't attend and will reach out individually.

I like to continue to attend portfolio reviews with new work. As mentioned above, many of my projects take on different subject matter, form, and content. I find it helpful to introduce a new body of work in person. Most reviewers enjoy seeing follow-ups as projects progress or get finalized.

23. Please comment on relationships that have developed from attending portfolio-review events.

We are participating in a very tiny part of the art world and in a small part of the photography world. There are overlaps, but I've never been around such a concentration of like-minded individuals with similar desires and goals. These relationships can grow into something akin to camp friendships, bandmates, or teammates—a collection of great humans I don't get to see often enough. Still, I can reach out to people comfortable with me to ask questions, seek advice, and make introductions. Some of my closest friends are people I've met at portfolio reviews, both reviewers and reviewees. I've found curators and editors I deeply trust with my work and words; we would never have crossed paths without the random draw in the portfolio-review lottery.

For example, I'm writing this while traveling for a new project. Looking at my calendar and contacts here, most people I'm meeting, joining for dinner, seeing exhibitions with, or photographing with are the same great people I've met at portfolio reviews. How cool is that? I can travel from city to city and have readymade friends to reach out to and break bread with, all because I put myself out there by attending a portfolio-review event. I am grateful for this community.

24. What is the biggest "no-no" for individuals attending portfolio-review events?

- Do not have too many prints (no more than thirty); make sure they are accessible and not on an iPad.
- Do not make larger prints; sizes bigger than 16" × 20" are hard to manage at the table. If the scale is essential to your practice, make a print showing the installation of the work as an illustration of the scale in a gallery space.

David Johnson

- Do not assume you will get a solo show or book deal offer at the table.
- Overall, just do not assume.

25. What one piece of advice would you pass on to first-time reviewees?

- Do your research on who you want to talk to and why. Always ask if your work is really a good fit for their organization.
- Practice! Practice taking your prints out of the box. Practice your elevator speech.
- Practice answering possible questions. Practice patience and being present.
- Practice with someone you trust to provide honest feedback. Seek out industry professionals and artists you respect to practice with and ask for feedback from.
- Know your work, and practice talking about the nuts and bolts, not just the specific subject or concept. You will be asked about material choices, edition size, price points, and shipping methods.
- Protect your heart with open ears. Do not take the criticism personally; take it with a grain of salt, but be willing to learn from it. If multiple reviewers comment similarly about your project, try to hear it because they are probably right.
- Reviewers also take time away from their lives, jobs, and families to meet and help you. Be patient, be kind, be helpful, and be professional. If they don't get it or don't respond well to your projects, that's okay. There is something very liberating when someone states that this work is not for them; your work can't be, nor should be, for everyone. This small rejection should help you better understand your audience and why the work resonates with them.
- Our household has a celebratory rap jingle when a new professional opportunity presents itself. My wife and I will say, "Put another line on the CV. Yo!" Yes, portfolio reviews can lead to exhibitions and publications, often the primary goal or focus for attending such an event. This should not be the case; if you go to a review only to get a gallery or book deal, you will most likely be disappointed and feel like you've wasted resources. Go to portfolio reviews with an open mind, and know that you will meet good people who are willing to help your path as an artist.
- I've never gotten an offer for book deals at the table, but I've met all the people who have helped me secure book deals at review events. Let your portfolio-review event be about understanding your practice and building sustainable relationships. If you do that, you'll get to put another line on the CV for years to come. It is not just about a twenty-minute conversation: it's about starting and maintaining the long game that is your art career.
- Remember to have fun; there is nothing like a portfolio-review event.

J

Hillary Johnson

Hillary Johnson

Chicago, Illinois

I worked for a few decades in photojournalism, long-form documentary work, and, later, advertising. During an extended hiatus from photography, I got my MFA in creative writing and spent a lot of time teaching writing in colleges and other settings but missed photography terribly. I knew I wanted to come back to it but wanted to do it in a whole new way.

These days I say I'm a slow photographer. I work mainly with large- and medium-format cameras, wet-plate collodion, paper negatives, and film, though I do use my digital Leica as well. The materiality and ritual aspects of process are critically important to me. I love to make artist books, work with handmade papers, and create immersive installations. I'm excited by the possibilities of combining nineteenth-century photographic technology with that of the twenty-first century.

I'm an MFA candidate in the Photography Department at Columbia College Chicago and a curatorial and education assistant at the Museum of Contemporary Photography. I'm interested in the tension between heartache and beauty; grief and joy; and longing and belonging that underpin the human condition. My work and research have their roots in twin threads of anxiety—a global cultural anxiety that developed during the Industrial Age in the mid-1800s, expanding exponentially in the Anthropocene era as our complicity in climate change was revealed, as well as my own quite personal existential concerns. My work engages the body in the process of coming to know a place through slow walking and mindful observation. My photographs of the landscape and my portraiture examine drastic upheavals that transform or destroy delicate beauty in both the environment and humankind. I believe that photography can be part of an expansive exploration of empathy, consciousness, and connection for positive social and cultural change.

1. What led you to attend your first portfolio-review event, and what stood out about the one you chose?

Returning to photography after so long away from it, I felt quite isolated. I didn't know anything about the photo community in the Midwest. When I was coming up in photography, portfolio reviews didn't exist. You just went to editors and showed them your book. I knew I needed to get feedback and guidance to help me develop. I was so hungry for that and for the community. When I learned about reviews and the whole process, I signed up for the next one that was available. I didn't really know what to expect, so I went in with zero expectations. I was honestly just happy to be in the room.

Lord, that first review was a hot mess in some ways. My work was all over the place. But people were so kind and so helpful, it really blew my mind.

What stood out was that I learned that there was a massive photo community right there for me to join. Everyone was really supportive, which felt like manna from heaven. I was also impressed at the diversity of reviewers, including those from museums, galleries, universities, different kinds of publications and curators, editors—people who could offer solid expertise and provide connections and, most important, relationships in an expansive, generous national photo community.

2. Please list, in order of importance, why you attend portfolio review events.

- Meet and initiate relationships with aligned reviewers, editors, curators, and publishers.
- Receive critical feedback and insight on my work from reviewers (especially now, outside my MFA program bubble).
- Meet other photographers to build relationships and foster community.
- Share work, knowledge, and opportunities with other photographers.
- Learn about opportunities for exhibition, publishing, funding, and teaching.

3. How do you go about choosing which photography portfolio-review events you want to attend and which reviewers you want to meet?

I think carefully about what I need or want to receive, given where I'm at for a particular body of work or other professional goals I may have. Different reviews have specific areas of focus, so I look at what that is for each one and consider how aligned it is to me and my work at the time.

When it comes to the reviewers, I do really deep research. I visit their websites and social-media accounts and look at what projects they've done. For curators, I look at their career paths, where they have been and whose work they've shown, and what research they've done, not only so I can sound like I know about them, but also to see if it makes any sense for us to talk to each other. I'm looking for shared interests or some kind of reasonable linkage to ground us. I want to love what they do and be able to speak to that cogently.

For book publishers, I look at what they've published and who the photographers they publish are. How do they do business? Is it a model that I like or not? Do they seem like nice people?

I don't want to waste someone's time if I get the feeling that there's no resonance. Overall, I really want to feel clear as to whether our interests are aligned or not. I also look at relationships—who knows who—and maybe sometimes I find that we know someone in common, and that can be really helpful for initiating a relationship and celebrating how small the world really is.

Hillary Johnson

4. What is your average cost per year to attend portfolio-review events, including event registration fees, travel, print production, and leave-behinds? Do you have a budget for self-promotion? If not using this amount for attending portfolio-review events, what do you think would be an effective, comparable use of funds in promoting your work in a different way?

I'm planning a budget for next year and moving forward after graduate school. Right now, as a grad student, I'm extremely fortunate to have access to financial support for attending reviews and conferences. My budget for leave-behinds is fairly simple because I love making small prints with hand-written notes on the back, along with a business card. My cards always have a photo on one side and my contact info on the other. Frequently, I have multiple cards—one for each project so I can give someone a very specific card at the end of the review. I like to leave reviewers with something unique, handmade, and personal. I know reviewers see a lot of photographers, so I try to leave them with something memorable. My budget for self-promotion includes the costs for making prints and business cards, or if I decide to create something else special to leave behind, and my website. I've also created experiences that I invite potential collectors, gallerists, and others to so they might experience my work in a highly curated way in order to shape their experience just the way I want.

J

5. What are the standout pros and cons of virtual reviews versus in-person portfolio-review events?

I've never attended a virtual review, so I can't really speak to this, except for what I've heard from friends and colleagues. So, I'll let them speak for themselves.

A potential con of virtual reviews may be that in the case of work that depends so much on in-person experience of the material qualities, a lot can be lost on screen and with a PDF. Obviously, a benefit is that we can bridge huge distances with virtual events, but there's something quite special about sitting across the table from someone and sharing actual objects, prints, et cetera.

6. For virtual reviews, please share your process for making a PDF version of your portfolio.

I have created a PDF for submissions for grants. I use Photoshop and drop the images in a sequence in which I would have shown them in person, one at a time. I include a list at the end of the document with titles and a statement or other supporting text. I am terrible at remembering tech details for such things, so I keep a file in my hard drive with specifics on how to do it. I asked people who know such things and got good advice, so I didn't waste a lot of time fiddling about. I try to repay the favor of help in meaningful ways.

7. How many photographs do you typically include in each project and why? How many projects do you typically show at a portfolio review and why?

I've been told the maximum number of prints to show in a review is twenty. Some advise bringing only one project to avoid confusion for the reviewer. I trust my intuition in the moment. Frequently a good reviewer will ask, "Do you have anything else?" because they know that sometimes the best work is that work you might not be inclined to show at first, but because you love it so much, it says a lot more about who you are as a photographer. A good reviewer will want to get to know you and not just look at your prints. I always have something to present as the main project, but I also have at least one and sometimes two other projects on hand and ready to go, especially since in my practice of making books and other special objects, my presentations aren't a simple "let's flip through the prints" experience. I think it's important to have work that is really close to my heart and shows who I am in a deep and honest way.

8. How do you make your prints or presentation materials? Do you do anything special to your portfolio to enhance the narrative of your project?

I always make my prints myself, whether digital or darkroom prints. I will sometimes include a text page that I strive to make easily readable and clear. Depending on what I'm showing, I will use a different kind of portfolio or presentation vessel. In 2023 I showed an assortment of interlinked handmade books. I brought them to reviews in a special case and had a specific order of presentation, which I hope worked to build a clear narrative and allow my reviewers to enjoy the work through a diversity of experiences that allowed the work to unfold its meaning, with multiple ways in.

I think of the portfolio as being part of the presentation of the work and am aware of how it can impact the experience for the reviewer. Because I like to create installations of my work that create experiences for viewers, I try to do that for my reviewers, too, both for their pleasure and to convey the extent of my thinking about the work. I want them to think, "Wow, not just a bunch of pictures, but a fully developed, nuanced concept, too."

9. What is your opinion about attending reviews with a body of work in progress versus a completed project?

I have done both and feel that it's really important to fully know what I want from the experience. What kind of feedback I want and the best time to seek it are important questions. It can be easy to feel pressured to go when I see other people flocking to an event, but sometimes maybe it's better to wait and know

Hillary Johnson

when I and the work are ready for a larger audience. I always do a gut check and trust that.

I don't have hard-and-fast rules. My process is quite personal and intuitive, but I do always want to show up ready internally. What I mean is that, since I never know how someone will respond to work, I need to feel confident and ready to show it. If I feel like the work really needs more time to sit before being exposed to criticism, then I listen to that and stay home or show something else. New work can be like a baby bird. I don't want to force flight too early.

On the other hand, if there are reviewers who I know are amazing at supporting a project in early stages, then I would definitely seek those people out for a review. Receiving wise counsel from a reviewer who really gets my work and wants to see me succeed is an incredible blessing. The right person might have an idea that sends the work in a magical new direction I would never have imagined.

With a totally complete project, my goals would be quite different, and, honestly, that is not a milestone I've yet crossed. I've gone in very raw, like at my first review, and more polished after a year of grad school. I do have a project that is ongoing and global, so it's something to think about bringing forward as complete in a certain way, such as ready for exhibition or ready for a book publication, which I will be doing at some point. Right now, it's still cooking. I'll wait and see what tips the scale for reviews.

10. What are your thoughts about "leave-behinds"? If you use them, please describe yours.

I think leave-behinds are essential. I want to give someone something they will love and put where they can see it each day, at least for a while, because they really love it. I make my own small handmade prints to leave behind. Once, I handed out prints and small stones from the place in which the photos were made. I usually have a variety of unique prints, and I fan them out, like a tarot card reading, and ask, "Which one grabs your attention?" And those answers are pure gold. Sometimes, I will go in with something a little extra special and just have it on hand to offer if it feels aligned.

11. Do you make time to see the work of other artists? If so, have you noticed where you are in the spectrum of work, experience, and education? How did it make you feel?

Of course! It's so important to see the work of other artists. They are not the competition, they are the community—and I love to see what they are doing and talk about it. I love to see work by other artists at various stages of career development because there is always so much to learn. If I can offer some support, as I received, then I'm happy to pay that kindness forward. I feel so inspired seeing the work, and even more so after those delicious conversations. I want to know how people a few years ahead of me—five years, ten years ahead—are doing. That is fantastic information, and to have a chance to see their work and talk is so important to me.

12. After looking at the work of your fellow reviewees, did you seek out any connections or collaborations, or were you simply inspired by their work? If so, how did you approach the person?

Yes, I absolutely do. This is one of the reasons I love in-person events. There's time to see work and hang out and really get to know each other and have those long wandering conversations that go everywhere. I realize that relationships take time to develop. Getting to see each other over time at reviews is like a big reunion all the time.

I am an introvert so I'm shy, but this is my life's work, so I push past my hesitation and just say hello. I usually start by introducing myself and saying what it is I love about the work. I've also trained myself to stand there and wait if someone is really getting a lot of attention. Maybe we won't talk right then, but later I might ask to connect via email or something.

13. Has there been any auxiliary programming (lectures, workshops, photobook fair, portfolio walk, et cetera) at a portfolio-review event that was exceptionally memorable for you personally?

I love a good lecture! Sometimes I hear just the words I need, which is so inspiring. Hearing about the journey of others who came before is like a good meal. Workshops have been too expensive in the past, so they are on my list to attend in the future.

14. Please share your most memorable portfolio-review experience (either positive or negative).

At my very first review ever, someone took the time to really talk to me and saw my potential. That led to many magical things—retreats and connections that still blow my mind, and all of that eventually became grad school at the one place I really wanted to study. That review and that reviewer changed my life in ways I could not have imagined.

Hillary Johnson

15. What is your favorite and least favorite part of portfolio-review events?

Favorite: when my work has been well received, and I feel so validated and beautifully challenged to make it better, and opportunities flow, and friends are seen and new ones are made. *The best.*
Least favorite: the cost. I realize how much I have to plan for travel, fees, lodging, et cetera. It's a major investment.

16. What do you think is the ideal length of time for a review session—twenty, twenty-five, or thirty minutes?

I've only experienced the twenty-minute review, and when things are going well, it never feels like enough time. I've had reviewers (when I'm last before a break) sit longer and talk, which is amazing. I feel like thirty would really allow for an arc: opening, viewing and talking, and some closure.

J

17. What are some positive outcomes you've experienced from attending portfolio-review events?

I've made great new friends. I've received invitations to stay in contact, show my work, and attend other events, all of which helped me grow. Relationships have been initiated that started professionally but led to real friendships and created new community connections. I think the outcomes have to be seen as a long game.

18. Have you met with a reviewer who was not a good fit for your work? If so, were you able to work around it and/or did you learn from the experience?

I learned what I could do to make my presentation better and more aligned the next time. I asked a lot of questions about what they wanted, what they were interested in, and how their process works. So, the review went well in that I learned a lot and left on a good note with that reviewer. I take everything as feedback with open curiosity.

19. Has a reviewer been disinterested in your work and clearly finished before the session was complete? If so, how did you handle the situation?

This really only happened one time. It was a real challenge. The reviewer was clearly not a fan. They were pretty aggressive in their challenges of my work, but I used the opportunity to find out why and hear them out, which felt like a growth experience. Rather than retreating with my tail between my legs, I challenged them to explain and challenged myself to sit there and listen. I learned I could stay open and not take it personally. This was about the work, not my own value as a human being. And that choice felt really sovereign.

20. What are your thoughts about public portfolio walk-throughs, and have you ever made a sale this way? Do you have any pointers for new reviewees about the walk-throughs?

[No response.]

21. How do you handle connecting—away from the review table—with a reviewer during an event?

I remember the manners I was taught growing up. I don't interrupt if someone is in the middle of something. I say hello and ask to introduce myself and if this is a good time. Usually, I will have a card on hand to offer. I have in mind clearly what I want to say or ask. (The introvert needs focus and direction!) I really take their lead energetically—one of the benefits of being an empath. If the moment is not good, I'll ask for a future time to chat if they have time and inclination. People are so nice and generous—in my experience.

22. Have you ever gotten to the point with your work when you don't feel the need to attend portfolio reviews? If so, why?

No. I feel like there is always something to learn. I know people whose work I love and who have years of experience, and they will sometimes seek out reviews even in mid- and later career stages, especially with new work that is significantly different from what people have come to expect from them.

23. Please comment on relationships that have developed from attending portfolio-review events.

The relationships are an essential part of the foundation of everything I'm doing now. I feel like one way to describe it is like creating the scaffolding or underlying supports for all the work, both in terms of personal support (the people who cheer me on) and in who I can give back to in a relationship based on reciprocity— the giving and receiving of gifts.

Hillary Johnson

24. What is the biggest "no-no" for individuals attending portfolio-review events?

Don't overtalk your reviewer. Listen.

25. What one piece of advice would you pass on to first-time reviewees?

Do your research so you know who is on the other side of the table, and be polite. It's a small world.

J

Ville Kansanen

Ville Kansanen

Martinez, California

My name is Ville Kansanen, I'm a Finnish multidisciplinary (or transdisciplinary) artist living and working in California. I work somewhere in the margins of digital photography, land art, installation art, and sculpture. I suppose you could say that I'm between emerging and midcareer. I've had a couple of solo shows, and my work was published as a monograph in 2021.

1. What led you to attend your first portfolio-review event, and what stood out about the one you chose?

Back in 2014, an artist/curator friend told me that they are great avenues for emerging photographers. She said that the Santa Fe review was the best one, so I applied and went in 2015.

K

2. Please list, in order of importance, why you attend portfolio-review events.

To foster relationships, to find new opportunities, to get professional advice, to get feedback for my practice.

3. How do you go about choosing which photography portfolio-review events you want to attend and which reviewers you want to meet?

I try to weigh costs with potential benefits. Smaller reviews are better than larger ones because you have more opportunities to connect and stand out. That said, I don't think it makes sense to go to a review that is very geographically specific in a market that is far away from you, or if the reviewers are limited in terms of their interests. My work is not political, so that always narrows the reviewers I choose—especially in the United States, where artists' identities are emphasized more. These days I try to pick reviewers based on the potential for tangible opportunities.

4. What is your average cost per year to attend portfolio-review events, including event registration fees, travel, print production, and leave-behinds? Do you have a budget for self-promotion? If not using this amount for attending portfolio-review events, what do you think would be an effective, comparable use of funds in promoting your work in a different way?

Approximately $2,000 to $4,000—but I make new work very slowly, so I do as many as I can once a series is completed. Otherwise, I do them here and there, and the costs are much lower. I don't have a budget for self-promotion. Currently I try to use Instagram more effectively, partly to grow an audience but mostly to keep existing connections interested in my work. If I were to spend the money elsewhere, it would go into making new work.

5. What are the standout pros and cons of virtual reviews versus in-person portfolio-review events?

Virtual reviews are fantastic because you can create a rich presentation of your work. Using video, sound, behind-the-scenes imagery, sketches, and animations can make a very strong impression on reviewers. Also, it allows you to construct a coherent script to present your work.

6. For virtual reviews, please share your process for making a PDF version of your portfolio.

I use PowerPoint for virtual reviews. I start with the sequencing I've determined for the printed version of my portfolio. My introduction includes behind-the-scenes images and video; from there I move into some conceptual sketches; and then, if appropriate, I'll present some background for the series with reference images, et cetera. After that, I present the actual body of work.

7. How many photographs do you typically include in each project and why? How many projects do you typically show at a portfolio review and why?

I try to keep it at twenty if possible. I think that's a manageable number. I keep some extra work in a box nearby, in case the reviewer is interested in seeing more. Recently I had great success merely showing my book, with the prints as backup to confirm the quality of my work.

8. How do you make your prints or presentation materials? Do you do anything special to your portfolio to enhance the narrative of your project?

I work with a local printer, who is extremely knowledgeable. I trust him to make small adjustments to the prints. I don't do anything special with the portfolio. It's just a black box. I think it's better not to distract with the case, unless it serves some specific purpose.

Ville Kansanen

9. What is your opinion about attending reviews with a body of work in progress versus a completed project?

There are smaller, friendlier reviews where I can show unfinished work. There are reviews where the setting is more intimate and budget-friendly, so I've used those to mine for feedback and constructive criticism. I wouldn't go to Santa Fe or Houston with unfinished work.

10. What are your thoughts about "leave-behinds"? If you use them, please describe yours.

I've made all kinds of leave-behinds in the past—from gated brochures to long postcards. It's the same as with portfolios—they should serve the work and not distract or detract. Right now, I have a postcard on thick card stock that functions kind of like a free print. I try not to make it too big or outside of standard sizing because the reviewers are burdened with everyone else's leave-behinds and cards as it is.

K

11. Do you make time to see the work of other artists? If so, have you noticed where you are in the spectrum of work, experience, and education? How did it make you feel?

I try to make an effort to see what people are working on. I'm often the odd one out due to the kind of work I make. Not being a photographer's photographer, it's challenging for me to find like-minded artists. I'm also self-taught. Strangely, I've found it rare to meet fellow autodidacts, so that also feels a bit lonely at times. In terms of experience compared to my peers, I think I'm somewhere in the middle.

12. After looking at the work of your fellow reviewees, did you seek out any connections or collaborations, or were you simply inspired by their work? If so, how did you approach the person?

I will chat between reviews and ask to see work. Sometimes reviews have opportunities to do that in a separate area. "Roaming" or informal reviews are also an easy way to see other artists' work.

13. Has there been any auxiliary programming (lectures, workshops, photobook fair, portfolio walk, et cetera) at a portfolio-review event that was exceptionally memorable for you personally?

I like attending lectures and seeing exhibitions, but I've never had the energy to do a workshop in conjunction with a review.

14. Please share your most memorable portfolio-review experience (either positive or negative).

I used to photograph myself in the nude, and a reviewer once said that they judge self-portrait work by their "desire to f**k the artist." I laughed it off as a joke at the time. But in retrospect, I probably should've said something to someone . . . Sometimes you get a reviewer who enjoys the power imbalance. There've been a few occasions where the process felt a bit dehumanizing.

15. What is your favorite and least favorite part of portfolio-review events?

My favorite, by far, is when a reviewer really connects with the work and offers deeper insight into it. My least favorite part is the anxiety and stress of having to repeat your pitch over and over.
In addition, a very negative part of reviews is the false hope that some reviewers will give you. I've had many promises broken by reviewers. Most reprehensible to me is when the reviewers will "ghost" you after the event. I know everyone has full inboxes, but I just find that to be rude to the most extreme.

16. What do you think is the ideal length of time for a review session—twenty, twenty-five, or thirty minutes?

Thirty minutes.

17. What are some positive outcomes you've experienced from attending portfolio-review events?

My first monograph was a direct result from a review. That was the most gratifying experience of all. Another was the opportunity to work with a museum to make physical installations, which was a first for me.

18. Have you met with a reviewer who was not a good fit for your work? If so, were you able to work around it and/or did you learn from the experience?

Yes, that happens at all reviews. As long as both of us act professionally and are constructive, it's no problem. Usually, a reviewer will have peripheral comments or advice that is really useful. I try to come up with one to two key questions tailored to the reviewer that have nothing directly to do with them liking or disliking the work.

Ville Kansanen

19. Has a reviewer been disinterested in your work and clearly finished before the session was complete? If so, how did you handle the situation?

Not yet. I've managed to salvage situations like that by trying to find out more about their criteria for judging work, or what their field of interest is. That helps me understand the overall landscape a little better.

20. What are your thoughts about public portfolio walk-throughs, and have you ever made a sale this way? Do you have any pointers for new reviewees about the walk-throughs?

I really enjoyed the opportunity to sell my book at one of the public events. But frankly, I hate the open-to-the-public events—it feels too commercial for my taste.

21. How do you handle connecting—away from the review table—with a reviewer during an event?

That's so tricky. Some of the reviewers are very gregarious, and some are not. Honestly, I try not to discuss my work with them and, rather, try to learn more about them and their work. I just try to relax and not expect anything from those interactions.

22. Have you ever gotten to the point with your work when you don't feel the need to attend portfolio reviews? If so, why?

Yes, I think once you've done a few and you realize that you're either not getting the traction you hoped for, or you are getting reactions that you already anticipated. Also, I try to consider the individual reviewers. After a while, you come to notice that they don't change much from event to event.

23. Please comment on relationships that have developed from attending portfolio-review events.

One of my most cherished connections was with my book publisher. Her encouragement came at the right time for me, and I've come to count her as a very special person. Another is a fellow artist who I met at my first review in Santa Fe. She has become a wonderful friend and a resource for wisdom.

K

24. What is the biggest "no-no" for individuals attending portfolio-review events?

Being overly emotional about your work. A review is a business event. The reviewers are there for the most part because they believe it helps them professionally. Your work may or may not fit into that. There are exceptions to the rule, obviously, but by and large, it's good to practice nonattachment to the work when you're at the event. Don't forget to consider the reviewer's point of view and their goals, so you can be more objective.

25. What one piece of advice would you pass on to first-time reviewees?

Make a hierarchy of goals. Let's say your primary goal is to get a solo exhibition. It's very unlikely to happen then and there, but there are stages toward accomplishing that. Figure out what those incremental goals are, so you don't feel demoralized. It's better to make small gains and celebrate them, rather than expect your "big break" with no nourishment along the way.

Ville Kansanen

Rania Matar
Boston, Massachusetts

Rania Matar was born and raised in Lebanon and moved to the United States in 1984. As a Lebanese-born American woman and mother, Matar's cultural background, cross-cultural experience, and personal narrative inform her photography. She has dedicated her work to exploring issues of personal and collective identity through photographs of female adolescence and womanhood. She works both in the United States, where she lives, and in the Middle East, where she is from, in an effort to focus on notions of identity and individuality—all within the context of the underlying universality of these experiences.

Matar's work has been widely published and exhibited in museums worldwide, including the Museum of Fine Arts (Boston), the Carnegie Museum of Art, the National Museum of Women in the Arts, and more. A midcareer retrospective of her work was recently on view at the Cleveland Museum of Art and at the Amon Carter Museum of American Art as well as in a solo exhibition *In Her Image: Photographs by Rania Matar.*

She has received several grants and awards, including a 2022 Leica Women Foto Project Award; 2018 Guggenheim Fellowship; 2017 Mellon Foundation artist-in-residency grant at the Gund Gallery at Kenyon College; 2011 Legacy Award at the Griffin Museum of Photography; and 2021, 2011, and 2007 Massachusetts Cultural Council artist fellowships. In 2008, she was a finalist for the Foster Award at the Institute of Contemporary Art/Boston and had an accompanying solo exhibition.

1. What led you to attend your first portfolio-review event, and what stood out about the one you chose?

I was attending a talk at the Photographic Resource Center in Boston and the lecturer mentioned portfolio reviews. Up to this point, I didn't know what they were. I applied to a juried one and got in. It was in 2005, and the experience was priceless. The place was magnificent; I met many people in the industry and made friends with photographers who I am still in touch with now. It also taught me to edit and learn how to present and talk about my work.

2. Please list, in order of importance, why you attend portfolio-review events.

- Make connections and meet people in the industry who I would probably not have the opportunity to meet otherwise: curators, publishers, gallerists, but also, very importantly, fellow artists and photographers.
- Start putting the work out into the world.

M

- Be in an environment solely focused on photography for a few days with like-minded people.

3. How do you go about choosing which photography portfolio-review events you want to attend and which reviewers you want to meet?

I have tried a couple but eventually decided to go to the one that included the most international pool of reviewers. I am from Lebanon, and meeting reviewers from all areas of the world felt important to me personally and to my work.

4. What is your average cost per year to attend portfolio-review events, including event registration fees, travel, print production, and leave-behinds? Do you have a budget for self-promotion? If not using this amount for attending portfolio-review events, what do you think would be an effective, comparable use of funds in promoting your work in a different way?

I do not attend them anymore, but I used to attend, on average, only one every other year. I made my own portfolio prints and produced postcards as leave-behinds, so the costs for me were essentially the cost of the review plus travel, hotel, and meals. I do not spend any other funds on self-promotion or marketing. I do it all myself via staying in touch with reviewers I have met, email, and now Instagram.

5. What are the standout pros and cons of virtual reviews versus in-person portfolio-review events?

I have not done a virtual review. For me, a big part of the reviews is the personal connection one makes at these events—the feeling of almost being on a retreat where one lives, eats, and breathes photography. I also love preparing a portfolio and presenting actual physical prints, but also seeing my peers' prints. For me, the physicality of the whole experience is important.

    I guess if there were no other options, virtual reviews are a good alternative, and definitely less expensive.

6. For virtual reviews, please share your process for making a PDF version of your portfolio.

I have not attended virtual reviews but have had to make PDF version of my portfolio when requested by galleries, publishers, et cetera. I do not have a special process. I just sequence my work, include a project statement, and create a PDF.

Rania Matar

7. How many photographs do you typically include in each project and why? How many projects do you typically show at a portfolio review and why?

I typically bring two projects: the most recent (could be in progress) and one that is finished. Depending on whom I am meeting with, I would show one or the other—or both if time allows. I aim to bring twenty images in each project—it is sometimes hard to edit down, but I found that having too many images to go through adds stress and takes away the time for conversation. I also always bring more images that I keep at the bottom of my portfolio, which I only share if people ask to see more.

8. How do you make your prints or presentation materials? Do you do anything special to your portfolio to enhance the narrative of your project?

I make my own prints and present them on 17" × 22" paper in a simple portfolio box. I am careful about how I sequence the portfolio to get my message across. I usually start and end with my favorite images. I keep in mind that the prints will be handled over and over, so I'm not too precious about them. I don't like adding protection on the prints or handing the reviewers gloves; I think it takes away from the intimacy of the experience.

M

9. What is your opinion about attending reviews with a body of work in progress versus a completed project?

There are both equally valuable. If the project is completed, I am usually looking (or at least hoping) for more tangible results in terms of publications, exhibitions, or gallery representation. If the project is in progress, I welcome the feedback.

10. What are your thoughts about "leave-behinds." If you use them, please describe yours.

I make postcards—a couple of different images—and ask the reviewer to choose one. Reviewers are usually traveling, so bringing something too cumbersome seems counterproductive, and chances are that it will literally stay behind.

11. Do you make time to see the work of other artists? If so, have you noticed where you are in the spectrum of work, experience, and education? How did it make you feel?

I love looking at the work of other artists. I love the communal aspect of the experience and the connections we make. The variety of work is enriching and inspiring. And there is a sense of democratization of the process—people could be at different stages of their careers, but we also all go through the same vulnerability of putting the work out there to be viewed and scrutinized.

12. After looking at the work of your fellow reviewees, did you seek out any connections or collaborations, or were you simply inspired by their work? If so, how did you approach the person?

I just love meeting other photographers and making friends in the industry. We compare notes about the experience and which reviewer we should reach out to, we go to lunch, et cetera. Some of the artists I met at these events are some of my closest friends, and we still help each other edit for submissions, books, et cetera.

13. Has there been any auxiliary programming (lectures, workshops, photobook fair, portfolio walk, et cetera) at a portfolio-review event that was exceptionally memorable for you personally?

Lectures, portfolio walks, and exhibitions are great when they are offered. Sometimes parties and events are hosted at homes of people who live locally, often collectors, and they are a wonderful way to all connect socially after a long day.

14. Please share your most memorable portfolio-review experience (either positive or negative).

Worst one was not during the review, but getting there and settled. My flight was delayed, and my hotel had given away my room by the time I arrived. They shuttled me to another hotel at midnight and set me up in the living room part of a suite on a tiny foldout bed. I had my first review at 9 a.m. the next day, and it was an unsettling start. It turned out great afterward, as the hotel went out of its way to make my stay pleasant.

The most memorable positive one was at that same review: it was meeting a museum curator for the first time who wanted to buy two of my photographs. That was early in my photography career, and a huge validation for me.

15. What is your favorite and least favorite part of portfolio-review events?

The stress of packing the portfolio at the end of the twenty minutes with the next artist (rightfully) looming over.

Rania Matar

16. What do you think is the ideal length of time for a review session—twenty, twenty-five, or thirty minutes?

I have only been to ones that have been twenty minutes. I guess thirty minutes would be great—twenty-five minutes for presenting and five minutes as a buffer to pack the work and give time to the next artist to set up. Twenty minutes all-inclusive with no buffer between artists can be stressful.

17. What are some positive outcomes you've experienced from attending portfolio-review events?

Exhibitions, publications, sales, gallery representations, and, again, very important long-term connections and friendships.

They don't always happen right away, so it is important for people to remember to be patient, and things could take their time happening while reviewers find the right time and venue for the work.

18. Have you met with a reviewer who was not a good fit for your work? If so, were you able to work around it and/or did you learn from the experience?

Of course—it is part of the experience. I actually prefer reviewers who are honest if they're not interested, especially if they try to find other ways to help with recommendations, referrals, or feedback, et cetera, to reviewers who are overly positive and promise things they have no intentions on delivering.

19. Has a reviewer been disinterested in your work and clearly finished before the session was complete? If so, how did you handle the situation?

No, but I have, unfortunately, heard of it happening. I think this is unacceptable. Artists pay a lot of money for those reviews and are often very emotionally invested, so some civility in the interaction is important from both sides of the table. The whole encounter is twenty minutes; one should find a way to turn it into at least a constructive encounter. I think sometimes we, as artists, also expect too much from a reviewer who is booked back-to-back all day long looking at portfolios, so giving the reviewer space and respect is also important. I have heard of artists following reviewers to the bathroom . . .

M

20. What are your thoughts about public portfolio walk-throughs, and have you ever made a sale this way? Do you have any pointers for new reviewees about the walk-throughs?

Portfolio walk-throughs are overall great. I personally don't love the experience of standing there and waiting for people to come to the table, but they can be very useful in connecting us with reviewers we didn't get a chance to meet with or with people from the community who are not present during the actual reviews. I currently work with a gallery because the owner saw my work at one of those walk-throughs.

21. How do you handle connecting—away from the review table—with a reviewer during an event?

If there are reviewers I really want to see and who I requested and didn't get, I would go to them and politely ask if they might have time to meet with me. Most people tend to agree, but not always. The reviewers also have a very long day, and some cannot look at more work after they have been doing it for seven hours straight. Often, just having a drink with reviewers or an informal conversation outside of the review setting can be a lovely way to connect with reviewers on a personal level.

22. Have you ever gotten to the point with your work when you don't feel the need to attend portfolio reviews? If so, why?

I haven't been to a portfolio review in a few years now. Maybe I am at this point? I honestly don't know. I just haven't felt the need to attend in a few years. That being said, I know that I would enjoy them, would enjoy meeting people, and would thrive on the energy of the whole experience. Maybe I will attend one again in the future, but at the moment I feel that I am at a good place to try to do it on my own for a bit. It is also always good to give the room to newer photographers.

23. Please comment on relationships that have developed from attending portfolio-review events.

I have met curators who have offered me museum exhibitions, collectors who have bought my prints, gallerists who have represented me, and photographers who have become dear friends. The reviews have been very good in putting my work on the map, and I am very grateful for all they have offered me over the years.

Rania Matar

24. What is the biggest "no-no" for individuals attending portfolio-review events?

Don't be too self-centered and entitled. Don't cut off other photographers. Don't be overcompetitive—it is a communal experience. Don't harass reviewers.

25. What one piece of advice would you pass on to first-time reviewees?

- Be thick-skinned. Some people will love your work. Others won't. It is reality.
- Take what you can from every review, then decide what you want to make of this information.
- Edit your portfolio tightly.
- Learn to talk about your work, but don't talk all the time. You are there to learn from the person across from you.
- Take notes.
- Follow up with a thank-you note a few weeks later. Stay in touch with reviewers who were positive, interested, and encouraging, but, again, without overdoing it.
- Be pleasant, enjoy the experience, and have fun!

M

Marcy Palmer

Marcy Palmer
Dallas, Texas

I grew up in the foothills of the Adirondack Mountains in the historic city of Saratoga Springs, New York. As a child, I spent time exploring the outdoors, which fueled my imagination and play.

My work explores themes of beauty, history, and social justice through the lens of art history and photo history, nature, and science. I often approach my work with questions that relate to research and with considerations of how the materials in my work can further communicate the ideas. Integrating various approaches to image-making, from contemporary to historical practices, I am particularly influenced by the earliest practitioners of photography and the Surrealist and Bauhaus movements.

I have an MFA in photography and related media from the School of Visual Arts and a BS in studio art from Skidmore College. My work has been exhibited at various spaces, including The Brooklyn Museum of Art, The Center for Photographic Art, The Griffin Museum of Photography, The Ogden Museum of Southern Art, and others. My work has been written about in *Lenscratch*, the *Boston Globe* Sunday edition, *D Magazine*, and other publications. I released a book with Yoffy Press titled *You Are Eternity, You Are the Mirror*, which was chosen as a Photo-Eye 2020 favorite photobook, The Luupe's Favorite Woman-Made Books of the Year, and Deep Red Press's Favorite Photobooks. The book is now sold out. I am an educator and teach photography at universities, nonprofit centers, and museums. I live and work in Dallas, Texas.

P

1. What led you to attend your first portfolio-review event, and what stood out about the one you chose?

I felt ready to share a project, and it seemed like a unique and interesting opportunity.

2. Please list, in order of importance, why you attend portfolio-review events.

I usually attend reviews to share work that I'm interested in showing or publishing, to get feedback on work, and to make connections with other photographers and reviewers.

3. How do you go about choosing which photography portfolio-review events you want to attend and which reviewers you want to meet?

I try to find reviews that will fit my schedule (timing is important) and reviews that host reviewers who I'm interested in seeing. If I'm not familiar with a reviewer, I research them and try to determine who might be interested in the work or who may have feedback that could help me.

4. What is your average cost per year to attend portfolio-review events, including event registration fees, travel, print production, and leave-behinds? Do you have a budget for self-promotion? If not using this amount for attending portfolio-review events, what do you think would be an effective, comparable use of funds in promoting your work in a different way?

It seems like it has been around $2,000 to $3,000 when considering the cost of portfolio production, registration fees, travel, hotel, leave-behinds, et cetera, although it seems like prices for everything are increasing. I keep things simple by printing postcards and business cards for self-promotion/leave-behinds for the reviews. I spend a yearly amount on my website and calls for entry.

5. What are the standout pros and cons of virtual reviews versus in-person portfolio-review events?

Virtual reviews are significantly less expensive, but there is something about spending time with people in person that is really missed. At in-person reviews, you have these wonderful spaces of time outside the reviews to connect with other artists or reviewers. Those times are not about your work, but about getting to know people that are a part of your community, and that I think is quite valuable.

6. For virtual reviews, please share your process for making a PDF version of your portfolio.

I have sorted through my images for each project, selected the order for the images, and included titles for each work. I think that keeping the design simple and focused on the work is important.

7. How many photographs do you typically include in each project and why? How many projects do you typically show at a portfolio review, and why?

I typically show fifteen to twenty images per project, and I like to bring at least two projects. One project may spark more discussion than the other, depending on who I am meeting with.

8. How do you make your prints or presentation materials? Do you do anything special to your portfolio to enhance the narrative of your project?

I tend to keep things simple and straightforward. I think that too many "accessories" can become distracting and the people you are meeting with will know if you are distracting from the work.

9. What is your opinion about attending reviews with a body of work in progress versus a completed project?

I prefer to bring completed or close-to-completed projects. I think that if the work is in progress, it should at least be at a turning point. One should be ready to receive feedback and thoughtfully digest it. If the work is still in its early stages, it can be hard for the reviewers to really help you, especially if you are still figuring out what you are trying to communicate.

10. What are your thoughts about "leave-behinds" and if you use them, please describe yours.

P

I like to keep it simple with a postcard and/or business card. The reviewers meet with a lot of people, most of them with leave-behinds, and the reviewers may not want to travel with something large, odd-sized, or heavy. I think that if you really want to send something to them later, you can.

11. Do you make time to see the work of other artists? If so, have you noticed where you are in the spectrum of work, experience, and education? How did it make you feel?

I think that seeing the work of other artists is one of the best parts of the in-person reviews. I look forward to who I can meet, ask questions about their work, and see what I can learn or who I can learn from—we're always learning, no matter where we are on this journey!

12. After looking at the work of your fellow reviewees, did you seek out any connections or collaborations, or were you simply inspired by their work? If so, how did you approach the person?

I tend to seek out connections, or I may just be inspired by their work. I think that meeting people between sessions, at additional events, or at the beginning or end of the portfolio walk can be helpful.

13. Has there been any auxiliary programming (lectures, workshops, photobook fair, portfolio walk, et cetera) at a portfolio-review event that was exceptionally memorable for you personally?

I ended up working with a gallery because of a portfolio walk at PhotoNOLA. It was totally unexpected, and I was thrilled. This is unusual and not something one should expect from portfolio walks, but it was memorable.

14. Please share your most memorable portfolio-review experience (either positive or negative).

One of my most memorable reviews was with a very kind and generous reviewer. I had met with that reviewer a few times over the years, I was comfortable talking with her, and she knew my previous work. I showed her a new body of work at this review, and she decided on the spot to put it in a show. This is the sort of thing that hardly ever happens at reviews, but the timing was right, the work was complete and presented professionally, and we had developed a relationship over time. I think that all those things were helpful, and a bit of luck was involved.

15. What is your favorite and least favorite part of portfolio-review events?

My favorite part is connecting with other artists and seeing/discussing so much work. My least favorite part is that I am an introvert, and I can get a little overstimulated by all the activity and interaction. I have found that small breaks are important, too!

16. What do you think is the ideal length of time for a review session— twenty, twenty-five, or thirty minutes?

I think that most of the time, twenty minutes is fine. I am not terribly verbose by nature, especially with people I don't know very well, so for me, twenty minutes is usually enough time to discuss the work and to get to know the reviewer a bit.

Marcy Palmer

17. What are some positive outcomes you've experienced from attending portfolio-review events?

I think that meeting and/or getting to know other artists and the reviewers has been one of the most positive things from these events.

18. Have you met with a reviewer who was not a good fit for your work? If so, were you able to work around it and/or did you learn from the experience?

Yes, I have. I steered the conversation away from concept to more practical questions that I had about the work, keeping in mind that I might be able to learn something from this person, even if the work was not a good fit for them.

19. Has a reviewer been disinterested in your work and clearly finished before the session was complete? If so, how did you handle the situation?

Once, I had an awkward ending to a review: the reviewer was finished and said "goodbye" before the end-of-session bell rang, but that was once. I think it's important to keep in mind that we're all human and we may be distracted for various reasons, and one should not take that personally.

20. What are your thoughts about public portfolio walk-throughs, and have you ever made a sale this way? Do you have any pointers for new reviewees about the walk-throughs?

I think that they can be very helpful in practicing your "pitch" as well as answering questions people may have about the work. I have made some sales at portfolio walks, and it's helpful to be ready for that (have the online payment method set up, cellophane bags or packaging ready, et cetera), although I wouldn't necessarily expect sales to happen. Portfolio walks are also a great time to see other artists' work and connect with them when it's less busy (either at the beginning or end).

21. How do you handle connecting—away from the review table—with a reviewer during an event?

I am friendly and polite, but I also respect their space, especially if they seem to be bombarded with attention. If I connect well with someone, I usually try to see them and continue a conversation. Some review events make it easier to connect with reviewers outside of the review table through various events (bus tours, exhibition openings, et cetera) and a good hotel bar, where people meet up after the reviews.

P

22. Have you ever gotten to the point with your work when you don't feel the need to attend portfolio reviews? If so, why?

No.

23. Please comment on relationships that have developed from attending portfolio-review events.

I have formed friendships over the years and have gotten to know others in a professional context whom I might not have the opportunity to otherwise. I appreciate that.

24. What is the biggest "no-no" for individuals attending portfolio-review events?

Be sure to respect others—your peers, the reviewers, and the people running the event. Sometimes people can feel very competitive and insecure, and they don't behave in the most respectful ways. This is your community, and developing relationships is a huge aspect of it.

25. What one piece of advice would you pass on to first-time reviewees?

It's a long game, and even if there isn't a direct outcome from one review event, it may lead to other things in the future—it's a cumulative effect. It's worth investing your time, money, and energy in engaging with your community.

Marcy Palmer

Lydia Panas

Kutztown, Pennsylvania

I am a visual artist working with photography and video. I have been making work for over thirty years about my experience as a woman. Becoming an artist was an act of defiance, giving myself permission to express what I was taught not to voice. All my work is made in the fields, forests, and studio of our farm in Pennsylvania, a property my husband and I reforested over time. The growth and beauty of this land is a metaphor for place and healing.

My work has been widely exhibited internationally, including at the Brooklyn Museum, Phillips Collection, Corcoran Gallery, National Portrait Gallery (London and Edinburgh), and Kunstlerhaus Bethanien (Berlin) and is represented in public collections, including in the Bronx Museum, Museum of Fine Arts Houston, Palm Springs Art Museum, Allentown Art Museum, Museum of Contemporary Photography Chicago, and Shanghai MoMA. It has appeared in the *New Yorker,* the *New York Times Magazine, Hyperallergic*, and the *Wall Street Journal*, among others. I have degrees from Boston College, School of Visual Arts, and New York University and am a recipient of a Whitney Museum Independent Study Fellowship and a CFEVA Fellowship. I have been an artist-in-residence at MASS MoCA and the Banff Centre for the Arts and a visiting artist at the American Academy in Rome. I have three monographs: *The Mark of Abel* (Kehrer Verlag 2012), *Falling from Grace* (Conveyor Arts 2016), and *Sleeping Beauty* (MW Editions 2021).

1. What led you to attend your first portfolio-review event, and what stood out about the one you chose?

P

My first review was Photolucida in Portland, maybe 2005? I remember thinking it was a great way to get feedback on my work from a number of curators, gallerists, editors, and photographers in one setting. Living away from a metropolitan area makes it difficult to get people to look at your work. The roster was extensive and interesting, and I had never been to Portland.

2. Please list—in order of importance—why you attend portfolio reviews.

- Meet people who might be interested in my work
- See/hear reactions to my work
- Meet other photographers

3. How do you go about choosing which photography portfolio reviews to attend and then your reviewers?

Reviews: Initially, I research the reviewers to see if there is a good number who might have interest in my work. I also consider location; some are easier to get to than others. I consider the number of reviewers—more is generally better, since the enterprise is expensive. I also went to some review events that friends were attending, so it was a nice way to meet up as well.

Reviewers: I research them to see what kind of work they are interested in and if they seem like a good fit. Although, sometimes the ones you think will be the least interested end up as the most interested and vice versa, so it's always a surprise.

4. What is your average cost per year to attend portfolio-review events, including event registration fees, travel, print production, and leave-behinds? Do you have a budget for self-promotion? If not using this amount for attending portfolio-review events, what do you think would be an effective, comparable use of funds in promoting your work in a different way?

I remember the cost was high—$3,000 to $4,000, at least. Purchasing a printer ended up being a huge savings. Initially, photographers were giving packages with CDs, cards, et cetera. At a certain point, the reviewers didn't want leave-behinds anymore, as they were too much to carry home, and information was much more available on the web, so that helped a little on time and budget.

Reviews are the best way to get eyes on the work, meet people, and start relationships. You want to try to keep up the relationships so you can stay in touch. Email services are helpful, and social media can get the word out as well.

5. What are the standout pros and cons of virtual reviews versus in-person review events?

I've only done one virtual review, so I'm not able to say much about them, but one pro is that they are much more affordable and, depending on length, they can be effective. Seeing the work online is never the same as seeing it in person, but it can be the beginning of a conversation. The lack of meeting up with other photographers is also a con.

Lydia Panas

6. For virtual reviews, please share your process for making a PDF version of your portfolio.

My online review was a while ago, and I don't remember how we viewed work. I think it was from my website.

When I send out PDFs to a curator, however (not at a review), I am careful to make them look attractive. I start with a simple and elegant cover page (I'm careful with placement and typeface), then a short but effective bio; next, a concise artist statement (this can go at the end as well); then I include maybe seven to ten images (depends on what an individual series calls for); at the end, I include a link to my website and an email; and at the very end, a copyright. It's important that the PDF is not too long and is clear and attractive.

7. How many photographs do you typically include in each project and why? How many projects do you typically show at a portfolio review and why?

I try to keep the edit to twenty images. The edit is super important; it needs to be tight, which can be difficult, especially if the project is still in progress. In both instances, it helps to have a variety of conversations and reactions. This is one of the main benefits of the reviews—to see how people are reacting and how you can improve, edit, or add more images to make the project come together.

I have shown two projects at times, but in retrospect, the twenty-minute time is too short for two. I think it's better to concentrate on one.

P

8. How do you make your prints or presentation materials? Do you do anything special to your portfolio to enhance the narrative of your project?

I try to make gorgeous and meticulous prints and present them in a professional portfolio case. It's important that the prints are good-quality finals. I make them all the same size, in a tidy presentation that can be opened for presentation and closed back up quickly and efficiently.

9. What is your opinion about attending reviews with a body of work in progress versus a completed project?

I think a completed project is probably best, but if you have enough prints to show where you are going, an in-progress project can work as well. A lot depends on how well you understand the project at the early stage, how you speak about it, and the interests of the reviewer.

10. What are your thoughts about "leave-behinds"? If you use them, please describe yours.

When I first attended reviews, everyone had "leave-behinds" (we used to leave CDs with images and cards, et cetera.), and some of them were gorgeous. But a few years in, reviewers started saying they couldn't travel home with them, so they went out of favor. Eventually, I used a simple card, one 5" × 7", with an image on the front and info on the back, and/or a few times I used a foldout card with multiple images. Each project calls for a different kind of card, so it varies depending on the project. I also sent cards as thank-you notes after the reviews instead of leave-behinds at the review.

11. Do you make time to see the work of other artists? If so, have you noticed where you are in the spectrum of work, experience, and education? How did it make you feel?

Definitely, and yes, I notice everything. I felt good.

12. After looking at the work of your fellow reviewees, did you seek out any connections or collaborations, or were you simply inspired by their work? If so, how did you approach the person?

There is always a lot of interesting work to see at the reviews, but my work is very personal and obsessive, so I mostly work alone. I did work on a fascinating collaboration during the pandemic, where we merged our two ways of working (and many thematic commonalities) into a beautiful thread. I would be happy to do something like that again. In general, though, at the reviews, I have found many interesting and inspiring projects that I admire, but I have not collaborated with anyone.

13. Has there been any auxiliary programming (lectures, workshops, photobook fairs, portfolio walk, et cetera) at a portfolio-review event that was exceptionally memorable for you personally?

All the programming is helpful, but I especially love the portfolio walks. You meet a lot of people you wouldn't have met otherwise and have lots of great and more casual and relaxed conversations. I have a lot of memorable experiences and conversations with people who really related to my work. I do remember a specific presentation/slide lecture that offered several ideas on presentation and getting the word out about the work.

Lydia Panas

14. Please share your most memorable portfolio-review experience (either positive or negative).

I remember many positive experiences and a few negative ones. One especially positive memory is when a reviewer connected to the complexity of the work with a combination of intellectual and intuitive enthusiasm without my saying anything. She spoke to the photographs individually and as a whole, and I could see that she grasped the complexities of the project in a meaningful way. Although she wasn't the only one to do this, for some reason, this memory really stands out.

A less-than-positive experience was when a reviewer told me to change the direction of an early-stage project. I felt she was not really looking and/or curious enough to try to understand my process. The advice was anathema to my interests. I disregarded it, and the project eventually became my most well-known body of my work. This memory stands out for me as well, and I have repeated the story often regarding taking advice.

15. What is your favorite and least favorite part of portfolio-review events?

Favorite part is when you connect with people who relate to the work and, of course, when someone wants to exhibit it, write about it, purchase it. I love meeting and connecting with other photographers and having so much to relate to on so many levels.

It is always a rewarding experience to meet with someone and discuss a body of work—its potential and where it is headed. If the reviewer is open and curious and kind, the experience is most often positive.

Least favorite: when a reviewer seems uninterested or distracted by something else.

Preparing to go to the reviews can feel stressful—so many decisions, prep work, travel arrangements, costs, worry about which/how many prints to take.

16. What do you think is the ideal length of time for a review session—twenty. twenty-five, or thirty minutes?

Twenty minutes is short, especially to try to get into any kind of depth when you are connecting with the reviewer; but if you're not, then thirty is too long. So, I guess twenty-five minutes might be best. There are small issues that can get in the way with the twenty-minute time—like if the person ahead of you takes up some of your time, then twenty is way too short. I try not to impinge on others' time, but not everyone is that way.

P

17. What are some positive outcomes you've experienced from attending review events?

Reviews have resulted in exhibitions, purchases, museum collections, work written about in journals—all of these both nationally and internationally. I have made connections with curators, writers, et cetera., and made lasting friendships with photographers from the reviews, which have all made me feel like I am part of a community.

18. Have you met with a reviewer who was not a good fit for your work? If so, were you able to work around it and/or did you learn from the experience?

I have met with reviewers who were not a good fit for my work. It's inevitable. Sometimes they are still open to a good conversation; other times they are not. I remember, once, the reviewer seemed like they were not even interested in being there.

So, sometimes you can work around it and still make it fun and worthwhile, and other times you can't. It's always a good learning experience on many levels.

19. Has a reviewer been disinterested in your work and clearly finished before the session was complete? If so, how did you handle the situation?

There have been reviewers who were disinterested in my work, certainly. I recall the conversation being sort of neither here nor there, but I do not remember one that did not last the entire twenty minutes. It's possible, but I don't remember any.

20. What are your thoughts about public portfolio walk-throughs, and have you ever made a sale this way? Do you have any pointers for new reviewees about the walk-throughs?

I love the public portfolio walk-throughs. I have made a few sales from them also connected with people who purchased prints later. Pointers? It's fun; just enjoy yourself and have cards to give out with your information.

21. How do you handle connecting—away from the review table—with a reviewer during an event?

I didn't do too much of that (I should have). It's complicated, as some of the reviews discourage it, so you must have a certain comfort level about it, which

Lydia Panas

I didn't. We did often meet up for drinks in the evenings, which is nice, but you generally don't talk shop at that point because everyone is tired at the end of a long day.

22. Have you ever gotten to the point with your work when you don't feel the need to attend portfolio reviews? If so, why?

I used to go to one or maybe two reviews a year, but I have not been to one for a number of years. Sometimes I think I might attend one again, but it really is a lot of work and expense, and I'm not up for it in the near future.

23. Please comment on relationships that have developed from attending portfolio-review events.

You must work to keep them up, as everyone is busy. They tend to last for a while but can get lost if you have not seen one another or kept the conversation going. Still, you can always reach out—send a note or a new book—to keep them informed of new projects.

24. What is the biggest "no-no" for individuals attending portfolio-review events?

"Don't corner a reviewer in the bathroom." A refrain heard at every review.

Be polite. Don't push or insist; reviewers are seeing a lot of photographers and feel some pressure to commit, which they mostly cannot do. Stay within your twenty minutes. Sometimes meetings go past twenty minutes, into the next photographer's time—sometimes it's the photographer, sometimes it's the reviewer; either way, it takes away from other people's twenty minutes.

The reviews are high energy, and you can feel a kind of anxiety running throughout. Everyone is feeling pressure—reviewers and reviewees—so be sensitive, polite, friendly and know when to back off.

25. What is one piece of advice you would pass on to first-time reviewees?

Be confident, but open.

P

Lou Peralta

Lou Peralta
Mexico City, Mexico

I am Lou Peralta. I am part of the family of the legendary HERRERA Portrait Studio in Mexico. I am its fourth generation. After more than thirty years as a portrait photographer, in 2017 I decided to devote myself full time to creating my own contemporary photography. In my work, I explore, through art, new meanings for the portrait. I fuse pre-Hispanic Mexican influences with contemporary culture, referenced in the fabrics and structures that I make manually with materials such as thread, cloth, wire, and others. The point is to capture the perception I have of whomever I'm portraying. So, after shooting it, I make it into a sculptural piece using those materials.

Right now, in my career I want to be part of the next stage in art photography. I want to proudly represent my culture in the world. I want to find the answer to why my family was dedicated for so long to portrait photography. I want to know what it really means to portray someone. I recently found out I could apply quantum physics to photography: the fact that we are only atoms made up of energy means that we can only see ourselves because of the reflection of light. I based all the work in my most recent stage of my Disassemble V Series: Portraits of the Invisible Vol. 2 connected on the exploration of portraiture as a reflection of energy and complexity of the human being.

1. What led you to attend your first portfolio-review event? What stood out about the one you chose?

My first portfolio review was one I'd known about for many years prior to going. Many friends of mine went there through the years and talked wonders, but at the time it wasn't my type of thing. Thus, when the time came to show my new work in 2018, I thought it was a perfect first choice for me in starting an international artist career.

Reviewers are the thermometers of what happens in the world of international art. Hence, they know what they're looking for, what's trending. Sometimes a single comment, idea, reference—or even a *word*—is worth all the cost of a portfolio review. You can get many reviewers, some of whom won't like your work and will openly tell you, others who will love it, and the "meh" ones: neither love it nor hate it. Only an expert in photography who has seen hundreds of thousands of images can say this type of thing. Consider that reviewers are linking your work with the thousands of artists they have in their memories. Through this perspective, after receiving their comments, you can also analyze what current trend or fashion to which you belong. There's no doubt that a reviewer's insight sometimes opens your eyes to things you would never have seen.

2. Please list, in order of importance, why you attend portfolio-review events.

- To show new work and find opportunities to exhibit it internationally.
- To widen my network with artists, curators, and people from the art world.
- To share experiences and see what other artists are making.
- To get out of a "creative block" by receiving feedback.

3. How do you go about choosing which photography portfolio reviews to attend and then your reviewers?

I see the list of reviewers and decide whether to be in it. I'll go if there are people I would like to be reviewed by. It depends on the work I'm doing at the time. With a few exceptions, if I am hoping to meet someone for a specific project, I don't want to repeat reviewers, so I check with whom I've already met in order to find new opinions. For these means, I have documentation with all information about who, when, and what happened in each portfolio review.

4. What is your average cost per year to attend portfolio-review events, including event registration fees, travel, print production, and leave-behinds? Do you have a budget for self-promotion? If not using this amount for attending portfolio-review events, what do you think would be an effective, comparable use of funds in promoting your work in a different way?

It varies from year to year. Since I live in Mexico City, I mostly attend online reviews to avoid travel expenses. As a promotion, I make postcards printed on Hahnemühle paper in my studio. While making them, I try to think about what kind of card I would keep on my board to see every day. I also carry a couple of catalogs of my most recent exhibition to give to the reviewer, but only if they show interest. I keep my website up to date, and I'm active on my social networks by uploading engaging content.

5. What are the standout pros and cons of virtual reviews versus in-person portfolio-review events?

About virtual reviews: I love them because they are like a visit to my studio! I can show my photo sculptures and their volume and dimensions (I wouldn't be able to carry them in my suitcase). I have everything at hand and can show even more things like sketches, tools, and framed work, rather than just a portfolio of printed photos. In addition, I can rest between reviews and have a good coffee next to me.

About in-person portfolio reviews: Meeting new artists is a definite pro. Going out for lunch, seeing museums and galleries, living for a brief period of

Lou Peralta

time among artists and reviewers. It's a fantastic experience, but it has its cons. For example, if you have jetlag, it can be very tiring. It can also be overwhelming, since a lot of information is received. One thing that can be either a con or a pro (depending on personal preference) is that, in person, one can have reviews with tons of people one after the other. Personally speaking, five reviews in an online event is more than enough, and if it is in person, I choose four in a day at the most. I prefer fewer reviews in order to really take advantage of them—absorb them, follow up on the references given, and take into account the recommendations.

6. For virtual reviews, please share your process for making a PDF version of your portfolio.

In order to make my PDFs, I think about what I want people to know about me when they see it. There are only a few seconds to catch the viewer's attention. So, the most important parts are the cover and the first few pages. I choose an attractive image for the cover and add my logo, my website, and my Instagram handle. Then I put the title and a short sentence describing my series. When that is done, I place the logo of the event in which it's showing (so in the future people will have the reference). Once I've finished the cover, I head on to the following pages. I write my project statement, technical data of the series, pictures of the pieces, and their technical sheet. Finally, I put the documentation: research, materials, and process. At the end, I like placing my bio, my picture, the galleries that represent me, my most recent exhibitions, my webpage, my email, and my social networks.

P

7. How many photographs do you typically include in each project and why? How many projects do you typically show at a portfolio review and why?

I show different pieces and in different ways for each reviewer. Most of the times I make up my mind on which to show right after introducing myself. I prepare multiple media. I take PDFs, individual photos, even a video with different descriptions about my work. Depending on my intuition on how the review is going, I may or may not show other work. No portfolio review is the same; that's what makes it exciting.

8. How do you make your prints or presentation materials? Do you do anything special to your portfolio to enhance the narrative of your project?

I do all my works' printing for portfolio reviews at my studio in a size that fits in my suitcase. I lay them in boxes that are covered with a color or design relative to the work I'm presenting. For example, for my Disassemble Series V, my boxes are covered with fine red paper because I use red copper to make my photo sculptures. For my Comalli Series, my boxes come dressed with the type of kraft paper with which tortillas in Mexico are wrapped. They always have my label on them. I care about having a good-looking presentation for my art, but through the years I've come to the conclusion that good work can be appreciated no matter the size, color, or the container fineness with which it's presented. If the portfolio review is longer than twenty minutes, I have also seen photographers who do very well showing 8" × 10" images to see on the floor or 4" × 6" images to display beautifully together on a table; both situations are so that the reviewer can help study and edit them. It honestly looks like a wonderful experience. I also encourage you to bring a photo that has all the images in a smaller size, like a contact sheet, so that at the end of the meeting, the reviewer has a complete panorama of the series.

9. What is your opinion about attending reviews with a body of work in progress versus a completed project?

I love to show work in progress because having feedback and insight while developing a series helps me. I'm always amazed about all the things you can learn about a theme when asking for feedback. Though, you obviously need to be prepared for both brutal and pleasant comments. At first it was difficult for me to listen to critical feedback, but now I ask for it. I appreciate knowing what resonates with the curators. It's very important for me to know the different reactions to what I am doing. It gives me a broader picture and helps me develop my series.

10. What are your thoughts about "leave-behinds"? If you use them, please describe yours.

For portfolio reviews, I only prepare a fine minimalist postcard. The work should be the protagonist and should be memorable on its own.

Also, I am aware reviewers do not want to carry much in their luggage, and if they ask to see more, I'll send them more material through a postal delivery service.

11. Do you make time to see the work of other artists? If so, have you noticed where you are in the spectrum of work, experience, and education? How did it make you feel?

Absolutely. It's wonderful to see other artists' work; I do it happily—especially when friends are showing theirs. Besides, when I see three-dimensional work showing, I feel good because I know we are pushing the limits of the medium.

Lou Peralta

It's clear to me that we must rejoice at the extraordinary work of others. At the end of the day, it's all about celebrating art.

12. After looking at the work of your fellow reviewees, did you seek out any connections or collaborations, or were you simply inspired by their work? If so, how did you approach the person?

I mostly use them as inspiration and motivation. However, I was approached by a colleague to collaborate in a "visual conversation"—a visual dialog with an artist whose work I admire. This collaboration came at a time when I placed special importance to it. It happened to be an unexpected, yet fortunate, project. Collaborations help you grow as an artist, so be open to them. There are more exciting collaborations coming, but they are yet to be defined.

13. Has there been any auxiliary programming (lectures, workshops, photobook fair, portfolio walk, et cetera) at a portfolio-review event that was exceptionally memorable for you personally?

Yes, these experiences normally happen on the portfolio walks. I remember one where I sold my first piece of my Comalli Series. A collector appeared in front of my assigned desk and said, "I want this piece." I replied, "Let me show you the rest." After showing him everything, he said, "I want this piece," as he pointed to the same piece he had chosen from the very beginning. I learned that people know what they want when they see it.

On another portfolio walk, a reviewer I hadn't had a chance to meet passed by my work and said that it was "compelling." I didn't know the translation for that word. I had to look for it immediately after in the dictionary! It's those kinds of things that stick to you.

P

14. Please share your most memorable portfolio-review experience (either positive or negative).

I remember the impression of being in front of a reviewer who had previously studied my work in detail. The specialist had taken notes from my website and my social networks. After saying hello, the person asked if I had my recorder ready and began to tell me something that completely revolutionized my practice as an artist. In twenty minutes, I received the keys to what I could do to improve my exposure, and I realized what wasn't helping me. It was unforgettable and invaluable.

15. What is your favorite and least favorite part of portfolio-review events?

The thing I like the least is that I end up mentally exhausted. It's so much feedback—when put together along with the pressure of time, it leaves you practically breathless. What I like the most is the variety of comments, insight, and feedback on my work. It's very interesting how each reviewer has such a diverse approach and perspective of what they do like and don't like. Of course, sometimes you get hung up on hard comments, but it's those comments—the ones that hurt—that I like best. I see that's where I have to dig and focus. That's where the deepest inspiration arises to continue with the development of my art.

16. What do you think is the ideal length of time for a review session—twenty, twenty-five, or thirty minutes?

For me, the ideal length is twenty-five minutes. I like to take a couple of minutes to meet and sense the person with whom I'll be talking. It's the same as when I was an editorial photographer and I had to go do a portrait to illustrate an interview. I had to connect with the person, create empathy. From there, I just show my work and listen to whatever said person has to tell me.

17. What are some positive outcomes you've experienced from attending portfolio-review events?

Unlike plastic artists who have no portfolio reviews, we in photography have an open space to show our work and get feedback. A positive outcome is that I've been able to show my work internationally, thanks to the fact that I met my gallerists outside my country in different portfolio reviews. That's an important aspect, but another one is that I've met many people from all over the world. They've become friends I admire.

18. Have you met with a reviewer who was not a good fit for your work? If so, were you able to work around it and/or did you learn from the experience?

Of course, I've had several. A reviewer once told me in a somewhat serious yet joking tone, "And what do I do with this?" I didn't even want to reply. I showed him another piece from my series, and even though he wasn't interested, he turned out to be someone with whom I had a very interesting talk about photography. He even recommended me to a very important person in the medium. So, the moral of the story is that you never know where a good thing is going to come from.

Lou Peralta

19. Has a reviewer been disinterested in your work and clearly finished before the session was complete? If so, how did you handle the situation?

Yes, but no. Time slows down when there's nothing to talk about. I understand that after reviewing hundreds of artworks, one gets tired, and if you don't match with the concept, it's difficult to stay interested. No reviewer has ever ended the meeting before the scheduled time, but for sure I felt every second go by s l o w l y.

20. What are your thoughts about public portfolio walk-throughs? Have you ever made a sale this way? Do you have any pointers for new reviewees about the walk-throughs?

It's like being in any store or market, and you have the opportunity to know your collector. I show my work as I'd like to be shown another person's. Sometimes you do sell pieces, and other times you don't. I think this is a good way to promote art and get fresh feedback from people. A thing that has worked for me is to bring small easels to put my work lifted on the table.

21. How do you handle connecting—away from the review table—with a reviewer during an event?

If I have a chance to come close without interrupting anything, I'll do it. First, I introduce myself and tell them something relative to what I like about what they do or the museum/gallery they represent, and then I give them my card. If they ask me something and we move on to have a proper conversation, fantastic. I always have my "elevator pitch" ready to use.

Never, ever carry your portfolio around and expect that somebody wants to see more pictures than they have reviewed through the day. So, unless you've been asked specifically, respect their leisure time.

22. Have you ever gotten to the point with your work when you don't feel the need to attend portfolio reviews? If so, why?

I feel I don't have the need to show my work whenever I'm in early stages of the development of a new series. There's no point in showing anything undefined and undeveloped.

23. Please comment on relationships that have developed from attending portfolio-review events.

I've met the most incredible artists, some who I even consider my close friends. I've also met invaluable consultants, mentors, curators, and, of course, my gallerists.

P

24. What is the biggest "no-no" for individuals attending portfolio-review events?

It's sad to see someone complain they haven't been given a chance to shine and questioning why someone else has. Celebrate those who have been given opportunities. Hopefully, in the future you'll be there, and someone will be happy for you. In addition, getting opportunities takes time. Some curators are developing projects that are to be made in two or five years from now. It's important to understand that they take you into account, but for future projects. Don't criticize colleagues or reviewers. Be nice; everyone's trying their best. Don't complain about mistakes or things that don't go well at an event. There are many people who work so that everything goes according to plan (sometimes they're only volunteers), and sometimes unexpected things happen. We as artists know that for sure. If you didn't get the reviewer you wanted, think it's fate. Sometimes you don't ask for a reviewer, and they turn out to be a life-changing person. It's happened to me in every portfolio review I've attended.

25. What one piece of advice would you pass on to first-time reviewees?

Prepare yourselves for criticism, and don't take anything personally. I find that practicing with a friend and asking them to give you the worst criticism helps. I say this from experience. In one of my first portfolio reviews, the criticism was too harsh for me. I remember going to my hotel room to cry. Nevertheless, I think this particular experience was one of the best portfolio reviews I've ever had. I noticed so many things and grew so much! From there, opportunities arose. Sometimes it hurts, but it's *nothing personal*.

One of the most important lessons I received from my family (all photographers) is that to learn how to portray, you have to become a model. When you change perspectives, you realize how terrible it is when the photographer goes to fix the camera, because the connection is lost. If you must ask that awkward question, "Where do I turn to now?" in that moment, the session is over. Or, if it's not timewise, at least the inspiration and excitement are gone. I also always recommend having a mock review, but this time, you're the reviewer and not the reviewee. Ask a friend or an acquaintance for help. Do a photo review. There, you'll notice how it feels when an artist begins to explain their work but you do not understand it. To finish, you have to have a clear understanding, and know it by memory, of what your art means and expresses and, most of all, why it's worth it. The key is *practice*.

When I was in my twenties, I was an amateur singer. There I learned that when you stand in front of an audience, you must be an energy magnet. You can't lose eye contact. The same thing happens when you are in front of a reviewer. You have to find a way to say and show your art in the clearest way possible. That

Lou Peralta

is how the magic begins. You need to be an artist on the stage. It is your time to shine. For this I ask myself: What do I want the reviewer to know about my art? That is all you need.

Besides, I write it as if it were an elevator pitch. That way I can engage with the reviewer and get their insight. We sometimes forget that portfolio reviews exist for us to meet people who think like us—people who can create an alliance to continue our work. If we get the shot there, we will take it.

P

Sara Silks

Sara Silks

Overland Park, Kansas

Sara Silks is a fine-art photographer known internationally for her work in alternative and experimental processes.

Silks received her BA in both visual arts and art history and her MA with honors in art history. Her research in her graduate papers led to the discovery of new provenance in museum-held pieces. Her graduate work with John Talleur for printmaking and her studies with Christopher James, Christina Z. Anderson, and Elizabeth Opalenik have inspired her continued work with alternative and historic photographic processes.

Silks has exhibited nationally as well as internationally in museums and juried gallery shows and had her first solo show in New York City at the Soho Photo Gallery in October of 2017. She was a featured artist with Lonsdale Gallery at Scotiabank Contact Photo Festival in Toronto in 2019 and 2020. Her current series, *Prairiefire*, has been exhibited in Lishui, China, at the Photography Museum of Lishui as part of the Lishui Photography Festival 2021–2022.

Silks is a five-time finalist in Photolucida's Critical Mass and was the international winner in two categories of the Julia Margaret Cameron Awards in 2017, resulting in a Barcelona exhibition. Both her work and her portfolio interviews have been featured in *SHOTS Magazine; Lenscratch; Diffusion Annual,* Volume IX; *L'Oeil de la Photographie; The Hand Magazine*; the Seities publication; *Fine Art Magazine*; DE (portfolio); and more.

Along with appearing in numerous museums, galleries, publications, and exhibitions throughout the United States and internationally, her work is held in major private collections.

She is a featured artist in both a Focal Press book, *The Experimental Darkroom* by Christina Anderson; and in *Platinotype* by Pradip Malde and Mike Ware.

1. What led you to attend your first portfolio-review event, and what stood out about the one you chose?

I attended a weekend retreat at the Center for Fine Art Photography in Fort Collins, Colorado, timed around the Center Forward Exhibition in the fall of 2016. Aline Smithson was generous with her time and reviewed the work I had brought. She encouraged me to attend portfolio reviews.

S

2. Please list, in order of importance, why you attend portfolio-review events.

I attend portfolio reviews to:

- Introduce my work to professionals in the field.
- Get information from professionals in the field based on their expertise.
- Practice my social skills and learn to present my work quickly and well.
- Meet like-minded people, artists, and others in the world of photography.
- Expand my understanding of the field and learn all about how photography is appreciated and used.

3. How do you go about choosing which photography portfolio-review events you want to attend and which reviewers you want to meet?

I read and research portfolio reviews to see which ones have a schedule that works for me, as well as reviewers who may have some interest in my work. The location of the review is also important to me, and I like reviews that have other cultural opportunities for me in museums, et cetera.

I look for reviewers who have some knowledge that I am curious about in an area of the profession (not necessarily about my work).

It is important for me to see a variety of people and to network.

I see the same reviewer more than once if I have developed a relationship and would like to show them progress on a project; otherwise, I try to see a reviewer I have not met before.

4. What is your average cost per year to attend portfolio-review events, including event registration fees, travel, print production, and leave-behinds? Do you have a budget for self-promotion? If not using this amount for attending portfolio-review events, what do you think would be an effective, comparable use of funds in promoting your work in a different way?

Each review is different in the way it is structured and with choices in the number of reviews.

Some reviews can cost $3,000 to $4,000, and others under $1,000.

Leave-behinds, print production, and other self-promotion work are all considered advertising, and the budget for that is tax deductible if you have a business (as is the travel, et cetera).

My budget depends on the work that I am presenting, but I never shortchange this. It is very important to stand out and show care and pride in the work.

Sara Silks

If I do not attend portfolio reviews in a certain year, my budget goes back into the work. The materials that I use are expensive, and the funds are applied to purchasing those and for research costs.

5. What are the standout pros and cons of virtual reviews versus in-person portfolio-review events?

Pros
- More reviewers are available.
- Location/geography does not matter.
- Reduced costs for travel, meals, et cetera.

Cons
- Lack of social time with reviewers and other artists.
- No sharing of thoughts, ideas, and work with others outside the review time.
- No portfolio walks.
- No roving reviewers/pick-up reviews.
- Technical issues can cause frustration.
- No standard procedure for all; each review requires different things.
- No auxiliary programming (lectures, workshops, photobook fair).

6. For virtual reviews, please share your process for making a PDF version of your portfolio.

I use Acrobat, or I export from the program I am working on as a PDF. There are many tutorials on YouTube and directions on the web . . . Each person has their preferences, and I do not always work the same way.

7. How many photographs do you typically include in each project and why? How many projects do you typically show at a portfolio review and why?

I think we have all been educated to believe that fifteen to twenty photographs in a project is a sustainable number. I also believe that the artist/photographer should prepare what is comfortable for them, depending on the way that they work, and this artificial standard is changing.

I typically take at least two projects, sometimes more depending on what I want feedback on as well as who the reviewers are. I bring cards that include work from the projects and introduce work that way, asking the reviewer if they have a preference about what they see.

8. How do you make your prints or presentation materials? Do you do anything special to your portfolio to enhance the narrative of your project?

Much of my work has alternative processes or hand-applied features and consists of unique prints.

Other work that can be reproduced is generally printed on my printer at home.

You did not ask about print size, but 13" × 19" is probably the largest I have felt comfortable with, although I have taken some unique pieces that are 16" × 20". These larger sizes can be awkward sometimes. I see many other artists with 8" × 10" or 11" × 14" work; that seems to be a good solution as well, and easier for the reviewer to look at on the smaller tables.

9. What is your opinion about attending reviews with a body of work in progress versus a completed project?

It depends on where you are in your career and what you want from the reviews.

If a photographer has a career that is new and is just introducing the work, I think it is essential to have a completed project and some good thoughts about it.

If a photographer is established, everyone loves seeing what might happen next.

10. What are your thoughts about "leave-behinds"? If you use them, please describe yours.

I have always budgeted more money for nice postcards and have designed them myself using Moo printing services. I have never been disappointed and have received many positive remarks from reviewers and other artists.

I have made small books of my project for reviewers at smaller reviews, and they respond well to the handmade aspect.

11. Do you make time to see the work of other artists? If so, have you noticed where you are in the spectrum of work, experience, and education? How did it make you feel?

I do not make seeing the work of other artists a priority, as I am focused on the reviewers and preparing and researching for that.

Many artists do share portfolios during breaks and at the portfolio walk if offered, so there are many opportunities to see work.

But to answer your question, it may serve to note the experience level of others and what they bring to the table if you admire their work. But stay true to yourself and your unique voice.

Sara Silks

12. After looking at the work of your fellow reviewees, did you seek out any connections or collaborations, or were you simply inspired by their work? If so, how did you approach the person?

I like getting to know the artist behind the work that I see, either at portfolio reviews or in open reviews that are outside the formal review sessions (roving reviews). I have approached others at social events or other programming and introduced myself and shared something that I liked about their work or their approach—and I go from there. It is thoughtful to bring your card with you to these events.

13. Please comment on relationships that have developed from these events.

Portfolio reviews that are held in person are like theater, where the main event is the review, but the side notes include all the gatherings before, the intermissions, and the after-theater get-togethers. I always felt that if I had bought a ticket to the show—at considerable expense—I should experience all of the goings-on to some degree to get the most from the experience.

    The people I talked with, shared meals with, and spent time in line with to see the next round of reviewers all became like family. It was nice to see a face and a name to associate with work, and I have stayed in touch with many of the reviewers and reviewees from these events.

14. Please share your most memorable portfolio-review experience (either positive or negative).

I had a successful dealing with a collector at one of the portfolio reviews, who had seen my work at the portfolio walk and contacted me later through my website. I sold three pieces to him!

15. Has there been any auxiliary programming (lectures, workshops, photobook fair, portfolio walk, et cetera) at a portfolio-review event that was exceptionally memorable for you personally?

The portfolio walks are well attended by the public, and I have sold work to collectors as a result of those. The keynote and lectures are always valuable, and I think many reviews do an outstanding job with their programming. I also enjoy the workshops that are offered, along with the ability to choose how many reviews you attend so you can schedule around workshops.

    I always love book fairs, and I love attending reviews in cities with bookstores that focus on photobooks and handmade books, like Printed Matter in New York.

S

16. What is your favorite and least favorite part of portfolio-review events?

I enjoy portfolio-review events when I am prepared with a project or projects that I need feedback on, and I have researched the reviewers adequately. So, if I feel unprepared, I suppose that is my least favorite part.

My favorite part is being around so many like-minded people talking about photography and art.

17. What do you think the ideal length of time for a review session is—twenty, twenty-five, or thirty minutes?

I have no preference, but the twenty-five-minute reviews that I have had seem to have the most natural flow.

18. What are some positive outcomes you've experienced from attending portfolio-review events? Please share your most memorable portfolio-review experience (either positive or negative).

I enjoyed talking with and getting to know so many like-minded and interesting people in one place at one time. So much can be accomplished in such a short time . . . I have so many good memories that it is impossible to single out one over another!

19. Have you met with a reviewer who was not a good fit for your work? If so, were you able to work around it and/or did you learn from the experience?

Sometimes I have been assigned a reviewer I did not request and who my research led me to believe would not be a good fit for my work. What is remarkable is that some of the reviewers can have personal interests that are very different from their job descriptions!

On the other hand, some reviewers who seemed to be a good fit may not respond to the work that I have brought, so it is helpful to know something about them and use that knowledge to ask a question about their jobs.

The best thing I learned is that twenty-, twenty-five-, and thirty-minute reviews go quickly, and it is important to have more than one body of work to show, as well as notes and questions in a small journal for each reviewer.

Sara Silks

20. Has a reviewer been disinterested in your work and clearly finished before the session was complete? If so, how did you handle the situation?

I have had a few reviewers who have struggled to connect with my work, but most are there to help or to network, and they do try to find something to talk about.

  I would generalize and say that the last reviews on the very last day are the most difficult (when everyone is tired), and it pays to prepare a bit more for those . . .

21. What are your thoughts about public portfolio walk-throughs, and have you ever made a sale this way? Do you have any pointers for new reviewees about the walk-throughs?

I struggle with showing my work in public walk-throughs, being a bit shy and nervous, but I have found the people looking at my work to be kind and very interested in photography.

  I have sold work as a result of people seeing it in portfolio reviews, and it has helped to have a "guest book" where interested parties can leave their contact information and interests.

22. How do you handle connecting—away from the review table—with a reviewer during an event?

I have a lot of respect for the reviewers and the hectic schedules that they keep, so I do not approach them outside the review if I see them. I will say that I scheduled a pick-up review one time on an elevator, but I already had a relationship with the reviewer.

23. Have you ever gotten to the point with your work when you don't feel the need to attend portfolio reviews? If so, why?

I have attended many reviews and have met with many different people in the photography and fine-art fields. Right now, I do not feel like I need to attend each one for the following reasons.

  When a review begins publicizing its event, I look to see who is available at the review and who may offer a different perspective for me. If there are enough new reviewers (or reviewers who have different positions in the field), then I may attend the review.

  I also think that a positive outcome of portfolio reviews includes the development of a personal network of mentors who can help with work individually. Because of this positive growth outcome, I do feel that I have "good eyes" who I can email and who will help me in this way, precluding review attendance.

S

24. What is the biggest "no-no" for individuals attending portfolio-review events?

I have seen artists attend reviews assuming that they will become stars in the field overnight. When they get discouraged, they leave. I find this unimaginable, as I am there to learn. Much of what happens as a positive outcome comes naturally over time!

Also, someone you are meeting with may move up in the field to be the next director of *Aperture*, so never burn bridges, and be a nice person.

25. What advice would you pass on to first-time reviewees?

Take notes in a small journal when you meet with reviewers …This shows interest and attentiveness and can also disguise nervousness. I kept notes and questions on the left side of each reviewer's section and that was helpful.

Keep your schedule printed and tucked into the back of your name tag lanyard, or put a screenshot as your wallpaper on your phone—always handy.

Get to know as many people as you are comfortable with, and attend programming events and pick-up reviews. Rest in your room when you can in order to process and have quiet time; it is unhealthy to go nonstop for too long.

Sara Silks

Heather Evans Smith

Chapel Hill, North Carolina

I am a photo-based artist whose work reflects my Southern roots, motherhood, womanhood, and a whimsical imagination relied on as an only child in a rural town. My photographic imagery explores the ideas of memory, loss, and family in conceptual settings. I shoot with natural light, creating sets in different rooms of my house. I consider myself a midcareer artist, switching from graphic design to photography thirteen years ago. My former design career has been an asset for using color and constructing images. My work is thought-provoking and at times heavy. To many people's surprise, my personality is much lighter and silly. My work is an avenue to express those heavy thoughts.

1. What led you to attend your first portfolio-review event, and what stood out about the one you chose?

I decided that Photolucida would be a good review to begin with when my work was accepted into Critical Mass Top 50 in 2014. People would already be familiar with my work, since the Critical Mass awards were part of Photolucida. It was intense, though I felt prepared. There were many reviews stretched over several days, and I hoped this review would get my work out to as many people as possible.

2. Please list, in order of importance, why you attend portfolio-review events.

- Opportunities for my work through the reviews and portfolio walk.
- Meeting new friends in the industry and catching up with old ones.
- Chance to explore a new city.

3. How do you go about choosing which photography portfolio-review events you want to attend and which reviewers you want to meet?

I take note of the reviewers to be sure that there are quite a few on the list who I want to put my work in front of, but I also look to see what other opportunities are available to the photographers. Is there a portfolio walk? Are there keynote speakers I am interested in? Money is also a factor—cost of the review, flights to the location, hotel rooms, et cetera.

S

4. What is your average cost per year to attend portfolio-review events, including event registration fees, travel, print production, and leave-behinds? Do you have a budget for self-promotion? If not using this amount for attending portfolio-review events, what do you think would be an effective, comparable use of funds in promoting your work in a different way?

Typically, I don't set aside a budget for reviews each year. I choose more strategically, based on when I have something to show and get out in front of people, which doesn't happen every year. I also want to make sure, if doing two reviews in one year, that there are many different reviewers in different parts of the country for a variety of opportunities and connections.

5. What are the standout pros and cons of virtual reviews versus in-person portfolio-review events?

I have never attended a virtual review.

6. For virtual reviews, please share your process for making a PDF version of your portfolio.

I haven't attended one yet.

7. How many photographs do you typically include in each project and why? How many projects do you typically show at a portfolio review and why?

I include around twenty images from one project, as well as a few images from another project as backup. If the primary project isn't resonating with the reviewer, then it's good to have another one in your back pocket.

8. How do you make your prints or presentation materials? Do you do anything special to your portfolio to enhance the narrative of your project?

I print my own prints. I show 16" × 20" because it's the typical size that I show in exhibitions. I create a 16" × 20" cover page so that when I open the portfolio, the reviewer can see the logo/title of the project first. This gives me a little time to talk about the project for a few seconds before moving on to photos. If I have had an exhibition of the work, I'll print out 8" × 10" prints of the exhibition to show the reviewer how this body of work looked in an exhibition setting.

9. What is your opinion about attending reviews with a body of work in progress versus a completed project?

I believe both are valuable. I tend to show work that is complete or nearly completed. At that point, I'm ready to put it out in hopes that galleries, publications, and online magazines might be interested. However, there have been occasions with certain reviewers where I've shown the beginning stages of a new body of work for feedback.

10. What are your thoughts about "leave-behinds"? If you use them, please describe yours.

I make two types of leave-behinds. One is by hand and more personal. My most recent handmade leave-behind was an envelope that unfolds with a set of small prints inside with the project statement. I always add a personal touch, such as a hand-sewn title or a little trinket that relates to the series. These are the leave-behinds for reviews that went well or seemed promising. I make a few extra to give to other people I might not have had a review with, but perhaps a side meeting or connection. I also make standard postcards to leave for reviews that might not have been a great fit, but I still want the reviewer to have my contact information. Postcards are wonderful for swapping with other artists and giving away at portfolio walks.

11. Do you make time to see the work of other artists? If so, have you noticed where you are in the spectrum of work, experience, and education? How did it make you feel?

I try to make time to share portfolios with other artists during breaks and view as much work as possible during the portfolio walks, though this can be a challenge while trying to man one's own table. I feel confident about where I am with peers in the industry. There is a difference in education, since I don't have a master's degree, though it doesn't particularly bother me. My photography journey happened by accident, although I have a degree in visual communications, which focused on photography along with graphic design. My fourteen years as a graphic designer prior to switching to photography was invaluable to my work. It's just a different path from others who went through a photography MFA program.

S

12. After looking at the work of your fellow reviewees, did you seek out any connections or collaborations, or were you simply inspired by their work? If so, how did you approach the person?

Most of the time, it's the breaks in between reviews where I'm able to see other reviewees' work. Sometimes it's just sharing a couch in the lobby that breaks the ice. There are some reviewees I'm aware of before arrival, and I want to be sure to have a chance to speak with them. I don't seek out connections or collaborations per se, but sometimes this happens organically while meeting and sharing work in an informal manner.

13. Has there been any auxiliary programming (lectures, workshops, photobook fair, portfolio walk, et cetera) at a portfolio-review event that was exceptionally memorable for you personally?

At the portfolio walk during Photolucida in 2015, so many people arrived that the fire marshal had to step in. Now that is a lot of people coming to see photographers' work!

14. Please share your most memorable portfolio-review experience (either positive or negative).

A reviewer looked at my work briefly and said, "People don't want to buy pictures of other people's kids." I tried to make the most of the situation and asked if the reviewer had any advice. They just repeated, "People don't want to buy pictures of other people's kids." I knew this clearly wasn't a good fit, thanked them for their time, and left. Sometimes it just isn't going to work out, and it's best to move on.

15. What is your favorite and least favorite part of portfolio-review events?

My favorite part of reviews is meeting other photographers. I create my work in a little bubble, so it's wonderful to have a few days to connect with other artists. My least favorite part is exhaustion from talking about oneself and one's work nonstop. By the end of the event, I don't want to talk about anything photography related for a few days.

16. What do you think is the ideal length of time for a review session— twenty, twenty-five, or thirty minutes?

Twenty-five minutes feels like an ideal length. If the review is going well, time really flies. Otherwise, it can seemingly last forever, especially if the review is thirty minutes.

Heather Evans Smith

17. What are some positive outcomes you've experienced from attending portfolio-review events?

During one review event, I met on the side with a reviewer (their idea) who I had spoken with in the past. They wanted to see what was new with the work since we last met, and I ended up getting a solo show from that encounter. I also received a short-term mentoring job because of a connection made with a fellow reviewee.

18. Have you met with a reviewer who was not a good fit for your work? If so, were you able to work around it and/or did you learn from the experience?

Yes, I have. This was a reviewer who was low down on my list. I knew there wasn't an opportunity there, but I had twenty minutes with this person, so I asked for their advice on approaching publications or galleries. Did they prefer emails or packets in the mail? I tried to think of basic questions that would apply to all artists wanting to maximize exposure.

19. Has a reviewer been disinterested in your work and clearly finished before the session was complete? If so, how did you handle the situation?

(This is a repeat from a previous answer—because it was so memorable.) A reviewer looked at my work briefly and said, "People don't want to buy pictures of other people's kids." I tried to make the most of the situation and asked if they had any advice. They just repeated, "People don't want to buy pictures of other people's kids." I knew this clearly wasn't a good fit. I thanked them for their time and left. Sometimes it just isn't going to work out, and one must move on.

20. What are your thoughts about public portfolio walk-throughs, and have you ever made a sale this way? Do you have any pointers for new reviewees about the walk-throughs?

S

Portfolio walks are a great way to get one's work in front of more people. I also found that reviewers I did not have a review with were able to see my work and engage with it. It's a long time to stand and talk about one's work. I suggest printing out one's project/artist statement and placing a few copies on the table. It can be loud and hard to hear, so having something everyone can read quickly is helpful, with several people at your table at a time. Always keep a bottle of water handy. You will be speaking nonstop, and my voice tends to go by the end of the night. If there's a book of the work, I always bring a few copies to sell publicly.

21. How do you handle connecting—away from the review table—with a reviewer during an event?

I realize that the reviewers have been looking at work and talking about work all day. I usually don't want to bother the reviewer while they're enjoying their downtime/social time. Saying a quick hello and "I would love to meet with you for a few minutes if you have the time" is all that I do. Then I hand out a leave-behind with my phone number/email.

22. Have you ever gotten to the point with your work when you don't feel the need to attend portfolio reviews? If so, why?

I still feel they're beneficial, but I am specific about which reviews to attend. If it's a series that has made the rounds a few times, I'll usually wait until I have something new to show.

23. Please comment on relationships that have developed from attending portfolio-review events.

I have found most of my opportunities have come from other photographers there who recommended me for jobs or other opportunities. I've also made wonderful friends at these events.

24. What is the biggest "no-no" for individuals attending portfolio-review events?

I feel the biggest no-no is being defensive to criticism about one's work. This is off-putting to the reviewer. In the end, you must go with your gut and decide which suggestions to take and which to ignore. Always be gracious.

25. What one piece of advice would you pass on to first-time reviewees?

You must go with your gut. You will receive a lot of advice and critiques, and some will conflict with others. Take the information that you feel works for you. Also, don't discount the influence and relationships formed with other reviewees. You may find your best opportunities will come from peers.

Heather Evans Smith

Rashod Taylor

Springfield, Missouri

I am a fine-art photographer, and my work explores family, race, legacy, and the Black American experience. I am an early-career artist, and what distinguishes my work is the love and tenderness that my images evoke while providing a dialog about the Black experience.

1. What led you to attend your first portfolio-review event, and what stood out about the one you chose?

What led me to attend my first portfolio review was the ability to get feedback on my work from industry professionals who were connected to the museums and publications that I wanted to have my work seen by. What stood out for this review was that it had top industry professionals, and it was free.

2. Please list, in order of importance, why you attend portfolio-review events.

Networking, feedback, and knowledge.

3. How do you go about choosing which photography portfolio-review events you want to attend and which reviewers you want to meet?

I make my decision based on the reviewer list and where I am in my practice. For instance, if I want to publish a book, then I look for reviews that have book publishers as reviewers. If I want to make more relationships and gain visibility, then I look for more museums and galleries. I will look for portfolio reviews that have several curators or gallery directors. Location and cost are also a factor in determining which portfolio reviews to attend.

4. What is your average cost per year to attend portfolio-review events, including event registration fees, travel, print production, and leave-behinds? Do you have a budget for self-promotion? If not using this amount for attending portfolio-review events, what do you think would be an effective, comparable use of funds in promoting your work in a different way?

I don't have a budget per year for reviews, but it would fall under my marketing budget, which is anywhere from $5,000 to $10,000 per year. Another way to look at funds for self-promotion would be promotional mailers and travel to industry

T

events and exhibitions for networking. Purchasing ads on social media and the cost associated with group exhibitions would also be included.

5. What are the standout pros and cons of virtual reviews versus in-person portfolio-review events?

Pros for virtual reviews would be time and money saved. The cons would be the lack of face-to-face interaction and the additional time to get to meet the reviewers and the other attendees. Pros for in-person would be time with reviewers and attendees, artist talks, training, and workshops that may be available. Cons would be cost and time away.

6. For virtual reviews, please share your process for making a PDF version of your portfolio.

My process for PDFs is using an editing software that has a contact-sheet feature. I include anywhere from fifteen to twenty images. I think about sequencing and how images flow together to tell a story.

7. How many photographs do you typically include in each project and why? How many projects do you typically show at a portfolio review and why?

Fifteen to twenty images I will show with each project. I want to show a good sample of the work without being redundant. I want to make sure I can show a depth of images that all work together. I try to show at least two projects, one project being more developed and nearly complete. I would want to get feedback on next places to take the work, what is missing, and where would the best place be for presentation. The other project is typically early and not finished. I want to get a sense of what images speak to them, whether my statement works with the images. I would also ask about feedback on other elements that I may be experimenting with.

8. How do you make your prints or presentation materials? Do you do anything special to your portfolio to enhance the narrative of your project?

Loose pigment prints in a presentation box. I like to go bigger with prints and show 16" × 20" prints.

Rashod Taylor

9. What is your opinion about attending reviews with a body of work in progress versus a completed project?

I think both are appropriate. I try to have both because if you get a little bit of time with influential people, you want to get your most important work in front of them, and often, as artists, we have more than one project we are working on that we want feedback on. Often, feedback on work in progress can help move us in one direction or another and give us clarity on ideas. Feedback on completed projects could be centered around exhibition ideas and/or publishing. Sometimes the reviewers could give suggestions on where the work could be shown or who may be interested in it.

10. What are your thoughts about "leave-behinds"? If you use them, please describe yours.

I like leave-behinds. They don't need to be fancy—just an image or two on a postcard with your contact information.

11. Do you make time to see the work of other artists? If so, have you noticed where you are in the spectrum of work, experience, and education? How did it make you feel?

Yes, making time to look at others' work is important. You can see where you fit in as an artist. In my case, the work of others around is always top tier. It gives you some validation that your work is on par with other artists who are exhibiting and showing alongside you.

12. After looking at the work of your fellow reviewees, did you seek out any connections or collaborations, or were you simply inspired by their work? If so, how did you approach the person?

I am always looking to make connections with people. You never know where your career may lead you, and relationships are very important. I approach people whose work I enjoy and want to know more about, or people who have accomplished things that I aspire to do. I approach them and always compliment them on why I like their work and congratulate them on accomplishments. I would say something like, "I see you have a book published by x publisher, which is amazing. I aspire to have a photobook at some point. In your opinion, what are some best practices you would be open to sharing about book publishing?" In my experience, most people are open and want to help.

T

13. Has there been any auxiliary programming (lectures, workshops, photobook fair, portfolio walk, et cetera) at a portfolio-review event that was exceptionally memorable for you personally?

Photo reviews that are around other, larger photo events are great. Some of the most memorable things are making new connections with other photographers and other industry professionals outside of the review setting.

14. Please share your most memorable portfolio-review experience (either positive or negative).

I received feedback from a museum curator that pushed me to think about my work in a different way. This made me think of a new way to approach exhibitions and a book project.

15. What is your favorite and least favorite part of portfolio-review events?

Favorite part is networking and getting feedback. I feel that sometimes I operate in a vacuum, and this is a way to get my work out in the world and in front of someone who can provide valuable feedback that can help me move the work forward. Least favorite part would be the cost around going to the in-person reviews.

16. What do you think is the ideal length of time for a review session— twenty, twenty-five, or thirty minutes?

Twenty-five minutes.

17. What are some positive outcomes you've experienced from attending portfolio-review events?

A new relationship with someone who is now one of my mentors.

18. Have you met with a reviewer who was not a good fit for your work? If so, were you able to work around it and/or did you learn from the experience?

Yes, I met with a reviewer who was a photo editor for a newspaper; it was not a great fit for the type of work that I do. However, they gave suggestions as to where my work could fit.

19. Has a reviewer been disinterested in your work and clearly finished before the session was complete? If so, how did you handle the situation?

I haven't had this happen before.

20. What are your thoughts about public portfolio walk-throughs, and have you ever made a sale this way? Do you have any pointers for new reviewees about the walk-throughs?

Not familiar.

21. How do you handle connecting—away from the review table—with a reviewer during an event?

I try to get to know reviewers away from the review table over dinner or separate meetings to get to know them on more of a personal level.

22. Have you ever gotten to the point with your work when you don't feel the need to attend portfolio reviews? If so, why?

No, I haven't.

23. Please comment on relationships that have developed from attending portfolio-review events.

Mentorship relationships and relationships with other photographers.

24. What is the biggest "no-no" for individuals attending portfolio-review events?

Don't ask for an exhibition.

25. What one piece of advice would you pass on to first-time reviewees?

Be open to feedback and don't be defensive about your work.

T

JP Terlizzi

I would consider myself a midcareer artist. My work is rooted in the personal and dedicated to exploring themes centered around memory, relationship, and identity. Home, family, lineage, and legacy continue to draw my interest. I am curious how the past relates to and intersects with the present and how the present enlivens the past, shaping one's identity. I enjoy creating images that come from the heart and that tell a personal story triggering an emotion.

1. What led you to attend your first portfolio-review event, and what stood out about the one you chose?

I was very intimidated attending my first portfolio review, I wasn't sure what to expect, it was all new to me. I decided that it was time for me to get out of my comfort zone, attend a review, and take my work to the next level and put myself out there, getting professional feedback, both good and bad. I had nothing to lose and everything to gain. My first portfolio review was a small and intimate one. I felt that a smaller and more intimate setting would be a good introduction to the world of portfolio reviews; I wouldn't feel so overwhelmed. What stood out was how quickly twenty minutes go by. You learn to edit your pitch very quickly. I loved being in the same hotel where the reviews were happening; it made things easier logistically, and so many valuable relationships were forged between and after reviews.

2. Please list, in order of importance, why you attend portfolio-review events.

I have a fully developed body of work that I would like to share with influential reviewers who have the expertise in providing genuine feedback and who are open to guide, offer suggestions, and help me push the work forward.

It provides me an opportunity to meet with reviewers I would never have had the chance to meet before—in a friendly environment where they are open to meeting new photographers and seeing new work.

It also provides a wonderful opportunity to meet talented photographers who you may only be aware of by name or have never met. You can get to know them personally and learn about their work and their process, get advice and recommendations, and forge lasting friendships.

T

3. How do you go about choosing which photography portfolio reviews to attend and then your reviewers?

I determine which portfolio reviews to attend by their reputation, the roster of reviewers I would like to meet, word of mouth, success stories, and overall costs. I choose my reviewers by reading their bios and paying attention to what genre of work they would and would not like to see. I do my research on the ones I am interested in by visiting their websites, checking out exhibitions they may have curated, looking at their social media, and, on occasion, Googling their names to see what comes up. I put my reviewers in three buckets: A, B, and C. This method helps when you need to rank your reviewers. A-list reviewers are the ones I really want to meet—those I feel are a good fit for my work and goals. B-list reviewers are ones I am on the fence about, reviewers who I think might fit but I'm not 100% sure. C-list reviewers are ones who my work isn't a match for what they are looking for, or I have no interest in meeting, or it's a reviewer who has already seen the work I plan to show and is very familiar with me.

4. What is your average cost per year to attend portfolio-review events, including event registration fees, travel, print production, and leave-behinds? Do you have a budget for self-promotion? If not using this amount for attending portfolio-review events, what do you think would be an effective, comparable use of funds in promoting your work in a different way?

Let's face it: review events are expensive for photographers, especially those on a tight budget.

I have spent on portfolio reviews anywhere from $3,000 to $4,000 for a three- to four-day event; this includes everything (registration, travel, hotels, Uber, food, prints, and leave-behinds). I don't budget for self-promotion. I spend what I can afford and what feels right for me. I think an effective, comparable use of the money in lieu of a review event could go toward hiring an editor or a curator to work with you one-on-one to achieve your goals; several are open to working with photographers individually. It provides an opportunity to really spend quality time with one another without the twenty-minute limitations.

5. What are the standout pros and cons of virtual reviews versus in-person portfolio-review events?

The pros of a virtual review are the low costs that you don't have like you do with an in-person event. In addition, access to reviewers who might be international and not be able to dedicate the time/expense for an in-person event. For me, the cons outweigh the pros in a virtual event. Virtual events feel cold. The warmth and camaraderie and all the things that happen between reviews and outside

JP Terlizzi

reviews in an in-person event are missing in a virtual event. There is a lot to be said for one-on-one face time and connecting with someone. You miss being able to touch and see the richness of a physical print. You miss out on a portfolio walk and all the special photography programming events that you see as a group with an in-person event.

The cons for an in-person event are typically the costs associated with travel, lodging, food, and registration. For me, the pros outweigh the cons in an in-person event. I put a lot of weight in meeting a curator or gallerist in person and being able to share a physical print. I like that they can feel my prints, see my paper choices and print size, and see how I present my work. I like to shake their hand and observe body language. I love all the stuff that happens outside the portfolio-review room. I love the camaraderie between photographers and getting to meet new people, going out to dinner as a group.

In-person portfolio reviews are much warmer, more intimate, and, hands down, my review event of choice.

6. For virtual reviews, please share your process for making a PDF version of your portfolio.

I create a high-res, multi-page PDF. All images are typically 18" on the longest side, at 300 dpi. There are anywhere between eighteen and twenty-one images in total. I start with a title page with the name of the series, where I introduce the series; it is then followed by the images—one image per page. I then finish with an "at-a-glance"—smaller thumbnails of the images presented in a grid format so they can be seen all at once. It makes it easier for a reviewer to see and speak about a specific image if I need to quickly go back to it.

7. How many photographs do you typically include in each project and why? How many projects do you typically show at a portfolio review and why?

I typically show eighteen to twenty-one images for a project. You only have twenty minutes. That number of prints seems to work; it gives enough time to present the work, get feedback, and pack up without being rushed. Eighteen to twenty-one images generally leave one minute of dialog per image. Granted, you may not talk about every image, but eighteen to twenty-one images give enough time to engage in a fully developed project.

I typically show one fully developed project when I attend a review; that seems to be my norm. However, I have at times brought a second portfolio of a project that was fully developed and that I think might be suitable for a specific reviewer I want to get feedback from. The downside is traveling on a plane with two portfolios. I've also had a reviewer not be interested in one body of work but totally interested in the other, so having a second portfolio helped. I have also shown a sampling of two bodies of work together. In that instance, I show ten images from one series and ten images from another series, with a title print dividing the two. That seemed to work nicely and is more manageable if you want to show two bodies of work. Remember you only have twenty minutes, so showing too much work from a variety of projects will not give you the feedback you might be looking for, and it's also a lot to ask of the reviewer.

8. How do you make your prints or presentation materials? Do you do anything special to your portfolio to enhance the narrative of your project?

Presentation is key, and the way you present your work makes a statement. I make my prints myself so I can control the color and the paper that I want the work to be viewed on. Paper choice matters: I use a heavier-weight paper, which works nicely with my images and feels good in your hands. My prints are 17" × 22". It's a manageable size to travel with and large enough to view the work comfortably, and it fits on the reviewer table without being cumbersome.

For completed projects, I commission custom-designed clamshell portfolio boxes. Clamshell boxes work wonderfully; they allow you to slide one print from one tray into the other. I print the title of the series, along with my name, on the outside cover of the box. I specifically will choose a book cloth and inner-lining colors that relate to or evoke the mood of the project that I am showing. My handmade leave-behinds are also consistent with the look of my portfolio box. This expense might not be necessary for everyone; it definitely elevates the presentation and sets the tone for what is about to be shown. When I first started showing my work, I used readymade black clamshell boxes that you could purchase online. That type of presentation box is totally acceptable and works nicely for portfolio reviews if you do not want to do something custom. Many photographers use a simple black clamshell box, which makes for a professional presentation.

9. What is your opinion about attending reviews with a body of work in progress versus a completed project?

I personally have never shown a body of work in progress. I am not against it; it's just not for me. If you were to go this route, I feel the idea needs to be somewhat developed and your thoughts around the idea realized. I would not show something half-baked, or something so loose, or something with multiple directions. I would be upfront with the reviewer and tell them you are sharing a work in progress, and I would be specific as to what I wanted to get from the review, be it things I am struggling with, sequence, or a direction on where to take the work. I would not say, "So hey, what do you think of this work so far? I'm still developing it."

JP Terlizzi

Personally, I feel a completed project that is fully realized, or close to being realized and developed, is a stronger route to go. I think you can speak about the work from a stronger and more authoritative place—you've already worked through your early decisions and thoughts. I also look at it as a chance to put the work out there for the first time and take advantage of the opportunity you have in front of you to meet with people who can help push your work forward.

10. What are your thoughts about "leave-behinds"? If you use them, please describe yours.

Leave-behinds are what makes you memorable and stand out from the sea of leave-behinds reviewers get. I spend a lot of time to make thoughtful, handmade leave-behinds for each of my reviewers who I have a good connection with. For those reviewers who I do not have a connection with or who are not interested in my work, I generally would leave a printed promo card.

Now, let's talk leave-behinds. Remember, your reviewer is traveling with lots of other leave-behinds, so a leave-behind that is too large is not ideal. Be considerate of their limited travel space. My handmade leave-behinds are small, accordion-style folios that feature one image. They are no larger than 6" × 4". I use book-cloth linen to make the inside and outside covers. I line the inside front and outside back as well, in a complementing cloth. The linens I choose tend to match my portfolio box that I am showing my work in. I place a hot-wax seal on the front cover, which has my initials embedded in an emblem. I choose a standout image from the series for the inside of the folio, which is then printed on very nice paper that can be folded into an accordion. I make approximately twenty-four leave-behinds in total, each with a different image on the inside in case a reviewer responds favorably to one image over another. In addition, I will supplement the image with hand-stitching or some other hand-applied application as it relates to my project. On the backside of the accordion page, I hand-sign each folio. I include the name of the series, the image title, my name, my email address, my website, and my Instagram handle.

Whenever I present a reviewer with my leave-behind, their eyes light up. Reviewers have shared my leave-behinds with other reviewers. They have used them in presentations of "memorable leave-behinds" when speaking about portfolio reviews. They've kept them in their arsenal of leave-behinds for years to come. In addition, I will often give my extra leave-behinds to other photographers I have met in the reviews who are big fans of my work—as a way of saying thank you and forging new relationships.

11. Do you make time to see the work of other artists? If so, have you noticed where you are in the spectrum of work, experience, and education? How did it make you feel?

I always make time to see other artists' work. It's one of the best parts of going to a portfolio review. I use it as an opportunity to learn and absorb and meet new people. It's a way of meeting other photographers whose work you may or may not be familiar with. I enjoy being exposed to and learning about their projects. I enjoy hearing how they talk about their work, how they physically present their work. It gives me ideas to improve upon my own presentation. I will be honest: yes, I do get intimidated by photographers whose work is more at an advanced level, or they are much more experienced or technical. I don't let that hinder me; I know my work is strong as well, and I speak to my strengths and my passion comes across.

One thing I have noticed across the board while attending several portfolio reviews: The fine-art photography community is a very close community. We all help and support one another. We genuinely are happy for each other's successes. I have always come back from a portfolio review feeling that sense of community and love from other photographers.

12. After looking at the work of your fellow reviewees, did you seek out any connections or collaborations, or were you simply inspired by their work? If so, how did you approach the person?

I have forged many strong friendships from portfolio reviews with fellow photographers. I have never done any collaborative projects with them, though. I stay connected with them through social media or email. I often will attend their openings to show support. I support photographers whose work I've seen at reviews and who are looking to get their book published through Kickstarter. If have a question or need an opinion or advice on something, it's nice to know that I can reach out to a fellow reviewee I have met to help me out.

13. Has there been any auxiliary programming (lectures, workshops, photobook fair, portfolio walk, et cetera) at a portfolio-review event that was exceptionally memorable for you personally?

Several reviews will arrange bus transportation to attend programming and exhibitions that are going around in their city. It's a great way to bond with other photographers and reviewers.

JP Terlizzi

14. Please share your most memorable portfolio-review experience (either positive or negative).

I attended one portfolio review where I brought two bodies of work. One portfolio was new work that I had just completed, which had won a couple of awards and which I had just begun putting out there; the other was work I had done a year and a half prior that was very successful, had been in exhibitions, and had won several awards. I wanted to get the latter work in front of people who may have not been familiar with it. Throughout the portfolio event, I became very intimidated by the caliber of work I was seeing from other photographers, and I was very reluctant to show my new work to anyone, for fear that it looked too editorial. I did share the new work between reviews with several photographers I knew and was comfortable around—all of whom asked what type of feedback and reaction from the reviewers I was getting on my new work. When I told them I hadn't shared the new work yet, and it was now the third day into reviews, they all asked why not and encouraged me to start showing it. My very next review was with a large gallery in Texas. I showed my first portfolio, and I could immediately tell that the work wasn't the right fit. I quickly went through the work and said I had a second body of work that was newer, and the reviewer asked to see it. There was much more engagement with the newer work. I left the review table feeling that the review went well and that the reviewer was super nice and encouraging.

Three months after the reviews were finished, I received an email from the reviewer of the gallery saying that they would like to represent me and the new work that they had seen in the portfolio review. Had it not been for the encouragement and support that I received from my fellow photographers at the review, I would have probably never shared the new work with any reviewer for fear that it would have been rejected and not accepted as fine art.

15. What is your favorite and least favorite part of portfolio-review events?

My favorite part about portfolio reviews is meeting and socializing with the other photographers during the breaks, in between sessions, and in the evening. It's a true bonding experience when you get to hang out together during lunch or dinner or for drinks at the bar. I enjoy meeting new reviewers, especially those I had a good connection with during my sessions, and keeping in touch with them outside the reviews.

My least favorite part of portfolio reviews is all the research that goes into looking up each reviewer and the prioritizing of reviewers that needs to happen before attending. In addition, the anxiety that builds leading up to the event—always second-guessing myself that the work I am showing is not going to be well received.

T

16. What do you think is the ideal length of time for a review session—twenty, twenty-five, or thirty minutes?

I have been in reviews with all three time frames. Twenty-five minutes seem to be best. Twenty minutes go way too fast, and sometimes the person ahead of me has run over their allotted time due to a good connection they made with a reviewer. I like to be respectful of that relationship and let them finish their discussion. Thirty-minute reviews can be painful if it's not going well. I think twenty-five minutes is more of the sweet spot.

17. What are some positive outcomes you've experienced from attending portfolio-review events?

I am extremely grateful that the opportunities given through portfolio reviews have provided me with gallery representation, exhibitions, print and online publications, and portfolio features.

In addition, I forged strong friendships with several photographers as well as with reviewers. I also learned how to better present and talk about my work in a group setting.

18. Have you met with a reviewer who was not a good fit for your work? If so, were you able to work around it and/or did you learn from the experience?

Not everyone is the right fit for your work at portfolio reviews. I've met with several reviewers who were lower on my list, and I could tell we were not a good fit for one another. I try to make the most of our time and ask for recommendations on how they think I can move my work forward, or if they can perhaps provide any recommendations on who might be the right person or type of institution that would be appropriate for the work. In most cases, the reviewers are very helpful.

The events have an exchange board where you can trade your reviewer and time slot with another photographer who puts theirs up for trade. I've also at times given my reviewer and timeslot, one I was less interested in meeting, to another photographer who really wanted to meet the person I had but didn't get them. It's a wonderful gesture to be helpful and supportive of your fellow photographers.

19. Has a reviewer been disinterested in your work and clearly finished before the session was complete? If so, how did you handle the situation?

Most definitely, a couple of times. It's so painful to sit through, and those twenty minutes seem to take forever. Even though you tried asking for recommendations or how to best approach moving the work forward, it still goes nowhere. In those cases, I've quickly come to accept the situation, and I politely thank them for their time, pack my stuff up, and tell them to enjoy the rest of their session. There is no reason to hang out. I'm a little uncomfortable saying this, but for those who are that disinterested, with zero connection, I don't leave anything behind, nor do I spend the time to write them a thank-you after the review is over.

For the most part, reviewers will always find something to talk to you about, even if they are disinterested in your work.

20. What are your thoughts about public portfolio walk-throughs, and have you ever made a sale this way? Do you have any pointers for new reviewees about the walk-throughs?

I personally have never made a sale in a portfolio walk, but I know several people who have. They make it convenient for the collector by accepting a credit card payment through Stripe or some other payment method like Venmo or Zelle.

Reviewers and collectors also walk around and attend these events, so you never know who is looking at your work. Just be yourself and be professional. It's very nice when a reviewer who you may not know says to you that they are familiar with your work. You have very limited space on a table in a portfolio walk—usually five to six feet—and you are flanked by photographers who are right next to you with limited space as well. Keep it clean and organized for easy viewing. I keep my prints in a box and will have some out on a table. I sometimes will include one small, framed piece that is displayed on a small easel. I always have my promo and business cards out for the taking.

21. How do you handle connecting—away from the review table—with a reviewer during an event?

I am always respectful of a reviewer's downtime and the time needed to decompress. If there is a reviewer who I really would like to meet and show my work to but I wasn't able to meet with them, I would ask politely if they would perhaps be up to seeing my work during a break or when they may have free time. Most of the time the reviewers are open and are extremely generous with their time and will accommodate the request. Ask politely, and don't hound or push; be respectful. If they can't meet with you, ask the best way, or if they have a preference, of reaching out to them. I've heard of a story from a reviewer where a photographer followed them into the bathroom and asked if they could meet with them. That takes a lot of balls. I don't have that kind of nerve, nor do I think it's appropriate. The reviewer was kind and did make time to meet with the photographer later during the event.

T

22. Have you ever gotten to the point with your work when you don't feel the need to attend portfolio reviews? If so, why?

I think you can always gain something from attending a portfolio review when you have new work or are working on a book, or with reviewers who are familiar with you, like when you share new work with them. I only attend a portfolio review when I have a fully resolved body of work that I would like to get exposure on and when I want to push the work forward. It's too costly otherwise.

23. Please comment on relationships that have developed from attending portfolio-review events.

I have met so many wonderful and talented photographers on all levels whom I have forged strong friendships with. They have always been very helpful to me in offering guidance, suggestions, and recommendations.

I have become friendly with many reviewers as well. Several have been so instrumental in helping me advance my career, and I am forever grateful. I am an active member of the galleries or museums they represent, attend their programming, and donate work to their auctions and fundraisers to support their generosity and contributions to the photo community.

The fine-art photo community is very warm, welcoming, and intimate. We are there to support and help one another. I think it's a community unlike any other I have encountered.

24. What is the biggest "no-no" for individuals attending portfolio-review events?

Speaking so much that the reviewer can't get a word in. Give a small introduction about you and your work and what you would like to specifically get out of the review in the beginning, then be silent. Let the reviewer absorb your work and ask the questions. You can add some thoughtful insights about the work as they view the images here and there if you like, but keep it brief.

Expecting you will get gallery representation or an exhibition from the review right on the spot. You are there to meet the reviewer and present the work; it's an introduction. Those opportunities will possibly come later—long after the review is over, when the situations present themselves. Sometimes they never happen.

Not doing your research beforehand. You can't know everything about every reviewer. Have a good general idea of who they are, what they do, and what type of work they represent. Keep notes in a journal or in a small notebook or on your phone, and bring it with you to the event to reference.

Bragging about all your accomplishments. Your successes are wonderful; offer them when asked.

JP Terlizzi

25. What one piece of advice would you pass on to first-time reviewees?

Be yourself, speak from your heart, enjoy the experience, and absorb. Meet other photographers, and share your work. Reviewers are people like us, and they enjoy hearing about work that comes from the heart, delivered with passion. Presentation is paramount: make sure your prints look their finest, and don't be afraid of people handling your prints.

Melanie Walker

Melanie Walker

Boulder, Colorado

I am a visually impaired, lens-based experimental artist invested in ideas. I was born legally blind in one eye. I see the world in two ways simultaneously, with uncorrectable double vision. My work gives voice to my blindness and the questions I have about what is real. As a metaphor for my visual challenges, I work with transparent materials, layering, and fabric—creating immersive installations as a metaphor for the elusive nature of memory and vision. My practice is haptic and multisensory due to my visual challenges.

In my photographic practice, I have been driven by contemporary sensibilities along with new ways of presentation. Louis Daguerre's 1822 immersive experiential diorama and a fascination for the prehistory of photography have been at the heart of my work. My approach to materials includes photographic media, alternative processes, digital art, artist books, sculpture, installation, fiber art, kites, printmaking, costume design, and public art.

I have received numerous grants and fellowships, including a National Endowment for the Arts Fellowship, a Colorado Council on the Arts Fellowship, Polaroid Materials Grants, and an Aaron Siskind Award. I have exhibited my work both nationally and internationally and have worked in more than twenty permanent collections, including the Smithsonian, the Los Angeles County Museum of Art, the San Francisco Museum of Modern Art, and the Center for Creative Photography in Tucson.

1. What led you to attend your first portfolio-review event, and what stood out about the one you chose?

I think it was curiosity that inspired me to sign up for my first portfolio review, as well as it being local. I had been aware of the opportunities friends had been given over years of attending reviews, and I was feeling that it was a necessary career step. What stood out to me, being an immersive photographic-installation artist, was that the event was oriented toward print-based work, and most of the reviewers didn't seem to have interest in other ways of experiencing photography.

2. Please list, in order of importance, why you attend portfolio-review events.

Feedback, exhibition opportunities, and getting my work in front of curators and other professionals in order to move forward with my projects.

W

3. How do you go about choosing which photography portfolio reviews to attend and then your reviewers?

Research, research, research . . . It's so important to research the reviewers and select based on your hopes for the reviews. Prioritize your selections based on your goals because it's usually based on a lottery system. I have only attended one review where every reviewer met with every reviewee.

4. What is your average cost per year to attend portfolio-review events, including event registration fees, travel, print production, and leave-behinds? Do you have a budget for self-promotion? If not using this amount for attending portfolio-review events, what do you think would be an effective, comparable use of funds in promoting your work in a different way?

I have been relatively sporadic about my participation in portfolio reviews, so it always depends on what my financial resources might be in any given year, but generally I try to keep costs down as I am not a wealthy person, and I haven't had many opportunities come from the reviews.

5. What are the standout pros and cons of virtual reviews versus in-person portfolio-review events?

I much prefer virtual reviews, without the distractions of all the other reviews taking place in the same room. Also, with virtual reviews there is the opportunity to record your sessions with reviewers (with permission) and the ability to go back and review feedback that was given.

6. For virtual reviews please share your process for making a PDF version of your portfolio.

I usually present my work in a PowerPoint presentation so I can include GIFs and videos. I have created PDFs from the images included in the presentation and included captions, a CV, artist statement, and contact information.

7. How many photographs do you typically include in each project and why? How many projects do you typically show at a portfolio review and why?

It really depends on the duration of the review. I have done reviews that were between twenty minutes and an hour. If it's twenty minutes, less is more—if you use all of your time explaining the project, there won't be any time for conversation or feedback.

Melanie Walker

8. How do you make your prints or presentation materials? Do you do anything special to your portfolio to enhance the narrative of your project?

I work primarily with immersive installations, and I have found that the way I work is best suited for online reviews—where I can share not only images but also video walk-throughs and GIFs.

9. What is your opinion about attending reviews with a body of work in progress or a completed project?

I have done both, and both situations have been helpful. I would say it all depends on your goals. Whether you want feedback on a project in progress or on a finished project that you hope to exhibit, if you select your reviewers carefully, it should be beneficial and worth your time and resources.

10. What are your thoughts about "leave-behinds"? If you use them, please describe yours.

I have created PDFs for virtual reviews and little one-page folded books for in-person reviews, which include contact information. Earlier in my reviews, I created business cards that included my images.

11. Do you make time to see the work of other artists? If so, have you noticed where you are in the spectrum of work, experience, and education? How did it make you feel?

I always try to see the work of others and learn more about how to better represent my work. I don't think about the hierarchy, because what is in vogue can change with the blink of an eye.

12. After looking at the work of your fellow reviewees, did you seek out any connections or collaborations, or were you simply inspired by their work? If so, how did you approach the person?

If you mean did I befriend anyone through the reviews, then yes, I have maintained long term friendships through the reviews. I have maintained long term connections with both compatriot reviewees as well as a couple of reviewers.

W

13. Has there been any auxiliary programming (lectures, workshops, photobook fair, portfolio walk, et cetera) at a portfolio-review event that was exceptionally memorable for you personally?

That is difficult to answer because most of my review experience has been online. I kinda like the zoom waiting room situations for online.

14. Please share your most memorable review experience (positive or negative)?

I have had two memorable review experiences, one positive and the other negative . . . The first was a reviewer who told me that my work was fearless. The second was a twenty-minute review, and I brought four bodies of work. The reviewer thumbed through everything very quickly, and we had about fifteen minutes of awkward exchange that was basically a waste of my time and money.

15. What is your favorite and least favorite part of portfolio-review events?

My favorite part is when it's over, and my least favorite part is the anxiety while preparing, to be quite honest. I am a shy person and have never been very good with promoting my work. I get self-conscious because my work is so unusual for the photo world, which seems to value prints rather than other ways of working.

16. What do you think is the ideal length of time for a review session— twenty, twenty-five, or thirty minutes?

For me and the complexity of my installation work, I think 30 works quite well because there's a bit more time for depth in the conversation. Twenty feels like speed dating and too superficial.

17. What are some positive outcomes you've experienced from attending portfolio reviews?

It was a few years after the reviews, but I did obtain gallery representation from one reviewer. Another review resulted in work being included in an exhibition in a New York gallery.

Melanie Walker

18. Have you met with a reviewer who was not a good fit for your work? If so, were you able work around it and/or did you learn from the experience?

Once I brought three bodies of work to a review, and one reviewer went through everything in a matter of minutes and had nothing to say. It was very awkward. I learned that there is a bias toward print-based work rather than anything that is based in installation.

19. Has a reviewer been disinterested in your work and clearly finished before the session was complete? If so, how did you handle the situation?

Unfortunately, I have had this experience. I usually use the time to ask questions and try to get some sort of feedback that can help with my work. It's pretty uncomfortable, but I always try to remember that I am paying for this session, and I try to get something out of it. I also make a note to myself to try to avoid meeting with this reviewer again in the future. In some reviews, you can indicate the reviewers you absolutely do not want to meet with.

20. What are your thoughts about public portfolio walk-throughs, and have you ever made a sale this way? Do you have any pointers for new reviewees about the walk-throughs?

Use the opportunity to engage with both reviewers and other artists. Spend some time not only sharing your work, but also moving through the space to see the work of other artists. It's a great opportunity to create a sense of community.

21. How do you handle connecting—outside of being in session—with a reviewer during an event?

Toward the end of the session in virtual reviews, I have asked if I can be in contact by email. Everyone has been kind and said yes. I have done follow-up emails thanking them, and sometimes they have written back.

22. Have you ever gotten to the point with your work when you don't feel the need to attend portfolio reviews? If so, why?

Absolutely not! I have always worked in very unusual ways, particularly regarding presentation, so my confidence level is not very high. I always am unsure about what I am doing, so I greatly appreciate getting feedback and having a conversation. Granted, 20 minutes is a very short time frame, but sometimes it can lead to a longer conversation over time.

W

23. Please comment on relationships that have developed from attending portfolio-review events.

Due to time constraints, financial constraints, and the complexity of my installation work, I haven't attended a lot of portfolio reviews so unfortunately, I haven't really had the opportunity to nurture long term relationships. I have many friends who have attended portfolio reviews for years and have developed very meaningful long-term relationships and have had lots of opportunities to exhibit their work.

I obtained gallery representation during one review and another review resulted in my work being included in an exhibition in New York.

24. What is the biggest "no-no" for individuals attending portfolio-review events?

Make sure that you edit down to the most meaningful work and distill down to what is essential. Don't bring all the work you have ever done. Remember, this is like speed dating and you only have 20 minutes.

25. What one piece of advice would you pass on to first-time reviewees?

Do your research and choose reviewers who align with your aspirations. Edit your work and do practice sessions with friends or other people when preparing for reviews. Remember that you are paying for this opportunity, and take it seriously. Stay open and listen to any feedback that is offered, and be respectful. Long-term relationships that can benefit your career can be established during reviews. And make sure that you don't talk the whole time so you can learn how people understand your work.

Melanie Walker

André Ramos-Woodard
Dallas, Texas

My name is André Ramos-Woodard, and I'm an emerging photo-based artist using my work to emphasize the experiences of marginalized communities and to shed light on the lasting repercussions of contemporary and historical discrimination. As a queer African American, my art serves as a platform to convey ideas of communal and personal identity—drawing inspiration from my direct experiences in life. My artistic focus lies in advocating for Black liberation and queer justice and in addressing the realities of mental health. Through my art, I aspire to give Power to the People.

I have had the honor of receiving the Denis Roussel Fellowship from the Center for Fine Art Photography in 2019 and was selected for Silver Eye's inaugural 2021 Silver List. I have showcased my work across the United States, including at the Silver Eye Center for Photography in Pittsburgh, the Museum of Fine Arts Houston, and FILTER Photo in Chicago. Equipped with a BFA from Lamar University in Beaumont, Texas, and an MFA from the University of New Mexico in Albuquerque, I am currently engaged as the exhibitions and programs coordinator at the Houston Center for Photography.

1. What led you to attend your first portfolio-review event, and what stood out about the one you chose?

The first portfolio-review event I attended was FotoFest in Houston, Texas. I didn't go as a participant, though; I went in 2018 through what was called the Student Observation Program, where I got to shadow a reviewer who was giving portfolio reviews one day. Phew—I honestly had no clue what I was getting into, but it was such a didactic experience! The reviewer I shadowed was so generous when it came to explaining her thought process behind her critique and what she was looking for in a portfolio. Also, FotoFest is one of the biggest photography festivals in the world, so, in hindsight, I was incredibly lucky to have that be my first experience.

2. Please list, in order of importance, why you attend portfolio-review events.

- Get feedback and new ideas regarding my work.
- Build connections with curators/gallerists/writers/et cetera.
- Meet other photographers.
- Panels, artist talks, and discussions.
- Learn about opportunities to share my work.

W

3. How do you go about choosing which photography portfolio-review events you want to attend and which reviewers you want to meet?

For me, which reviews I attend depends on accessibility and reviewers. As far as accessibility goes, I like to ask: Where is the event located? Maybe the event is close to home, which would make attending more affordable. Or maybe the event is home to other photography and contemporary art institutions that I'd want to visit. Second, are there any scholarships available that I could apply for? Portfolio reviews are typically multiday events, which means that on top of your entry fee, you'll need to account for travel, stay, and food. I try to look for opportunities that will lessen any financial burden.

And for reviewers, while I always appreciate feedback on my artwork in general, my selection depends on what I want to mostly get from the portfolio review. For example, at a portfolio review where I am presenting a near-complete body of work, it's more likely that I'd want to meet with reviewers who could direct me to opportunities for exposure: exhibitions, grants, publications, et cetera. I look directly at what institutions reviewers work for and how their missions align with my photographic endeavors, along with what people and places I aspire to put my work in front of. On the contrary, when I'm presenting a body of work that is new or in progress, I look more toward reviewers who have some sort of expertise in what I'm creating. So, if I come to a portfolio review with work about the Black diaspora, the highest people on my list would be those whose work involves themes of Black identity.

4. What is your average cost per year to attend portfolio-review events, including event registration fees, travel, print production, and leave-behinds? Do you have a budget for self-promotion? If not using this amount for attending portfolio-review events, what do you think would be an effective, comparable use of funds in promoting your work in a different way?

I don't attend portfolio reviews every year. I would love to, and I apply for scholarship opportunities when they come up, but I don't currently have the means to put aside money for that sort of thing, unfortunately.

Since I'm currently not in the best place to save for a lot of portfolio reviews, I put more money into opportunities like open calls that include exhibitions (both solo and group), grants, publications, and residencies. Applying to open calls may not be as direct as talking with someone about your work, but you do get eyes on your work nonetheless.

André Ramos-Woodard

5. What are the standout pros and cons of virtual reviews versus in-person portfolio-review events?

Virtual portfolio reviews are nice because you can literally get out of bed, turn your computer on, and voilà—you're ready for your portfolio review (give or take a little freshening up). You also have the benefit of sharing digital work, so, unlike bringing in your physical portfolio, you have an easier option of sharing different forms of image-based media, like video, GIFs, AI-involved imagery, and things of that nature. Not to mention, virtual reviews are significantly less expensive.

Having a portfolio review in person has tons of perks, and I'm willing to bet that most photographers prefer in-person reviews. Though you don't have the benefit of sharing video or digital photo-based media with ease like you would in a virtual portfolio review, it's not impossible; I've brought my iPad before to show digitally dependent media. On top of that, having the physical print can really change how your work is perceived. Sometimes size and paper type can play a huge role in your portfolio, and those things can easily get lost behind a screen. Also, meeting other photographers in person in a lobby or waiting area is so much better than sitting in a Zoom waiting room with them. You really can't beat the camaraderie cultivated between the photographers at an in-person review.

6. For virtual reviews, please share your process for making a PDF version of your portfolio.

I think it's best to keep it simple, and always sure to include title, series title, year, size(s), and medium. I tend to make my PDFs in Adobe Photoshop, since that's the software I'm most familiar with (gosh, I know I should be using InDesign, but we won't talk about that), and while there isn't a rubric in place like in some other software, it gives me a huge amount of versatility with small things that I can use to make my PDF stand out, like typeface, background color, and composition.

You should probably add prices, too, but I don't add prices in the portfolio I'm sharing during the virtual review; I only add those to the one I send via email after the review.

7. How many photographs do you typically include in each project and why? How many projects do you typically show at a portfolio review and why?

For a review, I tend to go with about twenty images from one body of work and about ten from another, with the intention of only talking about the body of work with the most images and the remainder as a backup. I do this because typically in a review, you've only got twenty to twenty-five minutes to introduce yourself, go through your body of work, and then hear what the reviewer has to say, which isn't a lot of time at all!

W

On very rare occasions, I'll have a review where we'll fly through the main body of work I have to present, or one where they'll be interested in knowing what else I'm doing. That's really the only time I'll pull out the last ten images, other than for the portfolio walk-through, of course!

8. How do you make your prints or presentation materials? Do you do anything special to your portfolio to enhance the narrative of your project?

I print my images myself using an Epson P800. I typically print my images for portfolio reviews on 13" × 19" paper, and I feel like that size is perfect for presentation work in that format. They're not too big as to where they become a nuisance to carry around, but they're big enough so that people can see detail in my imagery.

On top of printed work, I usually bring my iPad with me. It's nothing fancy, but it's perfect for showing any video work or installation shots along with the photographs that I'm presenting.

9. What is your opinion about attending reviews with a body of work in progress versus a completed project?

I think there is room for both, but you should know what you want from your reviewers and be able to explain where you're at with your project.

10. What are your thoughts about "leave-behinds"? If you use them, please describe yours.

I don't use them, but I think they can be a good idea if you do them correctly. At the end of the day, I feel like you just need to have something that stands out, and I personally feel like my business card does just that. As far as sizing goes, it's a bit of a double-edged sword; "leave-behinds" are typically bigger than business cards, giving you more room for information and artwork in comparison, but they're harder to fit into a bag and impossible to stuff into a wallet.

11. Do you make time to see the work of other artists? If so, have you noticed where you are in the spectrum of work, experience, and education? How did it make you feel?

Oh, yes, I always try to see other artists' work when I'm at portfolio reviews. It's the best part!

I don't really think much about how I compare to all the other makers. I mean, c'mon, who am I supposed to do that with in a group of artists who come from different experiences and backgrounds, all making work about different ideas using different techniques? I'm more intrigued by what's around me. It's inspiring to see artists owning themselves and sharing their work with the greater community!

12. After looking at the work of your fellow reviewees, did you seek out any connections or collaborations, or were you simply inspired by their work? If so, how did you approach the person?

I don't really seek out any collaborations as far as creating artwork. Not only do I typically make collaborative photographs with my art-partner-in-crime, Jennifer Marion, but I'm a bit too timid to ask a person I don't know well to create artwork together.

I do love speaking to people about their work, though! It's seriously an honor to get to know more about a person's practice, ya know? Not only do I love getting to learn more about contemporary photography styles and ideas, but seeing someone's heart and brain melt together when they talk about their work is just so energizing!

13. Has there been any auxiliary programming (lectures, workshops, photobook fair, portfolio walk, et cetera) at a portfolio-review event that was exceptionally memorable for you personally?

When I was at Medium Photo Festival during the portfolio walk-through, I had the privilege of meeting an incredible photographer, writer, and human being who expressed a great amount of enthusiasm in the work I was presenting. Even though he wasn't one of my reviewers, the dialogue we engaged in was easily some of the best I had during my time there; his words were both insightful and thoughtful, and speaking with him just came so naturally! After the event wrapped up, I reached out to him via email to thank him for his time, and he asked if we could continue our conversation on the podcast he hosts, and that was just as fun as speaking to him at the portfolio walk-through for the first time!

14. Please share your most memorable portfolio-review experience (either positive or negative).

I remember the first time I had a portfolio review with someone that didn't go too well. It would ultimately end in the reviewer telling me that my work needed more clarity and was difficult to understand, and I didn't get through many images without being interrupted for comments on their lack of accessibility. Not only was I getting negative feedback, but the delivery was a little sour.

W

At first, I was a bit bothered by the interaction, but I quickly realized that it was simply one person's subjective opinion on what I was making. Plus, I wasn't hearing that from other people or reviewers who experienced the work, so I had no reason to think that it was something to critically internalize for the longevity of the work. At the end of the day, I'm glad it happened. For me, it put into perspective that not all feedback can be great, but feedback doesn't have to change the trajectory of what I'm making.

15. What is your favorite and least favorite part of portfolio-review events?

My favorite part is definitely experiencing other artists' work and getting to know them. I talked about this a little bit earlier, but I am such a sucker for getting to look at what everyone else is making and presenting.

My least favorite part is waiting for the reviews to happen. My anxiety just climbs until the minute my reviews are over. In fact, the day of reviews, the anxiety that festers inside my stomach is so discomforting that I typically hide away in my hotel room in between reviews if I can!

16. What do you think is the ideal length of time for a review session—twenty, twenty-five, or thirty minutes?

Twenty minutes is too short in my experience, but thirty minutes, I imagine, would be too long—so I'm going with twenty-five.

17. What are some positive outcomes you've experienced from attending portfolio-review events?

I have had my work collected after sharing it with a reviewer during a portfolio review on behalf of Month of Photography Denver, along with getting a solo exhibition opportunity in Denver through the same portfolio-review event!

18. Have you met with a reviewer who was not a good fit for your work? If so, were you able to work around it and/or did you learn from the experience?

Most definitely. The experience I gave earlier wasn't the only time I've met with a reviewer who ended up not vibing with my work (though usually they're not necessarily negative experiences). That's okay though; I mean, there's no way every person I share my work with is going to like it or be able to get into it. When that's the case, it's pretty easy to adopt what I was told in graduate school critiques by one of my professors: "Take what you need and throw out the rest."

André Ramos-Woodard

19. Has a reviewer been disinterested in your work and clearly finished before the session was complete? If so, how did you handle the situation?

I think only one time, and in that case, I just thanked them for their time and left. If a reviewer doesn't want to share their time with me, then I find no point in dwelling over it. For that one disinterested person, I'm confident that I'll find another who will respect my time and practice.

20. What are your thoughts about public portfolio walk-throughs, and have you ever made a sale this way? Do you have any pointers for new reviewees about the walk-throughs?

A sale? People make sales through portfolio walk-throughs? I don't really look at it as any opportunity to make a sale, but maybe that's just because I haven't made any yet! As far as pointers go, portfolio walk-throughs are typically really casual environments, so I would just say be yourself; be prepared to talk more casually about your work. It's nowhere near as nerve-wracking as meeting one-on-one with a curator or leader in the photo world.

Oh, and go around and look at everyone else's work! If you have some time, don't just stand behind your own table; pack up your work and look around!

21. How do you handle connecting—away from the review table—with a reviewer during an event?

If the reviewer is alone or occupied with another person, I'll simply introduce myself with my name and let them know why I have respect for what they do. In my opinion, there's no reason to just do this with a reviewer you don't know about, so be sure to have good knowledge of what their role is and who they work for.

22. Have you ever gotten to the point with your work when you don't feel the need to attend portfolio reviews? If so, why?

Nah, I am still figuring out how to take better pictures, and I will be for probably my entire life.

23. Please comment on relationships that have developed from attending portfolio-review events.

So I've only been to two in-person reviews as a reviewee, but a few great friendships have managed to blossom between me and some of the people I've

W

met at these events. Some relationships are as small as keeping up with their work and an occasional message through Instagram, and others I've managed to pull in for events like the Print Auction at the gallery where I currently work. It's all over the place, but all fruitful!

24. What is the biggest "no-no" for individuals attending portfolio-review events?

Do not go into a review expecting a show!!! Please, do not expect to sweep the ED of the Whitney off their feet and be in the next biennial. Asking a reviewer, "Would you show this?" just sounds kinda greedy and unprofessional. If it's meant to happen, it'll happen.

25. What one piece of advice would you pass on to first-time reviewees?

Take time to chill and relax in between all the art speak, for sure.

André Ramos-Woodard

Jonas Yip

Los Angeles, California

I am a fine-art photographer and musician based in Los Angeles. Born in Princeton, New Jersey, to a poet-writer-professor father and an art historian mother, I was raised in a creative environment steeped in art and music, poetry and performance, design and architecture, and plenty of world travel. Yet, for some reason, I decided to become an engineer, building a successful career in Silicon Valley startup companies. Over the years, however, I never stopped pursuing my creative passions: music, design, and photography. I have since left the high-tech world to concentrate exclusively on these smaller, more personal projects.

My work explores themes of personal identity and memory: the anticipation of nostalgia, the haziness of recollection, the ephemerality of childhood, the sense of place and comfort of home, the pain of loss and displacement—fundamental concepts of human experience that form the building blocks of my identity, ultimately coalescing into an intimate record of the self.

As a photographer, I've explored the endless possibilities of photographic techniques, mastering the methods but ultimately embracing the wonderful potential in "incorrect" technique. The unpredictable effects of homemade lenses, manipulated photo materials, misaligned planes of focus, and aberrations have become my palette for photographic expression.

I have published two books, *Somewhere Between* (National Taiwan University Press, 2017) and *Paris: Dialogues and Meditations* (Nanjing University Press, 2008), in collaboration with renowned poet and scholar Wai-lim Yip. An exhibition, "*Paris: Dialogue*," featuring photographs and poems excerpted from the books traveled through Asia and was also exhibited at the San Diego Museum of Art. My work is in the permanent collections at the San Diego Museum of Art, the National Museum of Chinese Literature in Beijing, and the California Museum of Photography in Riverside, as well as in numerous private collections.

1. What led you to attend your first portfolio-review event, and what stood out about the one you chose?

Although I had been photographing since elementary school, having received my first SLR in sixth grade, it wasn't until many decades later that I began to more seriously approach my work from a fine-art perspective. To fill the gaps in my knowledge and photographic skill set, I started taking workshops at a local photography center. Around the same time, this organization had its first portfolio-review event. I didn't really have a cohesive portfolio at that point, but given the proximity and ease of participation, I went ahead and signed up. Although a little nerve-wracking, the event was an excellent experience, and what stood out for me was how open and generous both the reviewers and fellow reviewees were

Y

in general. This is not specific to this particular review, of course, but that overall experience encouraged me to search out and sign up for other portfolio-review events.

2. Please list, in order of importance, why you attend portfolio review events.

For me, the most important reason is the preparation: signing up for a review event forces me to wrap up a project, consider the edit and sequencing, and finalize my statement. There's nothing like a deadline to make things happen. After that: (a) have an opportunity to practice talking about the work, (b) gauge other people's response to the work, (c) connect with both reviewers and reviewees and generally get on people's radars, and (d) have an opportunity to spend an intense few days thinking and talking about art.

3. How do you go about choosing which photography portfolio-review events you want to attend and which reviewers you want to meet?

I've generally only gone to reviews that are relatively close, either local or within driving distance. Having a child in school and a schedule built around that, this helps to minimize the expense and the time commitment. There is one out-of-town review that I've attended regularly, but that was close to my parents' house, so I had a place to stay. Being able to get there by car also affects the size of work I can bring—and how much of it. When I did a review that I had to fly to, I actually reprinted everything at a smaller size and combined multiple portfolios into a single box. It was just logistically easier.

    I tend to look for reviews events that are geared more toward fine art rather than editorial or commercial, as I don't do much of the latter. As for reviewer choice, I'll prioritize reviewers with an obvious path for whatever work I'm showing. In my case, that's usually gallerists or curators or, perhaps, book publishers. That said, I'm not at all opposed to speaking to anybody on the roster. Everyone there potentially has useful feedback, and, as is often pointed out, people move around, know other people, and so on. You never know when, somewhere down the line, a connection you make might think of you when an opportunity arises.

4. What is your average cost per year to attend portfolio-review events, including event registration fees, travel, print production, and leave-behinds? Do you have a budget for self-promotion? If not using this amount for attending portfolio-review events, what do you think would be an effective, comparable use of funds in promoting your work in a different way?

I actually don't have a budget specifically for reviews. I've never done more than one or two in a year, and I minimize costs by choosing reviews that are local or

Jonas Yip

at least require minimal travel. I don't need to produce prints or leave-behinds specifically for a review, as those are things I tend to already have.

I'm not sure what would be an effective, comparable use of funds. I suppose one could enter a lot of calls for entry for that price or do individual consultations. But reviews are such an efficient way to share work and meet people that it seems like a worthwhile expense.

5. What are the standout pros and cons of virtual reviews versus in-person portfolio-review events?

Despite several years now of hosting online artist talk events myself, I personally haven't done any virtual reviews. But clearly there are pros and cons. Pros: We can talk to someone from anywhere in the world. Also, we can save on travel and housing expenses, which is significant. Cons: A PDF presentation is very different from a box of prints. I have a certain way of moving through my portfolios, often with a reveal pulled out of the back of the box at the appropriate time, which may vary with each reviewer. This does not work online. Also, my work often has a certain tactility to it, an important component that cannot be conveyed virtually. And finally, with a virtual event, you miss all of the in-between socializing and chance connections that can be so rewarding. Indeed, these are all reasons I haven't rushed to do virtual reviews.

6. For virtual reviews, please share your process for making a PDF version of your portfolio.

Having done much design work and laid out many books, I'm comfortable with making PDF presentations. My process depends on the complexity of the layout required. For most layout and design work, I'd use a page-layout program like InDesign (or, more recently, Affinity Publisher), but if it's really simple, I'll just pull up something like Apple's Pages. There's less control, but it's quick.

7. How many photographs do you typically include in each project and why? How many projects do you typically show at a portfolio review and why?

If the series is large, I'll choose around twenty images to present. That seems like more than enough to give an idea of the project without overloading the viewer. However, I may very well have more available in the box in case someone wants to see more. After all, we can stop flipping at any time. On the other hand, many of my projects are smaller and may have fewer than twenty images total.

I'll usually go to a review with two main projects to show, and I may choose to start with one or the other, depending on the reviewer. But I'll always have

Y

another box of smaller prints with me containing a few other projects. That way, if time permits or if one of those projects is a good match for that reviewer, I can pull them out. I also always have a copy of my book on hand and may, to give context to the work I'm showing, sometimes quickly flip through it first if I feel the reviewer could benefit from an overview of my past work.

8. How do you make your prints or presentation materials? Do you do anything special to your portfolio to enhance the narrative of your project?

I print my own work and tend to have specific papers for each project. I also print some of my promotional materials or leave-behinds myself, but specialty items, like postcards, I'll have printed. I always have plenty of postcards of the current work and the old work with me at portfolio reviews.

Presentation-wise, I don't use a fancy portfolio box, as I feel that can distract from the work itself. I prefer a simple black clamshell box, but always one that fits the print exactly. I want it to feel like it's a box that goes with the prints, as opposed to a bunch of prints thrown into an available box. When I was showing one series with nonstandard-sized prints, I made my own clamshell box rather than use an ill-fitting one. It just makes the presentation cleaner.

One thing I always do once I finish a series is create a carefully considered title page, often featuring one of the images. The title page is the first thing you see when you open the box, and it sets the tone for the work within. It's like a stamp of completion and it ties the series together.

The other thing I do is treat the print itself as an object. The papers I use for each project are carefully chosen for their tactility or surface properties to support or enhance the work. I have some work where the fragility of the paper itself is a critical part of the meaning.

9. What is your opinion about attending reviews with a body of work in progress versus a completed project?

I can see the value in getting feedback on work in progress. But I don't really work that way, and for me, a project—or at least the concept—needs to be finished before I let anyone else see what I'm working on. I may still be adding to the project, but the idea has to be pretty solid before I share it. A lot of that stems from insecurity, I suppose. I've always been reluctant to share work in progress, which is odd because I love to see other artists' unfinished work and get a peek behind the scenes into their creative processes. Sometimes I find that peek more interesting than the finished work.

10. What are your thoughts about "leave-behinds"? If you use them, please describe yours.

Some people make special handmade *objets d'art* for each presenter. I don't do that. Instead, I'll have a variety of things that the reviewer can choose to take: postcards, a "contact sheet" of the work we discussed, a thin self-published book, or, in some cases, a copy of my "real" book. I also have a thin compendium that includes all my other work. Basically, I don't want to give the reviewer something that's difficult to pack. In general, something flat and light is good. Otherwise, your "leave-behind" may just get left behind, especially if the reviewer has to fly home.

11. Do you make time to see the work of other artists? If so, have you noticed where you are in the spectrum of work, experience, and education? How did it make you feel?

Absolutely. I try to see everyone's work and hear how they're presenting it at the reviews. As for the spectrum of experience, there are always people at different points in their journey, and I don't worry too much about where I am relative to anyone else. I am glad to see work from artists at all stages of experience and am happy to engage and perhaps offer advice to the less experienced, as well as ask questions and soak up knowledge from those who have more.

12. After looking at the work of your fellow reviewees, did you seek out any connections or collaborations, or were you simply inspired by their work? If so, how did you approach the person?

Personally, I find that the time in between reviews—hanging out with fellow reviewees, sharing work, chatting, and networking—is as important a part of the review sessions as the reviews themselves are. So, I absolutely make the time and effort to connect with everyone. Most people at these events are open and approachable during the sessions, but if someone is focusing on their next review or reworking their portfolio or just taking a breather, then, of course, give them space.

13. Has there been any auxiliary programming (lectures, workshops, photobook fair, portfolio walk, et cetera) at a portfolio-review event that was exceptionally memorable for you personally?

There isn't necessarily any single event that stands out. But the auxiliary programming is important and usually worth participating in. The portfolio walks are great, as many more people get to see your work and ask questions or hear

Y

your story. I like when a review event gets all of the reviews out of the way during the first few days, then has lectures and events on the days following. That way you can get the stress out of the way and fully participate in the rest of the events.

14. Please share your most memorable portfolio-review experience (either positive or negative).

I'll share a negative one: I had a reviewer who seemed to have no interest in looking at the work and instead spent the time just talking about random things and looking around. I had to watch their eyes and note when they'd glance down and then move through the pictures at that point. It wasn't just me or my work. Others noted the same thing, and in the following years, that reviewer was no longer invited. But that was a waste of everyone's time, not to mention the loss of an expensive review slot.

15. What is your favorite and least favorite part of portfolio-review events?

Favorite? Making connections with reviewers and reviewees alike. My least favorite part is perhaps when I have three or more reviews back-to-back with just a few minutes in between to reset and to remember who the next person is. I also am irked when you send reviewers a thank-you note after the reviews and they don't respond at all, not even with a quick "Nice to meet you, too." It only takes a moment.

16. What do you think is the ideal length of time for a review session—twenty, twenty-five, or thirty minutes?

Twenty minutes often feels too short. I think twenty-five minutes is good. Of course, with some reviewers you wish you could talk much longer; with others you can't wait to move on.

17. What are some positive outcomes you've experienced from attending portfolio-review events?

First, I never go into the reviews with expectations that I'll see any immediate results. The most positive outcomes I seek are the connections to be made and an expanded network. That said, I can note some specific outcomes. In one case, I reviewed with a gallerist who shortly afterward offered to represent some of my work. In another instance, I was invited to participate in a museum show a few months after the reviews. However, that wasn't even from someone I reviewed with, but rather someone I talked to in the lobby while hanging out in between reviews. An opportunity came up at his museum, and he thought of our casual conversation and reached out.

Jonas Yip

18. Have you met with a reviewer who was not a good fit for your work? If so, were you able to work around it and/or did you learn from the experience?

You will always meet people who don't connect with your work or don't get what you're saying. That is an unavoidable and important part of getting the work out there. It's a good chance to figure out how to present your work to different people and the various approaches you may need, depending on the response. It's also a good time to remind yourself that your work doesn't have to, and in my view shouldn't, appeal to everybody.

19. Has a reviewer been disinterested in your work and clearly finished before the session was complete? If so, how did you handle the situation?

Other than the distracted reviewer I mentioned earlier, everyone has seemed to be able to at least feign interest for twenty minutes. But in the event that there's really no connection, I always have another portfolio box ready to go with a few alternate projects inside. I'm perfectly happy to put away the projects I'm pushing and pull that out. The top page in that box is an index page with the title and an image from each of the projects. I can just say something like, "Let's try one of these. Any of these catch your eye?" and easily go to that project.

20. What are your thoughts about public portfolio walk-throughs, and have you ever made a sale this way? Do you have any pointers for new reviewees about the walk-throughs?

The portfolio walk-throughs are great. We're all there with our work anyway, so let's lay it out and share it, right? I've probably sold some books. I've certainly made some connections. One downside as a reviewee is that you're unable to see the portfolios of those who are showing during the same shift.

One pointer for new reviewees is that this is the time to have your business cards, postcards, and other paraphernalia out for people. You never know who might grab a card and find you later. Many times, I've wanted to take something to remind me to look up or connect with an artist later, but they've run out of cards or, perhaps, only have enough for their reviewers. Make yourself easy to remember and easy to find.

21. How do you handle connecting—away from the review table—with a reviewer during an event?

Well, the reviewers are just other humans, so . . . talk to them like you would anyone else? That said, be respectful, don't monopolize their time, and don't try to

Y

get them to look at a portfolio or otherwise conduct business unless they ask to. Let people, reviewers and reviewees alike, have their downtime, and gauge how social they want to be. I find that joining groups for meals is a good time to relax and connect.

22. Have you ever gotten to the point with your work when you don't feel the need to attend portfolio reviews? If so, why?

As long as I have new work to share, I can see the desire to attend a portfolio review. Sometimes I don't feel the need to go to specific reviews, not because of my work, but because I may already know most of the reviewers, and I don't necessarily have something new to share with them. I guess I need to start going farther afield!

23. Please comment on relationships that have developed from attending portfolio-review events.

There are many reviewers who are friends now or with whom I connect online, at least. And similarly, there are many reviewers I may never see or connect with again and who may not even remember meeting me. The same applies to fellow reviewees. What's great about these events is that they provide an opportunity to find and start these relationships in the first place.

24. What is the biggest "no-no" for individuals attending portfolio-review events?

Bothering reviewers outside of session times when they don't want to be bothered. Hounding them to look at your portfolio at inappropriate times.

25. What one piece of advice would you pass on to first-time reviewees?

Don't get too worked up about what any one reviewer says and feel the need to constantly rework your portfolio in between sessions. After all, the next reviewer might agree with your original instinct. Who knows? Personally, I tend to stick to my presentation and, at the end, take an average of what the reviewers say, see if some suggestions pop up regularly, see if some are outliers, and then decide what can be incorporated in a way that works best for me.

Also: Have fun.

Jonas Yip

Portfolio Review
Organizers

Scott B. Davis

Scott B. Davis

Medium Photo Festival

Since the 1990s, I have worked with large-format cameras and the platinum/palladium process to explore the edges of photographic sensitivity. My work with photography is rooted in a thorough technical understanding of darkroom processes and a unique interest in the medium's history. Incorporating photographs of extreme darkness and light, working with in-camera paper negatives, and employing experimental darkroom formulas, I create multi-panel works that reinterpret the Western landscape. The finished works are one-of-a-kind objects that use scale and the limits of human perception to create playful juxtapositions of iconic landscapes.

I was born and raised near Washington, DC, and have had an uncanny fascination with desert landscapes since childhood. After relocating to California in 1989, I began making photographs of unremarkable wilderness corridors and anonymous urban spaces across the American West. Since that time, I've worked in landscapes from Mexico to Canada and, most favorably, in the nearby Sonoran Desert.

In 2021, I published a monograph with Radius Books. My photographs are found in private collections and museums, including the J. Paul Getty Museum, Los Angeles County Museum of Art, the Nelson Atkins Museum of Art, the Santa Barbara Museum of Art, the Center for Creative Photography, and others. Critical reviews of my work have appeared in the *New York Times, The New Yorker, Los Angeles Times, The Village Voice*, and online media outlets.

My website, www.scottbdavis.com, contains additional exhibition and project information.

1. Why did you become a portfolio-review event organizer?

Our community needed new opportunities to support the careers of creative photographers. A festival was organized, and many of the guest speakers suggested we include a portfolio review so as to offer additional services that would round out the planned events. We built a small review and watched it grow organically.

2. What is the most rewarding aspect of organizing portfolio-review events?

Every year feels like the best parts of a wedding. Friendly faces, new connections, and people leaving with more than they brought.

3. What is the most difficult aspect of organizing portfolio-review events?

Coordinating the timing of dates that don't conflict with other events such as art fairs, festivals, and publishing events nationwide. It's a bit like threading a needle to avoid overlapping at least one academic or industry calendar.

4. Please give an overview of your portfolio-review events, including location, frequency, and numbers (that is, number of days, reviewers, photographers, scheduled reviews).

The Medium Review happens annually in San Diego, California. We have historically held a two-day review that welcomes sixty-five photographers and an average of twenty-five reviewers. Photographers receive eight reviews, with opportunities to pick up additional, open meeting slots. The review is preceded by a welcome evening and includes an open portfolio night that brings out an eager community of people who love photography.

5. How do you go about selecting reviewers?

We select reviewers based on their ability to place the work of photographers. By "place," we mean to give it agency on the wall, in a publication, or on a platform that elevates the photographer's commitment and career. We infrequently host reviewers who are unaffiliated, and when we do, it is because they are actively engaged in the field and/or they have a track record of providing valuable insight that photographers should find useful.

6. How do you go about selecting reviewees/photographers?

We have an open-registration period that is filled on a first-come, first-served basis. We offer early registration for members of Medium Photo and have two scholarship programs for photographers who are historically underrepresented in review events.

7. What are some of the auxiliary events that happen at your festival in addition to the review meetings themselves?

We present an annual keynote lecture by a renowned figure in photography, in addition to artist talks, exhibitions, and film screenings. San Diego is the largest border city in the United States, so we work with colleagues in Tijuana, Mexico, to welcome participants on a bus tour of artist studios and exhibitions spaces south of the border.

Scott B. Davis

8. What are some essential, behind-the-scenes elements of organizing a successful portfolio-review event that attendees might want to know about?

Booking a reviewer to attend a portfolio review is rarely as easy as making a call and extending an invitation. The number and diversity of reviewers is based on many external factors, including personal and professional schedules, as well as questions about how a review can advance their own work.

9. What is the most-asked question you get from reviewees/photographers?

How can I get a meeting with a specific reviewer?

10. What is the most-asked question you get from reviewers?

What external events can I see during my visit? Reviewers are often interested in seeing exhibitions and making the most of professional time away from work.

11. What is your policy for filling empty review spots during sessions?

We hold an open sign-up before each review session (morning, noon, afternoon) to fill open slots. Attendees are told when the spaces are offered each day and can claim one slot on a first-come, first-served basis. For photographers who miss a scheduled meeting, we wait for two minutes after the meeting start time, then announce the open meeting to photographers waiting in our lounge area.

12. Do you offer roving reviews? Why or why not?

We allow reviewers to use unscheduled time as they see fit. Some reviewers want to engage with as many photographers as they can and will spend time in the lobby looking at work. We don't have a formal "roving review" element, primarily due to the scale of the review itself and a tightly scheduled event in general.

13. How has COVID changed portfolio-review events?

COVID raised the bar for what is expected from photographers. Taking a good picture and making a superb print used to be the name of the game. This still matters—a lot—but learning about an artist's process and the opportunity to see "behind the scenes" has become a reasonable expectation and a great way for artists to expand a conversation beyond the review table.

14. How do you feel about virtual reviews versus in-person reviews?

Both types of reviews have tangible benefits that can't be overlooked. Virtual reviews offer photographers a degree of flexibility in how and what they present to a reviewer. However, the dynamics of in-person meetings carry intangible benefits that can't be replicated online. These include physical presentation of yourself and your work, body language, and "soft skills" such as personality and communication, along with the opportunity for spontaneous connections that help humanize each of us as individuals.

15. What advice do you have for photographers?

Understand that photography is a long game. Embrace the joy of photography as a career, knowing it will take you places and introduce you to people who will enrich you and your work.

16. Can a project be presented, in your opinion, as underdeveloped or overdeveloped?

It's easy to have an underdeveloped project, but presenting one is unlikely to do you any favors. It takes an investment of time, experimentation, and failure to build a body of work that has merit. One criticism directed at some photographers attending portfolio reviews is that the work follows a formula and lacks the dynamic interrelationship that comes from thoughtfully developed work—both visually and conceptually. You see this in a lot of "typologies," where a subject has been chosen and photographs made without a sincere feeling of connection to the photographer's personal life, interests, and understanding of the medium.

17. What is the biggest "no-no" for a reviewee?

Don't gloss over advance communications from the organizers. We put a lot of effort into making sure each participant is fully prepared for everything the Medium Review offers. When we receive inquiries about the review process that have been covered in our communications, it feels like we're being asked to work twice because the photographer didn't want to do the work once.

18. What is the biggest "no-no" for a reviewer?

Don't be late. It's a big undertaking to arrange so many unique schedules and to know who is where and when.

Scott B. Davis

19. How do you feel about reviewees and reviewers socializing away from the table? If your opinion is favorable, what advice do you have for reviewees?

Socializing away from the review table is another way sincere connections are born—when both parties aren't in business mode and present themselves as a person. Reviewees need to keep in mind that a reviewer is meeting with dozens of photographers in a short period of time and often need to disengage from others (or engage with colleagues) so they can be fully present for other scheduled meetings. Know how to read nonverbal communication. If you're not skilled at that, it's a good idea to skip "off-table" opportunities to connect with reviewers.

20. As an organizer, what, in your opinion, is the best "leave-behind"?

The best leave-behind shows a clear extension of your commitment and is a reminder of what you and your work are all about. A QR code or link to something they've already seen (or is already on your website) can fall flat. Similar to social media that is used well, a successful leave-behind should reward the viewer with a feeling of exclusivity.

21. As an organizer, have you seen certain trends in photography subject matter over the years?

This is a fascinating topic, because we do see trends that connect artists from different generations and regions. These include subject matter, materiality, scale, and other topics that demonstrate the power of zeitgeist.

22. What is the single most important piece of advice you would give to a new reviewee/photographer versus a seasoned reviewee?

Set your expectations low. This is good advice for life, but in the field of reviews, there is a lot going on that's invisible on the surface. It's good to talk with peers who have attended reviews before and get a sense of their experience, particularly with a specific review event, since they all have different elements and atmospheres.

Samantha Johnston

Samantha Johnston

Colorado Photographic Arts Center

I am a wearer of many hats and always have been. I studied photography as an undergraduate at Alfred University and later earned an MFA through Lesly University's low-residency program. I have loved photography for as long as I can remember. In high school, the darkroom was a safe space where I could just be and create. After college, I taught middle and high school art and photography for twelve years while pursuing my MFA and making my own work on the side. My work was about my home—how light changes in my space—and finding ways to pause and quiet my active mind.

In 2015, I left my teaching career and was initially unsure of my next steps. I had completed a certificate program in arts development and program management at the University of Denver. In the fall of 2015, I took over as the executive director and curator of the Colorado Photographic Arts Center (CPAC) in Denver. At the time I was still making work, but as the position grew, I found myself making less formal work. I still find time to make pictures, but I don't always share them.

My position as director has challenged me in all sorts of exciting ways, but the job allows me to stay connected to photography and to consider our community both locally and nationally. It allows me to be a mentor, to teach, and to learn. In my career, I'm in a place where I'm challenged again and learning all the time, which is super important to me.

1. Why did you become a portfolio-review event organizer?

Honestly, the first reason is because I took over an organization that ran portfolio reviews during the biennial Month of Photography Denver festival. The second is that I believe portfolio reviews are a great way for photographers to make connections and build networks. Reviewers can also make connections with their colleagues. Additionally, CPAC offers portfolio reviews throughout the year (with me as the only reviewer), and through our monthly PhotoVox programming, we facilitate two to three print shares, where the public provides feedback on select artists' work. As a curator with a photography background, I've participated in reviews for my own work, and I've found them beneficial. I have experienced sitting on both sides of the table, which I often feel gives me a different perspective.

2. What is the most rewarding aspect of organizing portfolio-review events?

The most rewarding aspect is the connections that are made between everyone involved, including photographers, reviewers, staff, interns, and volunteers. For me, it's rewarding to watch everyone share their work—not just at the table with the reviewers, but also in those moments in the hallways, at lunch, or at receptions. All of that matters, and it's how we all make deeper connections to the work. Seeing the development of photographers' work after the reviews is another huge part—exhibitions or book-publishing opportunities that develop from the reviews. Many of the exhibitions I curate are works I've seen at portfolio reviews or those from juried exhibitions. I think a lot about the mix of reviewers we bring in and how they can be helpful to photographers. Providing opportunities for students to register for reviews at a discounted rate is also something I feel is very important. Creating space for access when we can is key.

3. What is the most difficult aspect of organizing portfolio-review events?

Balancing all the moving parts: photographer schedules, reviewer schedules, interns, volunteers . . . when it's all working, it's a beautiful symphony. But it takes lots of organization and communication and a great team to pull off long days. You can never make everyone happy, but we work to give photographers as many of their top reviewer choices as we can. Running the lottery to place reviewers and photographers together takes a full day to schedule. We do not have a computer program that does all this work; much of it is manual.

4. Please give an overview of your portfolio-review events, including location, frequency, and numbers (that is, number of days, reviewers, photographers, scheduled reviews).

Month of Photography Denver (denvermop.org) is a biennial celebration of the art form. The monthlong festival includes exhibitions, events, and programs. CPAC hosts two days of portfolio reviews. The event occurs in March of odd years, so March 2025 will be the next event.

In 2023 we had two days of reviews, with twenty-five reviewers each day, including a mix of local and out-of-state reviewers. We had seventy-seven photographers and eight students registered. Students received three reviews, and photographers could sign up for six, eight, or twelve reviews. We scheduled around 300 reviews each day. That number really shows the level of organization needed to pull off the event.

5. How do you go about selecting reviewers?

We have a mix of about half local reviewers and half out-of-state reviewers. I look at reviewers who have attended in the past and make adjustments each year. I need to adjust reviewers slightly for each festival so that there are new reviewers for photographers to receive feedback from. For instance, say a local

Samantha Johnston

photographer signed up in 2021, and then they registered again in 2023; they may have new work to show or a project that has been further developed. In this scenario, we find that most photographers are interested in having a new set of eyes or fresh perspective on the work. I look for reviewers with a mix of backgrounds and expertise, such as editorial, book publishing, gallerist, nonprofit spaces, museum curators, and independent curators.

6. How do you go about selecting reviewees/photographers?

Our portfolio reviews are open to those who want to sign up. We do not have a jurying process for the reviews. Many photographers who are also members of CPAC sign up for the reviews.

7. What are some of the auxiliary events that happen at your festival in addition to the review meetings themselves?

We host a portfolio walk that is open to the public. Usually, this walk takes place the evening of the first day of reviews, and photographers can opt in to share their work. Each photographer is given a table on which to display their photographs and engage with the public. Since it's just a two-day event, we don't currently have talks and lectures. However, since the reviews take place during Month of Photography, there are lots of photographic events and talks happening around Denver and the greater metro area. We provide a detailed listing of these events and talks in welcome packets for reviewers and photographers.

8. What are some essential, behind-the-scenes elements of organizing a successful portfolio-review event that attendees might want to know about?

Organization is everything to executing a smooth and successful event. There are a lot of moving parts. Collecting reviewer information, requesting details from photographers, and scheduling 600 twenty-minute reviews over two days is no small feat. We have hotel contracts that get negotiated over a year before the event, and we spend a lot of time setting up spaces and coordinating travel and other logistics well in advance.

9. What is the most-asked question you get from reviewees/photographers?

Who will the reviewers be? When will I receive my schedule?

10. What is the most-asked question you get from reviewers?

What's my schedule for the day?

11. What is your policy for filling empty review spots during sessions?

If we have extra reviews, we sell those extra spaces à la carte. Each day, a list of available reviews is put out on the registration table.

12. Do you offer roving reviewers? Why or why not?

We have done this at previous portfolio reviews for Month of Photography. We did not in 2023, as it's more people to organize. The open portfolio walk is a place where more reviews can happen.

13. How has COVID changed portfolio-review events?

I think COVID changed many aspects of review events and photography, among other things. In March of 2021, we had planned to host in-person reviews, but as the world readjusted, we shifted to a completely online platform. Then in 2023, we went back to in-person reviews. I think online reviews can be great, and I often participate in them, but I also think there is value in connecting with people in person. I also think that online reviews have created more opportunities for universities to bring in reviewers for end-of-year grad reviews. People ask, "Why not do both online and in-person?" But running a hybrid option is very challenging. While online reviews cut down on travel and space costs, there is still the organization of the event, creating all the Zoom rooms, and moving reviewers and photographers into those rooms—on top of organizing all the details for in-person reviews.

14. How do you feel about virtual reviews versus in-person reviews?

I think both create different options for photographers and reviewers. Online has just the cost to participate and does not include the travel expense, but establishing a personal connection on Zoom can be challenging. Virtual reviews also create a space that is quieter, one that the photographer and reviewer can control more. In-person reviews include added travel expenses, but reviewers then see the work in person, and reviewees have other opportunities to network in the hallway, photographers' break room, et cetera.

Samantha Johnston

15. What advice do you have for photographers?

Do your research and read bios of reviewers beforehand. At the event, consider your expectations and what you hope to get out of your meetings with reviewers. Being as prepared as you can is important. Ask questions. If you have not participated in reviews before, volunteer for the event, and/or go to talks and workshops that help you prepare for the event. Consider your goals as a photographer.

16. Can a project be presented, in your opinion, as underdeveloped or overdeveloped?

In my opinion, I meet with photographers who have work at all different stages, under- and overdeveloped. I feel there needs to be space for those who are new to reviews or making work to share it and receive feedback. I also think there are photographers whose work is more developed and who know what they are looking for in getting the work out there.

J

17. What is the biggest "no-no" for a reviewee?

Not doing your research and not understanding who you are talking with.

18. What is the biggest "no-no" for a reviewer?

Being late to reviews.

19. How do you feel about reviewees and reviewers socializing away from the table? If your opinion is favorable, what advice do you have for reviewees?

I think it's fine. We are all humans making connections. It can be challenging when you are first at an event for photographers and reviewers. I remember when I started going to reviews, I didn't know that many people. For many reviewers or photographers, it's all about making connections. But networking and putting yourself out there, no matter what side of the table you're on, can be challenging. I became an executive director, but before that I was a photographer. I've always loved looking at pictures and talking about them.

20. As an organizer, what, in your opinion, is the best leave-behind?

I've received beautiful handmade leave-behinds, original pieces created for the reviews, books, et cetera—but, honestly, I think a business card is just fine. A card with your information, and maybe an image of the work I looked at, works great. I think follow-up is also important.

21. As an organizer, have you seen certain trends in photography subject matter over the years?

Yes. Over the years, I would say trends often shift to what is happening around us: the pandemic, inequities in our society, the environment, to name a few. There will always be trends or popular subject matter; some work is very poignant at certain times, based on the surrounding cultural climate, while other projects can take further time to grow in their power and profoundness.

22. What is the single most important piece of advice you would give to a new reviewee/photographer versus a seasoned reviewee?

You never know where a conversation will lead. That goes for seasoned photographers and those who are new to reviews. I see photographers not sign up for certain reviewers because they think a reviewer can't "do something for" them—but I'm a firm believer that you never know where conversations will lead or what new connections can happen.

Samantha Johnston

Laura Moya

Photolucida, *Former Executive Director*

I have been honored to serve as the director of Photolucida for the past eighteen years (from 2004 to 2023); as such, I organized nine portfolio-reviews events with the support of additional staff and volunteers. For ten-plus years, Photolucida spearheaded Portland Photo Month, a citywide celebration of photographic exhibitions and events.

My job duties were largely administrative and organizational, yet I had a lot of freedom to try new things. It was rewarding to develop programming ideas like the Lunchtime Chat series and the Photobook Fair during the review event. Participants loved being based at the Benson Hotel—an elegant, historic, twelve-story hotel in downtown Portland adjacent to the Pearl District. In addition, I was honored to serve as a reviewer at other review events, including PhotoAlliance (San Francisco), ACP (Atlanta), LensCulture (Paris), GuatePhoto (Guatemala), and FestFoto (Brazil). It was rewarding to work on developing opportunities connected to Critical Mass, including monograph awards, solo-show awards, residencies, grants, and scholarships, and collaborating with venues in the United States and abroad on the Critical Mass Top 50 Exhibition.

I was always excited when asked to jury, write an intro to someone's book, or curate a show. My favorite curatorial projects were The Early Works Project (cocurated with Laura Valenti), HUMAN/NATURE (Lishui Art Museum, 2021 Lishui Photo Festival), and PERSEPHONE'S EDGE (Benaki Museum, 2022 Athens Photo Festival). Nothing gives me greater satisfaction than using photographic imagery as the beautiful language that it is to tell a story and make people think a bit differently than they did before they walked into a space.

1. Why did you become a portfolio-review event organizer?

When I became the director at Photolucida in 2004, organizing the biennial portfolio-reviews event was part of my job description. It was a learning curve for me—I had not heard of this thing called portfolio reviews, but knowing some foundational history was helpful, and thus, I was happy to share.

Fred Baldwin and Wendy Watriss went to Les Rencontres d'Arles in 1983, after Wendy won an Oscar Barnack award. This trip was the major impetus to create FotoFest. They were also inspired by elements of Le Mois de la Photo in Paris; namely, how that festival used municipal museums and buildings to stage their exhibitions. The first FotoFest Biennial occurred in 1986 and has continued every two years since. The first Meeting Place also occurred in 1986 at the Warwick Hotel, with 110 reviewers over 14 days. Though, as the lore goes, the earlier Meeting Place portfolio reviews were more "loose" than they are now—

no predefined preferences or schedules, just first-come, first-served—but still a very large program with a lot of participants.

Photolucida adapted the portfolio-reviews model in 1999 as a version in the Pacific Northwest. Review Santa Fe began about the same time as part of CENTER's programming in the Southwest. For many years it was only FotoFest, Photolucida, and Review Santa Fe in the United States that were offering review events; then a second wave of photography organizations began producing them as part of their programming.

2. Please give the numbers on your portfolio-review events (that is, number of days, number of reviewers, number of photographers, and number of reviews).

Photolucida has operated on a biennial schedule opposite FotoFest, always held in April at the Benson Hotel in Portland. It is traditionally a 4-day event involving 60 reviewers, 160 photographers, and a small roster of roving reviewers. Photographers would get four to five scheduled reviews a day, for a total of eighteen reviews on average. So that works out to be roughly 2,880 twenty-minute meetings over the course of four days.

3. How do you go about selecting reviewers?

At Photolucida, it was important to have a well-rounded grouping of reviewers representing different areas of the photography world—curators, publishers, editors, gallerists, consultants, and photo-festival and nonprofit directors. Most of the reviewers were returning—I would ask for feedback from photographers right after the event (to see how meetings had gone) and a year afterward (to see if any opportunities had been offered). I was focused on having reviewers who were able to give opportunities, but I also recognized that some reviewers were amazing at giving strong feedback and suggestions without the possibility of tangible opportunities. I would focus on bringing new reviewing talent in as well—maybe some lesser-known names in reviews-event circles or people starting new photographic endeavors and who were looking for new talent.

4. How do you go about selecting photographers?

In the early days of Photolucida, registration was "first come, first served," and 160 spots would fill up in the first 20 minutes of registration opening—it was crazy! At some point, we decided to make registration "vetted," which meant we would open registration for about a week, look at the websites of everyone who was interested in attending, and if their work was strong enough, put the name in a group. Then we ran that list of names through the "randomizer"—computer

Laura Moya

programming that would choose the 160 names for the slots; the rest would become the wait list.

5. What are some of the auxiliary events that happen at your festival, in addition to the review meetings themselves?

Photolucida has always had a portfolio walk, which takes place in the Portland Art Museum's Sunken Ballroom—a gorgeous space that accommodates the large amount of people waiting at the door to get in! We produced a Lunchtime Chat series at noon every day—where reviewers, and sometimes artists, would give talks on relevant topics. For years we had public lectures at the Portland Art Museum by well-known photographers. Some years we had the Pearl District gallery walk, where galleries showing photography for Portland Photo Month would stay open late and welcome our participants and the public. At the last few Photolucida events, we had a Photobook Fair, along with book signings, that was very popular for our participants and the public. Our closing parties were phenomenal events as well!

6. What are some essential, behind-the-scenes elements of organizing a successful portfolio-review event that attendees might want to know about?

The basis for a successful review event is having photographers effectively choose who they would most like to meet with. After receiving reviewer bio information and figuring out who makes the most sense for them to connect with, photographers enter their reviewer preferences online before the event, and Photolucida's programming assigns almost 3,000 meetings. It is very complicated, and the system must perform very accurately. If photographers get most of the reviewers they requested—say, sixteen of their top twenty—that is a great success rate. Photographers should know that there are usually four or five reviewers everyone wants to meet with, so statistically their names can't pop up on everyone's assigned list. Reviewer assignments are always going to include one or two people who were not high on someone's list, but there is always the opportunity to do trades, and one may be pleasantly surprised by a terrific conversation with a reviewer one was not expecting to meet with. So, an accurate system of assigning preferred reviewers to photographers is very key to the success of the event.

Also, it is paramount that the reviewing room is run in a very organized, efficient way—a great reviewing-room manager and volunteers make this happen. Things are wound very tightly, making sure people know where they are going, that they are not late, and that they don't stay longer in conversation than they are supposed to. If people are not attentive to these things, it can get messy fast!

Order in the reviewing room makes for less stress for everyone.

7. What is the most rewarding aspect of organizing portfolio-review events?

I think it always hits me at some moment during the closing party—the realization that we *all* pulled it off! Photolucida staff, reviewers, photographers, volunteers—we all worked hard to get to this specific moment in time. It is the feeling of real community at the end of the four days together—everyone is connected by the shared experience, and it is kind of amazing.

8. What is the most difficult aspect of organizing portfolio-review events?

Logistically, after all this time I would have to say, things that happen at the last minute. Specifically, cancellations (photographers and/or reviewers) after people have already been integrated into the scheduling system. It's nothing that can't be accommodated, but it can produce a lot of administration during a very busy time!

9. What is the most-asked question you get from photographers?

Photographers want to know how to navigate meeting with reviewers outside scheduled meetings. It is a bit tricky—some reviewers look forward to looking at work all hours of the day and night, and some reviewers want to reserve their energy for scheduled reviews only. The trick is to approach the reviewer and not make them feel cornered; put the ball in their court. Say something like, "If you have any extra time, I would love to meet with you. Here is my card with my cell phone number—please let me know if/when this might work!" And this gives the space for the reviewer to say something like, "How about at 5:00, after the last session?" or they can graciously just take the card if they are not into it.

10. Any advice for photographers?

If you are new to the review-event world, consider doing a two-day instead of a four-day event as an introductory experience, so it is not too overwhelming. Remember that relationships with reviewers take time to build—sometimes immediate opportunities are offered during a meeting, but more often it takes time for a reviewer to get to know you and your work before offering the opportunity. Don't hound or be pushy with a reviewer—they will remember you, but not fondly! A follow-up thank-you card is nice to send to a reviewer after the event, and always ask if they mind if you add them to your mailing list. Make the time to socialize with your peers—they can be a great support system and, potentially, connect you with opportunities down the line (and you should think about how you can do the same).

Laura Moya

11. What is your policy for filling empty review spots during sessions?

If Photolucida was working with a last-minute cancellation or someone not showing up for an appointment, we had a designated area near the reviewing-room entrance where people could wait for the opportunity to jump into an open spot. We would let photographers know of the availability and who with. If there were several people waiting, it might be that one already had an appointment with the reviewer, or maybe their work was not a good fit. Then it would go to the person most appropriate. If several people wanted the spot, we would do an impromptu "rock, paper, scissors" to let fate pick the person for the spot.

12. Do you offer roving reviewers? Why or why not?

Yes, Photolucida has always had a roster of roving reviewers as part of our event—it has added a terrific extra layer to the event experience. Comprised mostly of people from the Portland area who want to participate in a more informal way as a reviewer, it allows, I think, conversations to occur that bring value to both sides of the table. We had a designated "roving room," where photographers could just hang out between scheduled appointments and converse with rovers and their peers.

M

13. How do you feel about virtual reviews versus in-person reviews?

They are two very different experiences. Virtual reviews are obviously more efficient (easier to organize) and less of a financial expense for both the organizer and the photographer—no one is paying travel or lodging fees, and or carrying any worries connected to COVID. But then the important social aspect of review events is not being experienced (in-person conversations, networking), and the auxiliary programming (talks, exhibitions, portfolio walk) is not an experience, either.

14. How has COVID changed portfolio-review events?

COVID irrevocably affected photography organizations doing review events. Often these events are the organization's main source of income, and to have to cancel them during the pandemic was detrimental. Photolucida had to cancel its 2021 event and work with that fiscal deficit. We decided to hold the event in 2022 in a reduced capacity (half the days, half the reviewers, half the photographers), with all participants showing proof of vaccination and being masked indoors. It was largely successful as such. At the time of writing, some review events are being held in person, some are hybrid, and some are strictly online still. I am not sure if the super-large versions of in-person review events are a thing of the past; I guess we shall see.

15. What is the most-asked question you get from reviewers?

There is not one I can think of! Most questions coming from reviewers have to do with logistics—travel, lodging, food—connected to the event. Sometimes someone wants to clarify if they are obligated to give reviews outside scheduled appointments, and the answer is—it is up to them!

16. Can a project be, in your opinion, presented as underdeveloped or overdeveloped?

Often, photographers intentionally take projects to review events that are underdeveloped, as they are looking for direction to move them forward. There are also projects that photographers feel are complete and they are shopping them around as such for opportunities. Ideally, a photographer can bring two projects: the first they feel is complete and the second one could be in development, and they would solicit more feedback on that one.

17. What are the biggest "no-no's" for a reviewee?

Being late to an appointment or not getting up when your time is up. Being too asking with a reviewer's time outside a scheduled appointment. Just sitting quietly during a review session and letting the reviewer do all the talking—have some talking points and questions at the ready.

18. What is the biggest "no-no" for a reviewer?

I can't think of any specific thing; Photolucida's reviewers have always been very professional and gracious. We have had just a very few reviewers over the years give blunt opinions about work without framing it in a constructive way. This leads me to note that reviewing can be a developed skill as such—even if the work does not resonate with you personally, you can be helpful with your choice of words and encouragement.

19. How do you feel about reviewees and reviewers socializing away from the table? If your opinion is favorable, what advice do you have for reviewees?

I feel it is totally fine. It is great to see both sides sharing a meal or a drink—I am sure many meaningful conversations happen this way. Reviewees should not use

Laura Moya

this time to promote their work, though, unless a reviewer specifically asks about it. Downtime is important!

20. As an organizer, what, in your opinion, is the best leave-behind?

Something graphically eye-catching and nicely produced. Not too much information; the point is to have an image that represents your work well and just contact info (name, website, social media), which is fine! Make it a nice-enough piece that someone wants to keep it/pin it on a bulletin board. Compelling leave-behinds can serve one well at the portfolio walk—with reviewers and with peers.

21. As an organizer, have you seen certain trends in photography subject matter over the years?

None specifically come to mind. I am more curious about (looking forward to) how AI imagery is going to disrupt/change the photography world.

22. What is the single most important piece of advice you would give to a new reviewee/photographer versus a seasoned reviewee?

Sometimes new reviewees are nervous about jumping into the event, and that is understandable; it can be overwhelming at first! Usually, after the first few hours, new reviewees get "the system" and are able to relax a bit. I would just say, don't be nervous, have fun—and ask if you have any questions!

M

Laura Wzorek Pressley

Laura Wzorek Pressley

CENTER Santa Fe

After receiving my BFA with a focus in photography, I moved to the Bay Area, where I was an artist-in-schools at the Richmond Arts Center. There I witnessed the positive impacts of public programs on marginalized communities, and I have remained in the nonprofit sector since. Now, I am a cultural producer and an arts administrator who has been at the helm of the not-for-profit organization CENTER in Santa Fe for over sixteen years. CENTER's mission is to support socially and environmentally engaged lens-based projects through education, funding, public platforms, and partnerships. In addition to producing high-impact, outcome-driven programs, we produce exhibitions highlighting some of today's critical issues, including The Dispossessed (2016); The Frontier (2016); Immigration, Migration, & Evolving Boundaries (2015); and Art & Oppression (2017), among others, collaborating with local and international venues. Providing leadership continuity and having increasing government grant contracts have proven to be strengths of the organization. I consider dedicated, evolutionary, sustainable growth to be a strategic and creative practice.

I recently began efforts to seek out how to make systemic changes, getting my master's in public administration toward that end. One of my first research projects was titled "Is There Evidence That Photography Directly Influences Policy Reform?" (the answer is yes). I started exploring how policy and impact evaluations diagnose and provide recommendations for institutional changes. In 2023, I became a senior fellow in the Policy & Evaluation Lab at the University of New Mexico, providing quantitative and qualitative analysis to build evaluation capacity in community organizations. My latest research project focused on the efficacy of diversity, equity and inclusion programs. I'm passionate about root-cause analyses and transformative evaluation.

1. Why did you become a portfolio-review event organizer?

It's something similar to what Ayesha Siddiq is attributed to saying: "Be the person you needed when you were younger." Part of the reason I became an organizer, and the reason I continue after all of these years, was that there was a gap between education and practice. The opportunities and the sense of community (nonprofit) review programs foster provide a bridge between the academy and the field.

2. What is the most rewarding aspect of organizing portfolio-review events?

We have heard that participating in Review Santa Fe has changed people's lives. Feeling understood and heard is an essential human need, and at the top of Maslow's Hierarchy of Needs is self-actualization. For many of those attending our program, it's a career highlight, and putting one's personal creative expression into the world is beyond rewarding. I think it is vital to our healthy communities that today's stories and personal truths are told and retold.

3. What is the most difficult aspect of organizing portfolio-review events?

Not all participants have transformative experiences, and although it can be so impactful for some, it's not for everyone. Also, fund-raising is an ongoing challenge.

4. Please give an overview of your portfolio-review events, including location, frequency, and numbers (that is, number of days, reviewers, photographers, scheduled reviews).

Historic downtown, Santa Fe, New Mexico, for 3 days—with 100 photographers, 45 reviewers, and approximately 1,000 one-on-one portfolio reviews, equating to a minimum of 9 reviews per photographer.

5. How do you go about selecting reviewers?

We focus on curators, publishers, and editors who are looking for new work.

6. How do you go about selecting reviewees/photographers?

Review Santa Fe is a juried process; there is a selection committee comprised of three professionals, usually a photographer who has participated previously and former reviewers. The selection committee scores the work individually, and the top-scoring projects are invited. The next thirty-five are added to the wait list. There are often very small numeric differences between the scores of those who are invited and those who are not. So, what one submits is very important: the edit, the wording of your statement—that can be that extra one point you needed to get an invite. That's why it's worthwhile to keep trying with new selection committees and new edits of your project. Small tweaks can make a difference.

Laura Wzorek Pressley

7. What are some of the auxiliary events that happen at your festival in addition to the review meetings themselves?

- Opening-night talk (in 2023, it was author Lucy Lippard)
- Opening- and closing-night receptions
- Portfolio Walk and Book Fair
- Scholar lectures
- Career-in-the-Arts Lecture for the student volunteers
- Coffee with an Editor for student volunteers
- Award-Winners Exhibition (year dependent)

8. What are some essential, behind-the-scenes elements of organizing a successful portfolio-review event that attendees might want to know about?

We prioritize the experience of the photographer. If there is a reviewer who has been overly harsh and unhelpful, we would like to know, and we ask for your feedback in our follow-up survey. We take feedback to heart. Reviewers fitting into the CENTER culture is important to us.

If you have any special needs or requests that require more time or attention for any reason, we ask that photographers let us know ahead of time so we can prepare. We are a small team with many demands on site, so preparation is key in providing accommodations (which we are happy to do!).

9. What is the most-asked question you get from reviewees/photographers?

Who should I see? Can I bring my oversized portfolio?

10. What is the most-asked question you get from reviewers?

Will I know who I am going to meet with ahead of time?

11. What is your policy for filling empty review spots during sessions?

We offer them to volunteers first and then will offer them for purchase to the reviewees. We can't give them away for free, as we can't fairly distribute reviews to all 100 attendees.

12. Do you offer roving reviewers? Why or why not?

We don't have a hard policy; anyone is welcome to do it, but we haven't invited roving reviewers for many years. Our reviewers tend to want to be in the review room and not outside of it.

13. How has COVID changed portfolio-review events?

There are more online review experiences; there's more online mentoring. In 2022 we required masks, and most of the feedback was appreciative of our concern for everyone's safety.

14. How do you feel about virtual reviews versus in-person reviews?

I think many people initially viewed it as a consolation, but they turned out to be really effective. I am in the process of conducting a full evaluation on in-person versus online review outcomes, but a cursory analysis shows there were also outcomes for online reviews for photographers. There are other metrics and benefits with in-person events, as many people indicate that the friendships built are such a valuable part of their experience, and the opportunity for socializing is diminished with virtual reviews. In terms of the reviews themselves, they were surprisingly positive. Because each person signs in from their home or office, they don't have to travel and can be even more present—less distracted—for the conversations. We saw several evaluations indicating that some reviewers and photographers found the experience to be more effective than in-person events.

15. What advice do you have for photographers?

Reviews are about building relationships and being patient, thinking in terms of the long game. The right moment will happen for you to reach an expanded audience. Your role is to ensure you have the network and the clear articulation of your idea to successfully put the work out into the world.

16. Can a project be presented, in your opinion, as underdeveloped or overdeveloped?

Work that is too new or not resolved probably will not as be competitive in the selection process for Review Santa Fe. I have seen unfinished, in-progress—but resolved—ideas being shown at Review Santa Fe when they are still being developed, and having key feedback at the right moment can advance the project and be really useful.

"Overdeveloped" is an interesting notion; I think that depends on the reviewer. Some reviewers appreciate the polish and seeing book layouts, for instance, but some prefer to see the prints and projects that have room to evolve.

Laura Wzorek Pressley

17. What is the biggest "no-no" for a reviewee?

Being dominating and aggressive is difficult for all involved. Attitude goes a long way. This is a human-centered event. There are going to be flight delays; there are going to be hiccups. Having a bad attitude in any interaction is likely going to backfire.

18. What is the biggest "no-no" for a reviewer?

Getting up from the review table before the end of the review. We encourage reviewers to try to be helpful and educational even if the work is not in their interest area.

19. How do you feel about reviewees and reviewers socializing away from the table? If your opinion is favorable, what advice do you have for reviewees?

If it's welcomed by both parties, of course socialize. I would advise to wait for the reviewer to ask about your work rather than initiating that conversation. Keep in mind that at Review Santa Fe, for instance, the reviewers will have had at least eight meetings in half a day, and on Saturday they can have up to fifteen meetings. It can be tiring for some people to have that level of interaction for extended periods. It's nice to relax and decompress during the non-review times.

20. As an organizer, what, in your opinion, is the best leave-behind?

A selection of cards or prints, then ask each reviewer to choose one of four or so options. It creates an opportunity to select a favorite.

P

21. As an organizer, have you seen certain trends in photography subject matter over the years?

I feel really fortunate to have this 30,000-foot perspective on the photographic zeitgeist of the past twenty years through our annual calls for entry. Our annual award-winners are often reflective of the emergent trends. Starting in 2002, following the 9/11 attacks, we saw Bill Hogan's work "Finding Sanctuary," which provides "a look at personal sanctuaries around the world to see how families in other cultures find security among the harsh realities." In 2003, we saw the new documentary style start to take hold as Alec Soth won the Santa Fe Prize for *Sleeping by the Mississippi*. In 2004, we saw more of these feminine fantastical or lyrical approaches; Maggie Taylor's project won that year, and Julie Blackmon's uncanny family tableaus won the following year. Fast forward to COVID-19—with a surge of interior images and more projects examining mental illness—and on to an increase in protest imagery the past three years. When describing the value of this to our grantors, we explain that the CENTER programs spotlight how the defining external factors—such as global events—shape, and, in turn, are influenced by the creative response.

22. What is the single most important piece of advice you would give to a new reviewee/photographer versus a seasoned reviewee?

It's all about timing with your work. Be patient. Note that editors of magazines sometimes show conceptual bodies of work or human-interest stories that can then reach audiences of thousands, if not millions (examples: *HuffPost* or *Wired*), and that opportunity can be leveraged for exhibition or book contracts. One opportunity leads to others.

Laura Wzorek Pressley

Juliette Wolf-Robin
American Photographic Artists

American Photographic Artists (APA) is an established not-for-profit legacy trade association of professional photographers working primarily in the commercial advertising, editorial, and entertainment sectors. APA's mission is to advocate, educate, and elevate the photographic community.

I have worked with professional photographers on their marketing and business development for more than three decades. As the founder of a series of print and online photographer directories, including *Found Artists*, Ad Age's *Creativity Spark*, and *Alternative Pick*, I have been both a speaker and a moderator at photo-industry conferences such as PhotoPlus Expo and the Palm Springs Photo Festival, focusing on topics about working in the industry. Additionally, I've hosted webinars with industry professionals for APA (these can be found on our *YouTube* channel), and I was the host of *Art Buyers Lounge*, a podcast interview series.

By working with photographers, and those who hire photographers, for so many years, I know the experience from both sides of the table. It has been twenty years since I helped set up the first in-person portfolio reviews for photographers at the Art Directors Club in New York City, and I've been a reviewer and facilitator of photo reviews at various events ever since.

1. Why did you become a portfolio-review event organizer?

I want to connect photographers to the people who can hire them. Portfolio reviews provide an opportunity to introduce and connect photographers with industry creatives, photo editors, and art producers. If they have already met, it's a way to showcase a new project and to build a stronger relationship.

It can be challenging for photographers to find and meet agency art buyers, photo editors, and creatives. Producing an advertising campaign is expensive, and there is a lot on the line for both the ad agency and the client. The creatives want to feel confident that the photographer will successfully bring their vision to life, and the client needs to know that they can produce the project on time and on budget. Everyone involved is looking for it to be a good experience, particularly if they will be traveling together or spending multiple days on the project.

For an editorial publication, especially for portrait work, the photo editor needs to have confidence in the person they will be sending on assignment—especially if it's to photograph a celebrity, or if there will be limited access to the subject.

The style of work is only one factor in choosing a photographer. A photographer is more likely to be hired if they already work with the firm or are known in the industry. Portfolio reviews build relationships and start a rapport with potential clients.

Additionally, in order to introduce new voices to those who hire photographers, American Photographic Artists (APA) has launched special programs, including "Bridge" and "Level-Up," that create opportunities for diverse talent to get exposure. We recognize the need to tell stories from a wider lens and understand that not everyone has had the same access to be recognized. We'll continue to work on ways to provide opportunities and showcase talent.

APA has also produced portfolio reviews with photo agents in order to introduce photographers to those who might represent them commercially. These reviews provide an opportunity for feedback to the photographer from someone who actively presents work of multiple photographers to buyers. Photographers want to know how their presentation compares to those of other photographers and might be looking for tips on what to include or omit from their portfolio or website.

Reviews with photo agents and photo consultants can provide the photographer with ideas on how they can better market their work. They also have the opportunity to learn about other industry sectors they may not have considered.

The key for photographers is to ask a lot of questions, listen to the ideas presented, then take the parts they like and leave the rest. Remember, it's just the reviewer's point of view at the moment. My advice to any photographer taking part in a review is this: Consider the input you receive and go with your intuition. What resonates with you? Combine what you hear from different reviewers with the opinions of respected voices in your life. No one else will have the right answer but you.

2. What is the most rewarding aspect of organizing portfolio-review events?

Making connections. It has become challenging for photographers to connect with people who can hire them. Photographers need to research agencies, brands, and publications they want to work for. Once they identify a potential audience, how do they get seen? Perhaps they send an email, but in a sea of emails, how can they stand out? What will the ask be? Will they know that their email has been read? Photographers use social media for awareness, but with so many platforms, where should they direct their efforts? They can't saturate them all, and there is no guarantee that a post will be seen by the right people. Physical mailings can be expensive, and with so many professionals working remotely these days, it's hard to know where to send them. Cold-calling is not always appropriate, or even possible, if you don't already have a relationship established. A portfolio review guarantees that the photographer will meet someone and will have an opportunity to show their work and tell their story.

Juliette Wolf-Robin

3. What is the most difficult aspect of organizing portfolio-review events?

Scheduling reviewers and adjusting to changes in their availability as we try to match reviewers to specific photographers.

Making sure there is a diverse group of reviewers. Specialties of APA photographers run the gamut—lifestyle, still life, food, celebrity portraiture, architecture, sports, travel, fashion, and other areas. We strive to find reviewers from a range of ad agencies, editorial, streaming services, and brands that can hire them.

Reaching potential reviewers can be a challenge. They may not receive our emails, and if they do, they may not respond in a timely way. Often, we can't find a direct phone number to contact them. Then, once we do, the date/time we have scheduled for reviews may not work for them. We face the same challenges that photographers have in trying to connect to buyers and show their work. This is why, once we have secured the reviewer, we have so many photographers interested in booking the time with them.

4. Please give an overview of your portfolio-review events, including location, frequency, and numbers (that is, number of days, reviewers, photographers, scheduled reviews).

APA is a national association with eight regional chapters. Most of the portfolio reviews are hosted by APA chapters, including those in Atlanta; Chicago; Washington, DC; Los Angeles; New York; San Diego; and San Francisco. The reviews are sometimes held in person and sometimes virtually through breakout rooms on Zoom. APA Los Angeles, for example, will try to host virtual reviews twice a year over a full day on a Saturday. Several of the cities producing in-person reviews have done so on a weekday evening to accommodate reviewers after work. Most chapters try to host a review once a year, and if not a full portfolio review with buyers, then perhaps a peer review.

There is no set schedule for the year, as producing the events is dependent on board members who volunteer their time. The number of confirmed reviewers will dictate how many review slots will be available. Reviews are then sold as singular meetings or in batches. There is usually a limit to how many reviews can be purchased in order to accommodate more photographers.

5. How do you go about selecting reviewers?

Our priority is selecting individuals who regularly hire professional photographers for brands or publications. We might include consultants who can advise photographers or gallerists and photo curators for those looking to cross into the art market. Each APA board is comprised of professional photographers who volunteer their time to help produce the reviews, and they reach out to their networks. APA directors also search LinkedIn, connect with jurors of APA photo competitions, and reach out to the photographic community to solicit reviewers.

6. How do you go about selecting reviewees/photographers?

Reviews are primarily available only to APA members. APA provides several membership levels, from Contributor to Pro-Plus, and each level of membership provides benefits incrementally. Because there are limited review slots available, we will often limit review access to those APA members who have purchased one of the higher membership levels—a level congruent for a working professional photographer.

Exceptions are granted through special programs designed to promote inclusivity and more diversity, but even for those individuals (who may not be members of APA), their portfolio is first reviewed by a panel to assure that the photographer is ready to produce a project.

Most of APA's portfolio reviews are designed for the photographer who is already established and looking to be hired rather than for those looking for a consultation on how to get hired. Most APA reviews require that the photographer be present themselves rather than their representative and that they attend the reviews by themselves.

7. What are some of the auxiliary events that happen at your festival in addition to the review meetings themselves?

APA produces events throughout the year, including educational and inspirational webinars that are available on the APA National website and on the American Photographic Artists *YouTube* channel. Producing portfolio reviews takes a lot of work and coordination. When one is being produced, it is the only event planned for that evening or day. It is the singular focus.

8. What are some essential, behind-the-scenes elements of organizing a successful portfolio review event that attendees might want to know?

Portfolio reviews are complex to organize because of the number of people involved and trying to satisfy various requests from both reviewer and reviewee.

APA—and I know this is true for many of the review events that take place—strives to connect photographers with the people they most want to meet. The scheduling chart takes into consideration which reviewers are available at what time and which photographers most want to see them. Priority is typically given to those who sign up first or to someone who has made it very clear who their first choice is.

When producing a portfolio-review event, it is essential to build in downtime for the reviewers. It can be overwhelming to go from meeting to meeting to meeting without enough breaks. Give reviewers the chance to reflect on the meetings. Reviewers also enjoy time to meet privately with other reviewers. Building a private break time among the reviewers can enhance their satisfaction with the event and help promote the photographers by having reviewers compare notes on who they have met with.

9. What is the most-asked question you get from reviewees/photographers?

I reached out to the APA Los Angeles director, Patti Silverstein, to ask which questions come up most from reviewers and reviewees.

The questions most asked by photographers are: When do we get to select our reviewers? Do we get our top choices? What will the flow be like? I have a commitment part of the days, so can I get all morning reviewers? What is the best format to show the work?

10. What is the most-asked question you get from reviewers?

What are the photographers looking for from the review? How long are the reviews? Is there compensation for the reviewers? What will the structure of the day be like—what is the flow? What is the expectation? Will there be a break, and if so, what happens during that break? Will reviewers be able to socialize with other reviewers? Will they know beforehand who the photographers are that they are meeting with? When will they know their schedule?

11. What is your policy for filling empty review spots during sessions?

Extra reviews that become available prior to the event are sold. If a photographer is a no-show at the last minute, another photographer who is present and available might be given that slot at no charge. In other words, if you find yourself free between reviews, it's worth letting the facilitator know you are around and ready for the opportunity.

12. Do you offer roving reviewers? Why or why not?

We have not done this because it is a lot of work to get reviewers, and when we do it, we want to make that reviewer available for all those who are signing up. There is a scramble if a reviewer cancels at the last minute, so it would certainly be nice to have a roving one available, but this has not been what we have done. I am open to it if someone wants to present themselves as a backup!

R

That said, at every portfolio-review event, another dynamic emerges: the connection between photographers at events. I have observed the exchange of helpful tips among photographers as well as seen the development of long-term friendships forged from these events. At the in-person events, photographers will show each other their portfolios and promos. If it is a virtual event, photographers will talk to each other in the waiting room between reviews. These relationships can be essential for a photographer's success.

13. How has COVID changed portfolio-review events?

During the COVID quarantine, all the reviews went virtual on Zoom. Now it's a hybrid of in-person and virtual, and we will continue to produce both types of review settings.

Access to editors, buyers, and creatives for in-person meetings has always been a challenge. Since COVID, many of the reviewers have not been in an office full-time, making it even more difficult for photographers to get in-office meetings. A photographer might plan a trip to a major city, paying for travel and a hotel in order to meet with, and show their work to, several potential buyers, but there is no guarantee of getting or keeping those meetings. Meetings with different firms mean scheduling all over town. It can be very expensive, and there is no guarantee of return. This has made the scheduled reviews even more valuable. The photographer is at least assured to have face-to-face meetings—sometimes without leaving their home!

14. How do you feel about virtual reviews versus in-person reviews?

Both have tremendous value. Virtual platforms have provided an affordable, convenient way for people to connect from anywhere, including photographers and reviewers who are not all located in major cities.

In-person provides a more personal, organic connection. The fabulous part about being in either review situation is that for that period of time (typically 20 minutes), the person you are meeting with is giving you 100 percent of their attention.

Make the most of it!

15. What advice do you have for photographers?

Be clear on your intentions. What is it you want to leave with? What would a successful exchange look like? Do you want this person to hire or represent you? Are you looking for critique and advice? Consider beforehand what you want to know about the person with whom you are meeting that you are not able to learn from their LinkedIn profile. For example: What are their hiring practices? What type of photographers do they hire? Who have they worked with recently? What type of budgets do they typically have? How often do they hire photographers? Once you have the answers you need, adjust your approach and presentation accordingly. Have several directions ready so that you can lead the conversation. The meeting is your pitch, and your presentation should be catered to their needs—as if what they need is exactly what you do. They don't need to know everything about you on the first meeting. What are the keywords you use to describe yourself and your work? Make sure to repeat those words when showing your work. This is your chance to build up their confidence in working with you. The more you know about them, the better you will know how to sell yourself to them.

16. Can a project be presented, in your opinion, as underdeveloped or overdeveloped?

A portfolio review is typically only about twenty minutes long, so to answer this question, it would be important to know what the photographer is looking to get out of the meeting. I suggest photographers start the meeting with a strong, confident presentation. Then, toward the end, they can present a few images of a new project (this would be an underdeveloped one).

I'm really not sure I know what an overdeveloped project looks like. Even the most seasoned, accomplished photographer is looking for new opportunities. Presenting how they managed a complex, fully developed project will show how they can do the same for another client. In either case, I would suggest watching the person you are meeting with and gauge their interest in the story. If it is not connecting, cut the story and pivot to another body of work.

17. What is the biggest "no-no" for a reviewee?

- Not being prepared and/or not being respectful of the time.
- There is a set amount of time that everyone knows before the review begins.
- Practice and time yourself ahead of the meeting.
- Be on time and be prepared to end when the set time is up.
- Know before you start what general direction you want the meeting to go. You are in charge.
- Avoid connecting to Wi-Fi for a presentation. If it is a slow or bad connection, the reviewer will be immediately put off, even though this will have nothing to do with your work.

R

- Your meeting is the first experience of what it will be like to work with you.
- If the review is virtual, consider how everything looks—the background in the room where you're sitting, the background of your computer screen, the ambient sound in your location, and the flow of your presentation. Does it feel organized and professional? If you have other work you may want to show, have it queued up and ready to open. It should feel seamless.
- If the review is in person, be respectful of the reviewer's break time. Avoid cornering them in the restroom to talk to them or dominating their time when others are also waiting to meet them.

18. What is the biggest "no-no" for a reviewer?

The APA diversity committee came up with a great list, which includes the following:
- Think of yourself as a resource for the photographer. Ask if there is anything they'd like to know while you approach their work.
- Choose to ask open-ended, neutral questions, using "how" or "tell me about" as prompts.
- Remember that not everyone has had the same opportunities or the same access or resources.
- Try to avoid using your own journey as a reference of what is possible.
- Avoid the words "you should" and replace them with, "You might look into . . .," or "I've found it helpful to . . ."
- Avoid additional advice beyond the scope set.
- Be thoughtful—it's a conversation of equals.

19. How do you feel about reviewees and reviewers socializing away from the table? If your opinion is favorable, what advice do you have for reviewees?

Socializing is key to building relationships; just be mindful and respectful of the room. Is the socializing keeping anyone from their timed review? Is the sound level disruptive to other reviews taking place in the room? Is anyone else waiting to talk to the person? Be mindful of the group setting and of your impact on others.

20. As an organizer, what, in your opinion, is the best leave-behind?

The answer will be based on who you are meeting with and where they are located. If in person, ideally you would create a small booklet with key images for them to keep. At the very least, have a printed card with a signature image. The quality of reproduction and design of your promo matters as well. When in doubt, produce smaller, higher-quality pieces, and keep it simple.

Juliette Wolf-Robin

If it's a virtual meeting, then a PDF designed with your logo, an "about" page, and a few images, along with the links to your site and social-media pages. Include key words about yourself.

Promotional items can be memorable but should relate to your work and be practical for the person to carry. If you want to give the reviewer a book, don't assume they want it—ask them if it is feasible for them to take it with them at that moment or if you can send it to them later. Sending it later creates another touchpoint and provides you with a mailing address—and they don't have to manage it while attending the event.

21. As an organizer, have you seen certain trends in photography subject matter over the years?

I would say the biggest change is not the subject matter, but the variety of formats people use to show their work, including printed books, websites, PDFs, and social-media platforms. When meeting in person, I still believe there is value in showing actual printed images. There will always be something special about touching a printed photograph—but not oversized, and not so many that they are cumbersome to view. You want to allow the person to appreciate the quality of your images on the printed page.

22. What is the single most important piece of advice you would give to a new reviewee/photographer versus a seasoned reviewee?

It's actually the same for everyone: Consider each meeting as an incredible opportunity. It's a one-on-one meeting where you get to tell your story and present your work to someone in the photo community. This person may or may not hire you, but the connection can be very meaningful. Try to learn as much as possible about who you are meeting, be prepared, and have a thoughtful presentation targeted specifically to them, if possible. Try to make a connection on a personal level, and end with how you will follow up with them.

Generally, it's best to sign up early, arrive early, and stay flexible should schedules change. Also, be clear about who you most want to meet. Look up all the reviewers who might be there and get to know who is reviewing. If there is a change or if a new opportunity presents itself, be prepared to meet with anyone, even those not on your list. Make yourself available all day. A review is essentially a job interview or pitch to sell your work. Be present and focused.

R

Reviewers

Timothy Campos

Timothy Campos

f/22 print & Catherine Couturier Gallery

My name is Timothy Campos, and I have been working in the field of contemporary photography for the last fifteen years. I have been fortunate enough to work in museums, galleries, and as a fine-art business owner. Prior positions include those at the Museum of Contemporary Photography (Chicago) and Catherine Edelman Gallery (Chicago). In 2021, I launched f22 Prints LLC, which is an online and pop-up gallery featuring affordable, limited-edition fine-art prints by contemporary photographers. I am also currently the director of loans and exhibitions at the Art Institute of Chicago.

1. What do you look forward to most and least about portfolio-review events?

What I look forward to the most with portfolio reviews is the opportunity to inspire artists and to be inspired by their work and craft. There can be a magical moment where the work really clicks with me, and I am in tune with the reviewee, and there is this incredible dialogue. That is what I'm always hoping to achieve. What I look forward to the least is when I can tell that the reviewee isn't really listening to any of my feedback but rather thinking about what they are going to say next. It drives me nuts!

2. Why do you attend portfolio-review events, and do you have any specific goals in attending?

I attend portfolio reviews because I have always loved talking with artists about their work, and hopefully I can hone their vision of the project. Or even help to expand it. I guess my goal is always to try and provide advice that will benefit the artist in any way I can. Not only the images, but their edit, statement, display method, editioning . . . anything that can add value to the project.

3. When you attend portfolio-review events, what kind of strain does this cause on your work schedule?

If it were to do so, then I wouldn't agree to do the reviews. I wouldn't want my mind to be somewhere else—thinking about other tasks and responsibilities while I'm supposed to be focused on the artist and their work; that's not fair to anyone.

4. If you receive the reviewee list from the organization prior to the portfolio review, do you look at their work online in preparation for the review, or do you like to look at it fresh? Why or why not?

I do like to look at the work in advance, and I jot down my initial reaction. The other main reason I like to look at the work early is because it also gives me more time to process my thoughts and to look over any statement that I may have received. I feel this gives us more time to dig in during the actual session.

5. What objectives do you recommend reviewees bring to the table?

I certainly wouldn't want to tell anyone what their objectives should be. Every artist has their own personal objectives for sharing their work during a portfolio review. I will say that whatever your objectives are, you should state them clearly and make sure you understand the response or feedback. If not, ask more or different questions.

6. Do you ask at the start of your session what the reviewee wants?

I don't ask the reviewee their wants. I assume they will guide the session or let me know their concerns.

7. What advice do you have for first-time reviewees?

I would advise a first-time reviewee to show only one body of work and practice editing their work so that their selects are appropriate and cohesive. I also recommend making sure the body of work and the artist statement are cohesive and complement each other. Occasionally, the selected images or statement can be doing a disservice to each other.

8. Who should lead the review—reviewer or reviewee? Why?

I generally let the reviewee lead the session unless they are struggling to lead or ask questions, and then I have no problem steering the conversation.

9. What advice do you have for reviewees on how to manage the allotted time during the session?

It's helpful if you have your questions or concerns written out. It is also helpful if they are prioritized by importance. Having them written down means that you can focus on each reply without trying to remember what else you are wanting to bring up in the appointment.

Timothy Campos

10. How do you feel about a reviewee recording your session?

I don't mind if the session is recorded, but ultimately, I think it is easier to jot down a few notes on the same piece of paper or document as your questions.

11. How many different projects do you think are ideal for discussion in an individual review session?

I prefer to just discuss one body of work. If you have multiple bodies of work that are ready to be shared, I suggest scheduling different reviews for each project with the appropriate reviewers. This makes each session more manageable and gives the right amount of time to each series. This also forces the artist to ask themselves if they are truly ready for a review and to edit each body of work for that particular session.

12. How important is it for reviewees to have their ideas completely fleshed out regarding their projects?

The more fleshed out the project, the deeper we can really dive into the material. On the other hand, if what they are looking for is advice on how to help flesh out the idea, that is fine, too. I just want to make sure that some time and effort has been put into organizing the project and statement for presentation prior to the session.

13. Can a project be presented, in your opinion, as underdeveloped or overdeveloped?

Absolutely, and this happens regularly. What I always hope for is that the artist knows that the work is under- or overdeveloped and they use the session as an opportunity to focus the work. I much prefer that notion to the artist who doesn't know or believe that the project is under- or overdeveloped.

14. How important is the technical quality of physical objects (prints?) being presented at the review session? How do you feel about work being presented on a tablet or computer?

If there are physical prints, I typically like to view them as they are intended to be viewed. I'm speaking in regard to the editing being complete, paper choice, and the like. The prints can absolutely be portfolio size. I'm also not against someone just sharing jpegs; that works as well, but I would certainly like to hear more about how the work is going to be presented.

15. How do you feel about virtual portfolio reviews versus in-person portfolio-review events (pros and cons)? Is your ideal review session length twenty, twenty-five, or thirty minutes?

I love meeting with people in person if possible, but at the same time, I have had some wonderful virtual reviews over the last few years. There is something really great about being able to connect with someone anywhere in the world without having to leave my house/office! The con with that is not being able to see a printed working portfolio. As for time for a session, I lean toward thirty minutes. Most appointments have so much to cover, and I love talking about the work, so the time really flies by, in my opinion.

16. Have you ever offered a commission, a show, a press feature, or representation during a review? Can you share a success story or stories with us that came from a productive meeting at a review session?

I have certainly worked in galleries where we were reviewing a new body of work by an artist for a future show. I have never offered anyone a commission or a show during a session, but I have certainly gone back to several artists to help facilitate sales or have included them in group exhibitions.

17. Have you ever purchased artwork from a reviewee? If so, what do you base the price on, and is it signed by the artist?

I haven't bought work from a reviewee. I have certainly spent a lot of time in sessions talking with artists about editions and print sizes. That sometimes seems to be one of the most difficult areas for artists to finalize.

18. How often do you connect or recommend a photographer who may not be right for you but a good match for a colleague?

I recommend or share work all the time! I'm always excited to help out an artist or to connect them with someone who is organizing a show in which the work would be a great fit. I also like to introduce artists to other artists who share a similar vision or content but are approaching the subject completely differently.

19. Can you share the best review you have been a part of, and why it was? (No names should be mentioned.)

Over the years I've been lucky enough to work with a lot of successful contemporary photographers, and it is always exciting when they share a new body of work for the first time, and for me to be a person they trust and come to for feedback has always meant a great deal to me and is a position I've never taken lightly.

20. Are you open to looking at work outside of scheduled reviews or not so much? If yes, how do you prefer a photographer approach you about the possibility?

I am always open to looking at work! How an artist approaches me doesn't matter much. What matters is that they have done the work and are respectful of my time and feedback.

21. How do you feel about reviewees and reviewers socializing away from the table? If you are comfortable sharing, what advice do you have for reviewees?

I'm completely open to socializing outside the review session as long as we are actually socializing and not trying to continue the review session. I understand it can be difficult to turn it off and change the topic. I find in my own life that when I step away from a project, it sparks inspiration when I least expect it and possibilities I had never previously considered.

22. How do you prefer that the individuals you meet with follow up with you, and how often?

I prefer to receive an email follow-up, and I think every three to four months seems reasonable with an update and/or news regarding the series.

23. In your opinion, what is the best "leave-behind"?

I once had someone make a small notebook with one of their images on the cover. I thought that was great, and I literally looked at that image for the next few months as I was using the notebook!

24. What are the biggest "no-no's" for reviewees?

Don't ask me which galleries you should contact to work with. I find this frustrating because our time should be used to focus on the work and developing the project. Several times, I've had reviewees just waiting for me to pause so they can ask me what gallery they should work with or if I'm interested in taking them on. I get it. I know everyone wants to advance their careers, but if I feel strongly that the work is ready, and if I know someone who would be interested, I will certainly bring it up. But typically the work isn't ready, and the guidance I am sharing in the moment is not being received because the reviewee wants to jump right to working with a gallery.

25. What one piece of advice would you impart to reviewees?

The one piece of advice is to keep pushing. Push the project in different directions to see where it might go, push yourself into areas that aren't comfortable, push yourself to listen and see, push through blocks, push through being uninspired, and push the viewer.

Timothy Campos

Debra Klomp Ching

Klompching Gallery

I'm the co-owner of Klompching Gallery (founded in 2007) in Brooklyn, New York; a freelance consultant working with collectors and photographers, an educator with twenty-five-plus years' experience in formal programs of study, a regular judge of photography awards, and a seasoned reviewer at select portfolio-review events. In 2020, I launched my now-sought-after online training webinars, focusing on the creative and business side of making, exhibiting, and selling fine-art photographs. Additionally, I'm the cofounder of the Fresh Annual Photography Exhibition and the Rhonda Wilson Award.

1. What do you look forward to most and least about portfolio-review events?

The most: meeting the artists and viewing photographs in-person. The least: knowing I won't be meeting everyone and seeing everything.

2. Why do you attend portfolio-review events, and do you have any specific goals in attending?

I'm looking for new talent and quality fine-art prints to exhibit and sell at the Klompching Gallery. It's a great opportunity to reconnect with colleagues in the industry, to conduct some business, and to get a sense of what's being made photographically.

3. When you attend portfolio-review events, what kind of strain does this cause on your work schedule?

As any small-business owner will tell you, you're never really off the clock. Maintaining communications, responding to sales inquiries, and closing deals continue unabated. The workday invariably extends late into the night.

4. If you receive the reviewee list from the organization prior to the portfolio review, do you look at their work online in preparation for the review, or do you like to look at it fresh? Why or why not?

I always look at it fresh. I view attending portfolio reviews partly as a way to donate my time and expertise. So, my time spent on this is limited to the time at the actual event.

5. What objectives do you recommend reviewees bring to the table?

Quite frankly, there's not much point for a photographer to attend a review event unless they know what they want to achieve from it. This provides the photographer with a clear plan for who to meet with and why.

6. Do you ask at the start of your session what the reviewee wants?

Yes. I always ask the photographer what they want from the review—in particular, what they want from me. The review is then tailored to the photographer's needs.

7. What advice do you have for first-time reviewees?

I have a lot of advice to give——too much to list here. That said, just remember that first impressions count. Be professional; be the best ambassador and champion of your work that you can be. Listen, be open-minded, be objective, and be flexible. Remember that everyone in the room shares the same passion—photography.

8. Who should lead the review—reviewer or reviewee? Why?

It's a conversation, which is obviously two-way. Who leads generally will be dependent upon the dynamics of the specific, unique conversation that is taking place.

9. What advice do you have for reviewees on how to manage the allotted time during the session?

In my twenty-five years of reviewing portfolios—at these formal events—I've always found it best if I manage the time. It helps the photographer to focus on their work and absorb the conversation.

10. How do you feel about a reviewee recording your session?

I don't like it, and I normally do not agree to it.

11. How many different projects do you think are ideal for discussion in an individual review session?

Based upon my experience, one project is enough for a focused review. That said, it's possible to look at more than one portfolio, depending upon the nature of the specific review itself.

Debra Klomp Ching

12. How important is it for reviewees to have their idea completely fleshed out regarding their project?

I'm impressed by photographers who are articulate about their creative practice, especially the specific portfolio of work being discussed in the review. This is particularly important if the photographer is pitching for an exhibition or representation. However, if a photographer is simply seeking feedback and/or advice, then this is less important.

13. Can a project be presented, in your opinion, as underdeveloped or overdeveloped?

Yes, of course.

14. How important is the technical quality of physical objects (for example, prints) being presented at the review session? How do you feel about work being presented on a tablet or computer?

At an in-person portfolio review, there's no point presenting a photographic project to me that is on a tablet, computer, or in book form. I'm a curator and an art dealer. I deal in photographic objects—that's what I want to see. I will assess print quality, scale, and paper type. I will make judgments about how those elements meld with the subject, concept, and intention of the photographer.

15. How do you feel about virtual portfolio reviews versus in-person portfolio-review events (pros and cons)? Is your ideal review session length twenty, twenty-five, or thirty minutes?

As a private consultant, I conduct portfolio reviews online on a regular basis. They work very well and are set at thirty minutes because there's invariably time needed to manage the viewing experience. At an in-person review, the twenty-minute time frame is a perfect allotment of time.

16. Have you ever offered a commission, a show, a press feature, or representation during a review? Can you share a success story or stories with us that came from a productive meeting at a review session?

The Klompching Gallery has many photographers on our roster whom we first met at a portfolio review! However, the offer to work together has generally come after the event.

17. Have you ever purchased artwork from a reviewee? If so, what do you base the price on, and is it signed by the artist?

No, I've generally not done this, mostly because the majority of photographers I have met haven't yet determined the final format, edition, and price. Your question asks, "what do you base the price on?" It wouldn't be up to me to price the work in this context, and I would never pressure a photographer to rush a decision on that for the sake of one sale.

18. How often do you connect or recommend a photographer who may not be right for you but a good match for a colleague?

Quite often!

19. Can you share the best review you have been a part of, and why it was? (No names should be mentioned.)

In terms of meeting individual photographers, there have been so many that I can't possibly choose.

20. Are you open to looking at work outside of scheduled reviews or not so much? If yes, how do you prefer a photographer approach you about the possibility?

Not unless I request it from the photographer. If a photographer wants me to see their work but did not succeed in being assigned a scheduled review, I strongly recommend they leave their business card on the review table with an appropriate note—I'll seek them out at the portfolio walk-through and take a quick look at their work.

21. How do you feel about reviewees and reviewers socializing away from the table? If you are comfortable sharing, what advice do you have for reviewees?

The socializing and networking aspect of in-person portfolio reviews is an excellent and enjoyable benefit. There is no specific advice, except to say that it's good to be mindful of being professional and respectful.

Debra Klomp Ching

22. How do you prefer that the individuals you meet with follow up with you and how often?

There isn't one answer that is applicable to all photographers. It really does depend upon the dynamics of the review session. That said, I don't like being added to a mailing list without my permission, and I don't think it's appropriate for a photographer to feel that the review can continue via email later on.

23. In your opinion, what is the best "leave-behind"?

Small and appropriate: a visual that relates to the portfolio under discussion/ review. If it's a business card, standard size is best, so that it fits into a standard business-card holder. I always advise photographers not to invest in a magnificent leave-behind at the expense of compromising on the quality of their portfolio of prints.

24. What are the biggest "no-no's" for reviewees?

I think it's understood that everyone attending these events is expected to behave professionally and respectfully. Any behavior contrary to that is a "no-no."

25. What one piece of advice would you impart to reviewees?

That's tough—view the portfolio-review event as an opportunity that you've invested in, in order to achieve whatever objective you have for attending. Stay focused, pace yourself energy-wise, enjoy the experience, and take advantage of being in the same room as so many other talented professionals in this wonderful photography world.

Alyssa Coppelman

Alyssa Coppelman
Oxford American

Alyssa Ortega Coppelman is an independent photo editor and photobook consultant based in Austin, Texas. She is an art editor for *Oxford American* magazine and an archival researcher on the Emmy-nominated PBS *NewsHour* series "Brief But Spectacular." She was previously the deputy art director at *Harper's Magazine*.

Alyssa loves connecting with undergraduate and graduate photography students, both as a guest lecturer and by leading photo-editing workshops. She advises photographers on how to get their best work in front of photo editors and how to know who to connect with.

As a photobook and portfolio consultant, Alyssa edits and sequences photobooks, zines, and portfolios and can provide oversight on design and editorial aspects of these projects, helping artists present their strongest work in the most cohesive way. In portfolio reviews, she shares insight about a number of topics, often touching on how to strengthen the project overall—the edit and sequence, design details, social media presence, and so forth.

1. What do you look forward to most and least about portfolio-review events?

Pre-portfolio reviews, I get most excited about interacting with real, live photographers and fellow reviewers. I love viewing work within the unique context of the intense twenty minutes of concentrated, one-on-one conversation with a photographer—something that rarely occurs in the same way outside of portfolio reviews. The knowledge that we've got a short amount of time forces a specific intensity of concentration so I can effectively express my gut-level reaction to, and feedback on, their work. I look forward to meeting with photographers whose work I didn't know or brand-new projects by photographers I did know. It's often most gratifying for me to view work before it's done—when it's mid-project or not yet in the can—because I can suggest edits and directions for fleshing out the project.

My least favorite element of reviews is being in a review with a photographer who did not do the research when signing up and is unfamiliar with the type of work I am interested in. Naturally, we can still have a conversation when these scenarios arise, but by default it tends to be more generic advice and is a missed opportunity for them to meet with someone more well suited to their needs.

2. Why do you attend portfolio-review events, and do you have any specific goals in attending?

Reviews are one of the most efficient, most enjoyable ways to be introduced to new work. Having work put directly in front of my face within the portfolio-review bubble—in the relatively undistracted setting away from my computer, with many windows and tabs open at all times—is one of my favorite ways of learning about work. I always encounter work I might not otherwise have come across, simply due to the vastness of the internet and the limitations of my waking hours. The steps between me sitting at my desk at home and coming across a photographer's work—on Instagram, on their website, with work at a gallery, via a mailing list— are considerably greater and, without exception, cluttered with a number of more pressing tasks at hand. Bringing me face-to-face with photographers, when I can hear directly from the photographers about their work, is the best way to learn about work.

3. When you attend portfolio-review events, what kind of strain does this cause on your work schedule?

Reviews generally put a heavy strain on my work schedule. I have almost never been able to be entirely off during reviews. Even if I am able to take time off, it almost always means I have to work long hours before attending and after returning home from reviews. Including the better part of two days for travel, reviews take from several days to almost a week that otherwise would've been occupied by work.

At worst, I'm cramming in work on breaks and after hours, as much as necessary, and then returning to longer hours to make up for taking time away from work. Although reviews are exhilarating and stimulating, the come-down is usually exhausting, and long hours are the last thing I want to do. However, it's part of the sacrifice, and it's worth it.

4. If you receive the reviewee list from the organization prior to the portfolio review, do you look at their work online in preparation for the review, or do you like to look at it fresh? Why or why not?

Because I don't want to develop preconceived notions of the work that are too fixed, I don't look. Aside from that, it's generally impossible time-wise to fit it in (accounting for the days spent traveling and reviewing).

Alyssa Coppelman

5. What objectives do you recommend reviewees bring to the table?

You have an expensive twenty minutes to squeeze the most out of your time at the table. Bringing to the table a healthy amount of knowledge about what I do will help ensure you get the most out of that time. I often ask reviewees what questions they have for me in particular, as this gives them the opportunity to get specific feedback according to my background—as a photobook consultant, as an editor of photo essays and portfolios, as someone in the publishing industry, and so forth. Reviewees should not assume that we'll be able to continue the conversation via email later; they should plan on hitting the most important points during the review. This is simply because when I'm back to my regular work schedule, I am inundated with email and busy with strict deadlines—not a lot of time to continue conversations, as much as I may wish to.

6. Do you ask at the start of your session what the reviewee wants?

I generally start out wanting to know about the reviewee in general: Do they have a day job, and what is it? What led them into photography, and when did they start taking it seriously? If photography is a secondary career or interest, does their primary career relate? And then, yes, it's great to know if they have a specific goal in mind, or aspects of their project they wish to discuss. If they don't bring this up, quite often I will ask.

7. What advice do you have for first-time reviewees?

I like knowing when it's a photographer's first review. I would encourage reviewees to let the reviewer know it's your first review, or if you're nervous, or even if you want feedback on how to make the most of the review. It's not naturally occurring knowledge to sail through reviews and get the most out of them. Reviews are a bit of a pressure-cooker situation—even just time-wise—and best-laid plans to ask this or that question can sometimes dissolve in the moment. Getting tips from reviewers who no doubt have done reviews with hundreds, if not thousands, of photographers is a wonderful way to maximize that precious time.

8. Who should lead the review—reviewer or reviewee? Why?

In general, I lead the review. Because I've done so many, I have goal posts of sorts to aim for, in terms of imparting knowledge they may or may not know to ask me about. This doesn't mean the reviewee shouldn't contribute, as they know all the essential details about their work. In terms of me looking for work to pitch to clients for publication—which I'm always doing at reviews—I know what type of work or subject matter will resonate, so it's important for me to manage the timing and make sure I see everything the photographer has that pertains to this. That said, it's important for the photographer to take the initiative and let me know which project and/or aspects of a project they're most in need of feedback on.

9. What advice do you have for reviewees on how to manage the allotted time during the session?

If you have more than one body of work with you, establish this right away. If I know this, I will structure our conversation accordingly and leave time to view both, unless we get deep into the first one, which happens. When this occurs, you can ask if it's okay to send me a PDF or images from the other body of work. I'm always happy to see the work, though after the review is finished, I cannot promise feedback as in the review, due to reasons already discussed (my regular workload).

10. How do you feel about a reviewee recording your session?

Although at first it can feel a bit uncomfortable to be recorded, I believe reviewers should always agree to it when asked. Between the stress and anxiety of being in reviews, combined with the hubbub of the review room, trying to hit your presentation's bullet points, moving prints around, reorganizing between meetings, making sure you're in the right place at the right time—it's hectic! Especially when a reviewee has back-to-back reviews, details of the conversation are sure to get lost. It also allows the reviewee to be that much more present if they're not also trying to take notes. Reviewees can also review a tape between reviews to hear themselves in a review, know if they hit all their bullet points, and hone their future review sessions—all of which leads to better future reviews for both reviewee and reviewer.

11. How many different projects do you think are ideal for discussion in an individual review session?

It completely depends on the projects, and reviewers have different thoughts on this (and, well, everything). If a photographer has two to three projects, it's good to bring them, as quite often I will be interested in one more than the other. I am always searching for work on different topics, made with a multitude of different techniques and styles, so I am a fan of seeing as much as possible, if there's time.

Alyssa Coppelman

12. How important is it for reviewees to have their idea completely fleshed out regarding their project?

Very important. Even if a reviewee is still exploring the main idea or doesn't have a completely formed "thesis," they should have a solid grasp on the project up to the point they're showing it and a grasp of—or specific questions about—what the project might still be needing to get it to completion. As an editor, I love getting my hands on a project when it's at this stage: when a photographer has not attached themselves to the final product. The possibility of enriching a body of work at this stage is exciting for me.

13. Can a project be presented, in your opinion, as underdeveloped or overdeveloped?

Yes. If the project feels underdeveloped, I can discuss specific images or work with an artist to get to the core of what they're trying to express. That can lead us in a good direction. If they don't have a grasp of what they're trying to express, or they have brought miscellaneous images rather than solid projects, the reviewee likely won't get as much out of the review as they would if they had a specific idea of the reviewer's wants and needs.

I don't believe I've encountered an overdeveloped project as of yet. I have reviewed final projects, in which case the photographers have wanted feedback on what I think they could have done differently for a stronger book edit and/or design. Those sorts of post-mortems can be valuable for me as well, as it gives me a chance to really fine-tune with the photographer and to discuss why specific choices were made with the design, edit, and sequence of their book.

14. How important is the technical quality of physical objects (prints?) being presented at the review session? How do you feel about work being presented on a tablet or computer?

In the first few minutes of the review, I form an opinion of the reviewee's technical capabilities. If I've got a relative beginner in front of me, I am delighted to give them the same attention as a more experienced photographer. But if I see unintentional jpeg noise or pixelation, it indicates that their attention to detail is wanting, as no such print should ever be included. I would rather see ten good prints alone than an additional ten spotty ones. Plus, don't waste your money on crappy prints!

Prints are lovely and delicious to commune with, and I can know the work on a different level than I can if I am only seeing images on a screen. A couple buts: As I work with print magazines and digital media, it isn't crucial that I handle prints. I also think it's crucial to work toward greater parity in the photo world, and making portfolio reviews more accessible is a crucial part of this. One way to make strides in this direction is for digital presentations to become more accepted. (If you are showing work to a gallerist or curator, this same advice does not apply, for obvious reasons.)

Let's be honest: Portfolio reviews are crazy expensive. On top of travel expenses, the cost of printing an entire portfolio can be prohibitive, and for those who have been led to believe that a beautiful, handmade, pricey portfolio box is mandatory (it is not), the expense skyrockets.

I would absolutely prefer to see a few select, exemplary prints taken out of a manila envelope, combined with a full on-screen presentation, if it means I will be able to see worthwhile work and meet with photographers I otherwise wouldn't have had access to because of the cost of these events.

15. How do you feel about virtual portfolio reviews versus in-person portfolio-review events (pros and cons)? Is your ideal review session length twenty, twenty-five, or thirty minutes?

Before participating in virtual reviews, I thought I'd hate them. In fact, I quite like them.

Virtual pros: A quiet room! No distractions! A greater sense of the passage of time, so I can better guide the conversation. As I can screenshot images I like, I have an immediate reminder of work I want to look at further or pitch to a client for publication. Perhaps the greatest bonus of virtual reviews is that they are suddenly much more accessible to a much wider array of artists—those who are abroad, or those who might not be able to afford the expense of in-person reviews.

Virtual cons: The potential for disconnect and technical glitches. The lack of ability to interface with the photographer and their prints in person. While my end product (on-screen or on a magazine page) doesn't necessitate seeing prints, there is still a lot of value added with a face-to-face meeting. There's a lot to be gained by meeting the photographer in person that can't be replicated online, including socializing or interacting outside of reviews.

In terms of the ideal length of each review, my muscle memory is trained for twenty minutes each, since it's the length at most reviews I've participated in. At longer events (four days, sixteen reviews per day), any longer than twenty minutes would feel too long; as they are, it's a nice churn that keeps the day moving. But, when the work resonates strongly, twenty minutes feels too short. And, if I want to completely re-sequence a portfolio, which happens sometimes, it's not enough time. It's a fun challenge, but more of a visceral than thoughtful edit (because there's no time). I would say that for the sake of the overall event, and to maximize the number of photographers I get to meet with, twenty minutes is my preference.

Alyssa Coppelman

16. Have you ever offered a commission, a show, a press feature, or representation during a review? Can you share a success story or stories with us that came from a productive meeting at a review session?

I don't have final say on commissions or publication, as a team is always involved. If I did, I wouldn't make this sort of offer on the spot. I would want a much more in-depth review of their work. What I have offered on the spot is the desire to see specific work if I think it might be a fit with a current project (e.g., publication, video production), or I have expressed the desire to talk to the photographer outside of reviews (usually via email once I'm back home) if I think we'd work well together and they want help with a project.

A good number of photographers whose work I saw in portfolio reviews have been published by my clients. Sometimes it takes years for a placement; other times, we're lucky enough that I can make a publication offer shortly after reviews.

17. Have you ever purchased artwork from a reviewee? If so, what do you base the price on, and is it signed by the artist?

Many times, I have wanted to. A few times, I have come close. As of yet, I have not. What would push me over the edge into making a purchase at a review? I would have to be flush with cash!

18. How often do you connect or recommend a photographer who may not be right for you but a good match for a colleague?

Quite often! Sometimes reviewers will discuss what work any of us is looking for at that moment, in case there's work in the room we should see but haven't. Reviewers will also recommend looking at a given photographer's work if they think it might be right for them. I will also share photographers' names with photo editors who weren't at the reviews but frequently commission, as they're always looking for new talent.

19. Can you share the best review you have been a part of, and why was it? (No names should be mentioned.)

The best review I have taken part in has been one in which the vast majority of the work I reviewed was completely in line with the type of work I look for. I saw a range of work: more photojournalistic work, which I rarely see at reviews and which I am looking for always; fine art; and work occupying the space in between. At this review, most of the work was new to me. The reviews ran exceptionally smoothly, the five-minute bell was loud enough without jolting us out of our seats (a virtuoso performance). Communications before reviews were clear and informative, but not so detailed that the information was difficult to locate once I was at the reviews and scrolling through emails to find the info I needed in the moment.

20. Are you open to looking at work outside of scheduled reviews or not so much? If so, how do you prefer a photographer approach you about the possibility?

When I first began attending portfolio reviews, I was hungry to see everything, including as much as possible on breaks. It only took one portfolio review (over the space of several days) to learn my lesson—burnout! It was exhausting not to have solid brain breaks from looking, thinking, or even talking about images, even though I sometimes regretted missing out on seeing work in person. Depending on my fatigue level, I will sometimes still schedule meetings outside of reviews, or try to see someone's work in particular, but it's usually best if I take the breaks we're given.

21. How do you feel about reviewees and reviewers socializing away from the table? If you are comfortable sharing, what advice do you have for reviewees?

I'm a fan of socializing across borders. It's completely possible to organically develop personal relationships outside of the official reviews. In fact, I've successfully pitched work to clients for publication by a photographer whose work I've never reviewed but whom I've gotten to know socially at several reviews.

When commissioning a photographer, I want to work with someone I have a good rapport and easy communication with. This is one way to establish that. When you find yourself in a social situation with reviewers, as one often does at these events, act natural! Don't bring up or pitch your work—unless I ask you directly. It can be a huge imposition to throw your work into the conversation in a social setting. Quite often, an opportunity arises anyway; you don't want to push it. Of course, it can come up naturally in these settings and, at that point, run with it (but not too fast).

To reviewees, I say this: Use your gut instinct, read the room, read the signs. Don't approach if you sense exhaustion or an unwillingness to engage. Sometimes I need to try to shut that part of my brain down—the part that analyzes, discusses intelligently, and so forth—or put a wall up at social events to ensure that I have enough time to recuperate before doing it all over again the next day.

It takes a lot of energy and focus to do twelve to sixteen meetings in a row. And you want reviewers to want to talk to you outside of reviews. One way to do this is to not bring up your work or talk about reviews. It may sound weird not to talk about reviews at reviews, but it's sometimes the last thing I can talk about once the day is done.

22. How do you prefer the individuals you meet with follow up with you and how often?

Email follow-ups are preferred. I do find there's sometimes a lack of understanding about whether the reviewee will get a reply. I do my best, but it can be difficult to impossible to stay on top of this, as it's outside of the realm of my normal, busy workload. I don't always reply in a timely fashion, and sometimes I don't have the time and energy to reply at all. Rest assured that if you put your email in my inbox with a post-review follow-up, it lives in my data bank/email search engine, and I can easily come back to it when I need.

23. In your opinion, what is the best "leave-behind"?

A small card with an image and all relevant contact info, for me, is the best. Most of us have no space in our carry-on suitcases to keep everything, and quite often no space at home either. In my opinion, the money is better spent elsewhere, no matter how cool the idea. If you have a book or larger leave-behind, I appreciate it when you ask if I would like it, rather than simply handing it over.

24. What are the biggest "no-no's" for reviewees?

Constantly interrupting. Not listening. Not asking any questions. Not having a grasp of what it is I do—this one is a total waste of your time and money. It's absolutely understandable and okay if you don't agree with my feedback. But the review will go better if you don't actively discard it during the review, as something I say might resonate later on. Sometimes this happens after you get the same feedback from different reviewers. You might get something out of our discussion that you couldn't foresee, so you want to be present and accepting during the reviews. A deep conversation about the work is great, but no one benefits if feedback is rejected (whether silently or loudly) on the spot.

25. What one piece of advice would you impart to reviewees?

Know your audience! Being familiar in advance with what I'm about will allow us to occupy those areas I have the most knowledge in, which should lead to the reviewee getting the most out of me, in particular, during the review.

Alex Decosta

Alex Decosta

Hyde Art Gallery at Grossmont College

I received my degree from NYC's School of Visual Arts in 2010, and after graduation I gained extensive experience handling artwork and curating exhibitions as a studio assistant for several artists and for various institutions around the city, including Gallery HO and Art MORA in Chelsea, the Armory and SCOPE Art Fairs, and the Jamaica Center for Arts & Learning. In 2012, I joined the New York Foundation for the Arts as part of their fiscal sponsorship program and, shortly after, became a full-time art handler for Sotheby's Auction House.

After relocating to San Diego in 2015, in addition to maintaining a personal art practice as an illustrator, I continued advancing my career in art curation and installation at Madison Gallery and Laguna Art Museum before accepting the gallery directorial position of the Hyde Art Gallery at Grossmont College in April 2016. As the first full-time director of The Hyde since 1980, I curate at least six exhibitions each academic year and have reestablished the gallery as a premier, award-winning East San Diego County art institution. This revitalization included moving into a brand-new, state-of-the-art gallery, now housed in Grossmont College's new Performing and Visual Arts Center. In addition to my work as a gallerist, curator, and educator, I am also the cofounder and executive board president of Front Row Center, San Diego's newest 501(c)(3) nonprofit performing arts company, which provides exciting theatrical opportunities that are accessible to all young performers.

1. What do you look forward to most and least about portfolio-review events?

By far, my favorite aspect of portfolio-review events is the comradery of like-minded creators and the communal events usually scheduled around these reviews. In most portfolio review-processes I've participated in, reviewees are asked to submit "leave-behinds," typically PDF documents that contain an abridged version of their portfolio. I hate seeing my reviewees work out of context, ahead of time, because another favorite moment is the initial presentation in which conversation surrounding the work can take an infinite number of routes.

Incidentally, my least favorite part, which isn't always a part of every review I've participated in, is when the avenues of discussion have reached dead ends and conversation with a photographer becomes overtly labored. This is almost always the case for work with shallow conceptual depth, or when the reviewee hasn't brought enough material with them to discuss.

2. Why do you attend portfolio-review events, and do you have any specific goals in attending?

I direct an exhibition program for an academic institution, and I am constantly looking for new artists to exhibit who showcase the wide array of practices taught on my campus. This includes not only photography but also drawing, painting, ceramics, digital arts, sculpture, and jewelry design. My goal is primarily as research to identify new, viable artists I feel would best engage the students we serve, through either exhibition programming or one-off events such as visiting-artist lectures or classroom workshops.

I have many goals as a gallery director, primarily focusing on increasing outreach and collaborative opportunities with various programs around campus, but I'm also concerned with developing exhibition programming that showcases a more equitable array of creatives and object makers—particularly the inclusion and elevation of BIPOC artists, both local and national. That is why these opportunities to meet new photographers through portfolio-review sessions are so important. Additionally, these sessions offer unique opportunities to edify working artists about my programming and the opportunities available for artists to exhibit.

3. When you attend portfolio-review events, what kind of strain does this cause on your work schedule?

Most semesters I am able to hire a student gallery assistant, either through our federal work-study or another internship program. As long as they are available to gallery-sit during the portfolio-review dates, there shouldn't be an issue. This is assuming that the portfolio-review event is local. It would also be an entirely different scenario if a portfolio review were scheduled at the same time as an exhibition installation, as the turnaround time between exhibitions in my particular program is fairly short. I would also like to add that it is important for any director or curator to exit the confines of their gallery or museum space and engage with working artists—this needs to be built into their work schedule.

4. If you receive the reviewee list from the organization prior to the portfolio review, do you look at their work online in preparation for the review, or do you like to look at it fresh? Why or why not?

In most critiques I've been a part of, both as an art-school student and as an educator, I am seeing artwork presented for review for the first time. When I'm visiting artists in their studio space for exhibition consideration or as part of the normal curation process, I'll rarely ask to see a digital facsimile of the work ahead of time. This allows me to give the critique recipient my initial response, which is incredibly important because all artwork, at least work displayed publicly, is seen

Alex Decosta

constantly for the first time every day. The public's perception of and imagined engagement with an artwork doesn't necessarily need to influence the work but it should certainly be considered at some point during its creation process. Any artist should be concerned with the visceral response their work instills in a viewer. Additionally, most work presented in either "leave-behinds" or on a website are almost always presented without enough, or sometimes any, context. At the beginning of every review, I expect the photographer I'm engaging with to give a short presentation of their work and process, anyway. The only resource that I might want to look at beforehand would be a biography or exhibition record of the reviewee.

5. What objectives do you recommend reviewees bring to the table?

Every reviewer has a different perspective, and photographers bringing their work to a portfolio review should expect their work not only to be perceived through different mentalities, but also for some of the more subtle nuances to be lost. As I said before, I enjoy diving into a portfolio without a statement of intent. With that in mind, reviewees should know how many photographs and bodies of work they want to cover during the incredibly short review. They should keep a mental stopwatch going so that our time together is utilized fully.

My own objective, as I've stated, is to learn about and possibly offer exhibition opportunities to photographers I meet with, but I don't think individuals should participate in the review process solely to find these opportunities. Photographers should be acutely aware of what they want to discuss with the reviewer. Think about what is missing or what isn't working about a particular body of work. If a photographer is experiencing a creative block, direct the dialog during the review to dig deeper into the conceptual possibilities surrounding a photograph's development. Since I work primarily as a curator and gallery director, I receive a lot of requests for input on art installation and framing. These review sessions end in the blink of an eye, so stay focused and be prepared with a list of every topic you want to cover.

6. Do you ask at the start of your session what the reviewee wants?

It depends, but this isn't usually necessary; reviewees typically come strapped to the nines with work that they want to present. Due to the short time frame we have together, it is important that they go through as much of their portfolio as possible so we can discuss their overall trajectory. Also, most reviewees, prior to meeting with me, have already mentally cataloged what they would like to discuss during our session.

One contrary example is when I met with a photographer, during a 2022 portfolio-review session, who was just starting their journey, and they presented a wide array of photographs that seemingly had no conceptual through line. They didn't identify a specific aspect of their work that they wanted to examine. They essentially threw all their cards on the table and asked me to read their fortune. In this case, it was important for me to break down the discussion into digestible sections: What are they working on now? What do they find fascinating about this imagery or subject matter? What ideas are they looking to further examine? How do they see this work being presented once the body of work is better defined? In this case, it was important to guide the reviewee to think about what they want their artwork to achieve, and it may have been something they hadn't considered before.

7. What advice do you have for first-time reviewees?

Understand that your work will be viewed from a new perspective. If a reviewer doesn't readily understand or perceive the nuances within a particular work, don't be offended. Keep your mind receptive to these new viewpoints. Some of the most powerful redirections of my own personal art practice were initiated through the discourse of a critique. A single person's perspective will always be myopic, and collaboration is necessary for the creation of successful artwork. I would also advise first-time reviewees to bring a large single body of work, multiple bodies of work that have either conceptual or thematic similarities, or an array of works that show progression. The least productive reviews I've participated in were when a reviewee presented work that was seemingly random.

8. Who should lead the review—reviewer or reviewee? Why?

In any critique or review, the participating artist should start each session by presenting themselves and their work in a sort of monologue format. It is the role of the reviewer to then speak upon aspects of the work and guide that conversation going forward. It's best to approach this opportunity as a conversation; there is no particular lead, and the process should be fundamentally collaborative. A successful review conversation ought to be casual, albeit extensive in its reach, and a quality reviewer should be able to direct that discussion. If a reviewee provides adequate material to look over, this should be easy!

9. What advice do you have for reviewees on how to manage the allotted time during the session?

Like any project, it's all about preparation. Before entering a review session, know what work or body of work you want to discuss. I would advise leaving behind older work and presenting pieces that are a part of a single conceptual body. You

Alex Decosta

can certainly bring additional work with you just in case you find that there is still time.

However, understand that these sessions are extremely short and go by quickly. If you come prepared and know ahead of time what works you want to discuss, it becomes much easier to keep a mental stopwatch going. Don't be afraid to purposefully cut a discussion short so that you can move onto another set of photographs. We as reviewers are extremely aware of how fast each session can go, and no reviewer worth their weight would be insulted if you politely said, "I see we are running out of time; can we please move on to the next piece?"

10. How do you feel about a reviewee recording your session?

In the age of Zoom, recording a remote review session seems obvious, but I would feel uncomfortable with what I said during a session being recorded. I do, however, expect my reviewees to take notes. During these somewhat casual conversations, there are often tangents or comparisons made from initial observations of the work. These options can, and often do, evolve over the course of the session, when work is further illuminated by the presenter. It is therefore imperative that any recording of a review session be rewatched with that understanding. I know in several past review sessions, I made a connection with a piece that was entirely reactionary, but after examining the work in more detail with the photographer, my initial observation might seem absurd or completely off base. To give an example, it is like when you are interviewed for a publication: if that session is being recorded, nothing is off the record, and therefore, any digression could be included in the final production. This may not always be desirable.

11. How many different projects do you think are ideal for discussion in an individual review session?

It depends on the allotted time for each review session. In most portfolio-review processes I've participated in, one well-conceived project can take up the entire session. I would say bring your most current, well-rounded body of work and one secondary grouping in case time permits. Before entering the session, every reviewee should be aware of the time constraints and expect that your discussion will be cut short. Therefore, it is imperative that you put your best work forward and have a tentative grasp on which aspects of that work you want to cover.

12. How important is it for reviewees to have their idea completely fleshed out regarding their project?

A photographer who doesn't have an idea or a project completely fleshed out might be the perfect example of why a photographer might attend a portfolio review. This is the discourse arena where they can gain clarity of vision. It's also important to note that while having a fleshed-out idea is valuable and can allow time during the review session to be more appropriately allocated, it doesn't mean the project cannot evolve or adapt based on feedback received during the portfolio-review session. The review process can provide valuable insights and suggestions for improvement. When a photographer starts with a clear and developed concept, this lends the session a strong foundation to build upon and increases the likelihood of a successful review.

13. Can a project be presented, in your opinion, as underdeveloped or overdeveloped?

I believe that the impetus for most portfolio-review participants to register for a review is the desire to seek additional counsel on projects that they feel are underdeveloped or lacking direction. A successful review happens when a reviewee leaves the process with a renewed sense of creativity and a more defined understanding of their work's trajectory. It may be difficult to engage a photographer with overdeveloped work because they have already invested so much executive function into that project; my advice would involve subtraction rather than addition. As with any other object-maker, artists impart a piece of their ego into all their work, and it can be easy to guide an artist toward a goal they have not yet discovered. However, it is much more difficult to explain to them, after they have overpoured themselves into something, that their endeavor needs to be amended or redirected.

14. How important is the technical quality of physical objects (for example, prints) being presented at the review session? How do you feel about work being presented on a tablet or computer?

I would always rather see raw, unframed works during a portfolio review. These prints being offered up for examination are not ready for exhibition. If a reviewee presents work that is immaculately matted and framed, it indicates to me, as the reviewer, that they have created a finished product and may therefore be less willing to amend or adjust the work. That being said, all photographers and artists should treat their work with respect in regard to storage and presentation. If you undervalue your own work, you can expect everyone else to as well. In almost all reviews I've administered, the topic of exhibition presentation comes up, and therefore, it helps in the discussion if those decisions surrounding mounting or framing have not happened yet. In regard to presenting the work digitally, some pieces in particular work with film or animated elements and may only be viewable in that format. However, reviewees should keep in mind that without physical prints available, their material quality and scale is undefined, and the conversation surrounding physical presentation is much harder to have.

15. How do you feel about virtual portfolio reviews versus in-person portfolio-review events (pros and cons)? Is your ideal review session length twenty, twenty-five, or thirty minutes?

I've participated in both in-person and Zoom-based portfolio reviews, but my preference depends on the context. Ironically, my portfolio reviews over Zoom were far more personal, as I would typically get a view of the photographer's home or studio. There also isn't the consistent distraction of other reviews happening at the same time and place. However, as I've said before, interpersonal acumen is paramount to the success of any artist, and in-person review events offer these additional socialization opportunities. Also, photographers can present physical copies of their work, which allows reviewers a better opportunity to comment on material quality and scale. My ideal review session is as long as possible—I would take thirty minutes, thirty-five minutes, or forty minutes! Each session I feel ends too quickly. When participating in a virtual review, it is much more abrupt and jarring when you are suddenly ripped away from your Zoom breakout room.

16. Have you ever offered a commission, a show, a press feature, or representation during a review? Can you share a success story or stories with us that came from a productive meeting at a review session?

In my own professional practice as the director of an exhibition program for an academic institution, it is difficult for me to operate with that sort of immediacy. At the end of a review session I found particularly stimulating with a photographer whose work I thought would engage the students I serve, I will mention that exhibition submission proposals are accepted on a rolling basis and where on our website they can find more information. A portfolio review isn't the place to examine a photographer's organizational expertise, but I will need to get a better sense of that through the submission of a proposal in order to assess if we can work with them. Also, most exhibition proposals are vetted through several committees, and it wouldn't be proper to promise something I couldn't rightly guarantee. Most photographers who are participating in the review process are looking for these opportunities, so I've received multiple, beautifully composed exhibition proposals after a session has ended. Some of them have been explored and offered, leading not only to full-scale exhibitions but also individual classroom workshops and lectures.

17. Have you ever purchased artwork from a reviewee? If so, what do you base the price on, and is it signed by the artist?

I have purchased artwork from a reviewee, but it was long after the review session had concluded. I don't think portfolio-review sessions are an appropriate place for selling work. Even though through the review process I become acquainted with an artist, and I might even jokingly request a friends and family discount, regarding pricing I will always leave that at the discretion of the artist. Since non-hand-embellished, standard photographic inkjet prints exist as multiples, I wouldn't expect to pay the same price as a one-off unique piece. I would also anticipate any print I purchase to be signed, dated, and possibly editioned if applicable.

18. How often do you connect or recommend a photographer who may not be right for you but a good match for a colleague?

The visual arts and photography, unlike other artistic modalities like theatre and dance, are fairly solitary practices; however, no one can be successful in a vacuum of self-reliance. Collaboration is the backbone of any successful artist. I will typically schedule my exhibitions a year in advance to give the artists I work with ample time to plan around other museum or gallery obligations and possibly create new work. This doesn't allow me much flexibility with scheduling, and if my gallery is unavailable, I will, of course, redirect that artist to another gallery in need. This doesn't happen often, but it is important, and I strongly believe that this approach has karmic repercussions.

19. Can you share the best review you have been a part of, and why it was? (No names should be mentioned.)

During a 2022 portfolio-review event in San Diego, I met an artist whose work conceptually spoke about their mental health struggles and who used their photographic process as a way of overcoming that adversity. I thought the work was incredibly moving and close to fully developed.

    The institute I work for always has programming for Mental Health Awareness Month in May, and my initial reaction was to mount an exhibition of their work to coincide with that programming. Although this process is still in progress, I have been to several exhibitions of their work, and we have developed a close friendship. It is amazing watching them develop their process further and, in doing so, find success. The greatest reward for any educator is seeing your students' accomplishments after you have spent so much time guiding them. Seeing a photographer take my recommendations and, in turn, for those recommendations to actually aid in that photographer's success is a good feeling.

Alex Decosta

20. Are you open to looking at work outside of scheduled reviews or not so much? If yes, how do you prefer a photographer approach you about the possibility?

I've been approached by several photographers after a session has closed to discuss their work further, either as an impromptu review or as an invitation to their studio or an upcoming exhibition. As I've said, the best follow-up I can receive is an update on their work, especially if they have utilized points from our discussion. I will always give feedback if I am able. Once a review has concluded, I don't feel like my job has ended, and the relationships that are developed during this process will remain long after the portfolio review has ended. Typically, I will recommend artists reach out to me via email for additional dialogue.

21. How do you feel about reviewees and reviewers socializing away from the table? If you are comfortable sharing, what advice do you have for reviewees?

The art world is built upon relationships between artists, gallerist, critics, publishers, and curators. It is imperative for an artist to engage in that social collaboration in order to advance their career; therefore, I am always delighted to socialize with reviewees outside of our sessions.

My main advice for any artist or photographer regarding this is simple: praise in public but criticize in private. This is one of the first pieces of advice I received in art school when we began our gallery visits in NYC's Chelsea neighborhood: don't trash talk while you are in a gallery—you never know who might hear you. The same advice can be applied when socializing away from the review table: you never know who is listening, so always be positive.

Another piece of advice I always give my students is that it cannot be overstated how important it is to be affable. You don't have to be the loudest or funniest in a crowd, but at least be likeable. No one will want to work with you if you are egocentric, gossipy, or downright negative.

22. How do you prefer that the individuals you meet with follow up with you and how often?

It is entirely at the discretion of the photographer I work with to follow up. The exhibition program I direct accepts exhibition proposals on a rolling basis, and when a reviewee is ready and has a viable proposal ready, they can submit at any time. All reviewees receive my contact information, and, of course, I love hearing from reviewees about new work, publications, and exhibitions. It makes me so happy to see them succeed!

23. In your opinion, what is the best "leave-behind"?

Every artist and photographer should have an up-to-date website and decent social-media presence. The best "leave-behinds" should therefore include their website and links to social media, but possibly a few images so that I can readily identify who they are. Ideally an artist's website would include all this anyway, so I like to think of the "leave-behind" as more of a business card—keep it short and put your contact and social-media information front and center.

24. What are the biggest "no-no's" for reviewees?

Number one: don't get defensive. I once had a reviewee who was unhappy because I couldn't readily identify the conceptual and symbolic nuances within their work. They became aggravated and felt that I was not seeing their vision or purposefully misconstruing what they were presenting to me. My advice to every reviewee is to come into the process with an open mind.

My job is not to reaffirm what you already believe; the conversations we have in these sessions are meant to open your visual dialogue and expose you to alternative thought processes. You will never grow as an artist if you aren't receptive to this. Your work and confidence as an artist should be able to stand up to slight criticism. Another thing to avoid during the portfolio-review process is to get intimidated by your reviewers or the process. We all suffer from imposter syndrome, and it is important to be able to open yourself up to conversations surrounding your work without feeling overwhelmed. You are the world's premier expert on your own artistic practice!

25. What one piece of advice would you impart to reviewees?

Success in the art world is predicated on your ability to be consistent—never stop producing work. It is better to produce lower-quality work than nothing at all. In addition to this, always continue experimenting. Although I've reiterated many times before the importance of keeping an open mind during the review process, don't let any advice deter you from pursuing your artistic goals.

Alex Decosta

Anne Kelly

El Zaguán Gallery

My (photography) origin story began when my mother started making black-and-white portraits of me; I was about fourteen years old. This experience inspired me to make pictures of my friends, using a 35mm Nikon. In high school, I continued to pursue my hobby and spent numerous evenings in the darkroom satisfying my curiosities. It was magic! Following graduation, I relocated to Santa Fe, New Mexico, to expand my understanding of photography at the College of Santa Fe, which had a strong photography program.

I started working at photo-eye Gallery in 2006. This gallery, established in 1991, was one I often visited during my college years. Working at the gallery has allowed me to indulge in the world of fine-art photography every day and gain valuable experience in the business aspect of it. Through my work at photo-eye, I have built lasting connections with esteemed photographers, aided up-and-coming photographers in advancing their careers, supported clients in developing and maintaining their photography collections, and educated the public about the artists we represent. I have also curated more than eighty exhibitions at our Santa Fe gallery and photography fairs throughout the country.

In fall 2020, I launched *Art in the Raw*, a podcast and YouTube channel dedicated to supporting the arts. Through engaging in discussions about practice and creativity, I aim to inspire and connect artists. This initiative has led to the creation of a second video series, *photo-eye Conversations*, as well as speaking engagements with various art organizations, including the Santa Fe Workshops. Additionally, I am an occasional contributor to *Analog Forever* magazine.

1. What do you look forward to most and least about portfolio-review events?

Portfolio reviews offer a unique chance to spend time among people who share similar interests. I appreciate the opportunity to view physical prints and chat with their creators during the formal reviews. This is not always possible when I am at the gallery managing daily logistics. It's a pleasure to be able to devote a few days to connecting with photographers and industry experts I wouldn't ordinarily meet. I have attended enough reviews to know that by the end, I will be exhausted, but I believe the experience is worth it.

2. Why do you attend portfolio-review events, and do you have any specific goals in attending?

I attend portfolio reviews with the hope of finding photographers to collaborate with in the future. However, not everyone I meet will be a good fit for my institution or current exhibition schedule. While I can't guarantee opportunities for everyone, I strive to offer helpful guidance to each photographer I meet with.

3. When you attend portfolio-review events, what kind of strain does this cause on your work schedule?

While I set aside time to participate in portfolio reviews, I still need to check work emails on my breaks. There is always something at the gallery that I need to attend to.

4. If you receive the reviewee list from the organization prior to the portfolio review, do you look at their work online in preparation for the review, or do you like to look at it fresh? Why or why not?

I don't because I prefer to approach conversations with a fresh perspective and no preconceived notions. However, I find it useful to have a list so I can easily find the artist's work online after our meeting.

5. What objectives do you recommend reviewees bring to the table?

Everyone is different and should have unique objectives. It is helpful to have a clear understanding of what you wish to achieve beforehand. Although seeking an exhibition or publishing a book is a common goal, I suggest diving deeper and identifying even more specific objectives to focus on during the review. This way, our conversation can be more productive and tailored to your specific needs.

6. Do you ask at the start of your session what the reviewee wants?

I ask at the beginning of the session because they pass quickly. I have a wide range of knowledge I can share, but I make it my goal to tailor the conversation based on the photographer's objectives, if possible.

7. What advice do you have for first-time reviewees?

When attending a photography review, it is key to have reasonable expectations. It's not common to be offered an opportunity on the spot, but there is much to be gained by building relationships with your reviewers and other photographers. Any knowledge you gain or improvements you make is a win.

Anne Kelly

8. Who should lead the review—reviewer or reviewee? Why?

It should be a two-way conversation.

9. What advice do you have for reviewees on how to manage the allotted time during the session?

It's crucial to be aware that sessions will fly by quickly. When attending a review, make sure you have clear objectives and communicate them at the start of each meeting. Allocate time for discussing your work and goals, and make time to listen and to address any new questions that may arise during the conversation.

10. How do you feel about a reviewee recording your session?

I can see how it would be helpful, but you should check with your reviewer first.

11. How many different projects do you think are ideal for discussion in an individual review session?

Usually, there is only enough time to review one project. However, occasionally it can be helpful to quickly view additional projects to gain a better understanding of the artist and their work's trajectory. If you have multiple strong projects, I would recommend bringing two or three, if possible; however, it's important to decide beforehand which project will be the best fit for each reviewer.

12. How important is it for reviewees to have their idea completely fleshed out regarding their project?

I highly recommend having a good sense of what your project is about, but also remaining open-minded. Sharing your work with various reviewers can provide diverse perspectives that might reveal aspects of your project you weren't aware of—potentially leading to a slight pivot in your idea. I suggest being receptive to feedback.

13. Can a project be presented, in your opinion, as underdeveloped or overdeveloped?

Portfolio reviews can be a helpful tool for project development. However, if, for example, you show up with twenty photos you made in one day that you haven't given much thought to (this is an extreme example), the project may not warrant the cost of attending a portfolio review. When it comes to completed projects, if the artist isn't interested in feedback on any level and is only seeking a solo show or book deal, the twenty-minute meeting may start to feel long for both the reviewee and the reviewer, so even if your project is complete, it is still good to keep an open mind.

14. How important is the technical quality of physical objects (for example, prints) being presented at the review session? How do you feel about work being presented on a tablet or computer?

When I attend portfolio reviews, I am aware that the prints have likely been made specifically for the review and may be smaller than usual and may not be pristine due to handling. However, print quality is of utmost importance in ensuring a professional and polished presentation of your work, so I would go as far as to say that it is crucial to prioritize it. I would also advise against presenting your work on a computer during portfolio reviews, unless necessary. Most reviewers, given the opportunity, will want to see the final product (the print) whenever possible.

15. How do you feel about virtual portfolio reviews versus in-person portfolio-review events (pros and cons)? Is your ideal review session length twenty, twenty-five, or thirty minutes?

Although I generally prefer in-person photo reviews, the virtual reviews that emerged in 2020 provided a valuable opportunity to connect with the photo community from the comfort of our own homes. I was pleasantly surprised at how well the virtual format worked. However, I believe most of us miss the socializing that typically occurs before and after in-person reviews. To this day, one of the advantages of online reviews is that they tend to be more cost-effective, as there is no need to travel, making the overall price point more accessible. I don't think there is an ideal blanket length of time. It depends on the depth of connection between the reviewer and the reviewee.

16. Have you ever offered a commission, a show, a press feature, or representation during a review? Can you share a success story or stories with us that came from a productive meeting at a review session?

Often. I have included artists in exhibitions after meeting them at a review, but I've never invited them mid-review. Collaborating with an artist, even for one show, marks the beginning of a new relationship, and I usually don't commit to any type of relationship after only knowing someone for twenty minutes! However, there was one instance where I was curating a group show, and I met a photographer at a review who was perfect for that show, so I contacted him shortly after our first meeting.

Anne Kelly

17. Have you ever purchased artwork from a reviewee? If so, what do you base the price on, and is it signed by the artist?

Based on my experience with reviews, the topic of making purchases has never arisen. Typically, we focus on discussing facets of the work. Furthermore, at the gallery, I am constantly exposed to art I would like to own, so it is necessary to give very careful consideration to any art purchases.

18. How often do you connect or recommend a photographer who may not be right for you but a good match for a colleague?

When I spend time with other reviewers in the evenings, it is common to suggest work to each other that we loved but was not a good fit for us/our organizations, but we believe would be a good match for others.

19. Can you share the best review you have been a part of, and why it was? (No names should be mentioned.)

I have been fortunate enough to attend many excellent reviews across the country. These reviews are all centered around one-on-one review sessions, but they also include social events, lectures, and exhibitions. They all have something special about them. I enjoy both small and large reviews, but I particularly like the smaller ones where everyone can interact. My first portfolio review was in San Francisco. I have fond memories of showing up at the welcome party, which kicks off the event, to find their director (and a prolific photographer and educator) serving homemade chili. I've been invited back every year since, which is a great honor. Every time I attend, it feels like visiting old friends—because in truth, I am.

20. Are you open to looking at work outside of scheduled reviews or not so much? If so, how do you prefer a photographer approach you about the possibility?

I don't mind the request, but unfortunately, it's not always possible. My schedule is typically booked with reviews throughout the day, with only short breaks and lunch. These breaks are necessary to be able to provide thoughtful feedback for all the scheduled reviews. That said, if it is possible, I will oblige, and if not, I will make it a point to seek out that artist during the public portfolio walk-through. Requests can be made before the review via email or in person.

K

21. How do you feel about reviewees and reviewers socializing away from the table? If you are comfortable sharing, what advice do you have for reviewees?

I am all for it, but it's important to be genuine and not try to manipulate them for personal gain or to get extra reviews. This kind of behavior is usually easy to spot and can be off-putting. It's better to approach socializing with reviewers as you would any other social interaction in life.

22. How do you prefer the individuals you meet with follow up with you, and how often?

It is a case-by-case situation and will vary based on the connection you form (or not) with your reviewer. I suggest sending a thank-you card or email about a week and a half after the review. Typically, immediately following the reviews, most of us are swamped catching up after taking time off to review—and it can be challenging to respond to follow-ups in that time frame.

23. In your opinion, what is the best "leave-behind"?

Something small and unique that includes both an image and your contact information. Keep in mind that your reviewers will likely need to bring all of their "leave-behinds" to the end-of-day events, plus travel home with it.

24. What are the biggest "no-no's" for reviewers?

Avoid behaving in a way that may make your reviewer feel pressured or cornered, as this can be very off-putting. Many reviewers have stories about unpleasant experiences with photographers who insist that their project is perfect for them or their institution and that no further improvement is necessary. This kind of entitled behavior should be avoided and will not take you anywhere positive.

25. What one piece of advice would you impart to reviewees?

Research your reviewers and the institutions they work for before the review, and consider what unique knowledge they have that would be most beneficial to you.

Anne Kelly

Michael Kirchoff

Forever Magazine/One Twelve Publishing

With a career as a professional photographer that spans over three decades, as well as a side of me that participates in the industry as what I would call a photographic artist (my fine-art work), the last ten years have seen me shift much of my time to "the other side of the table" as a reviewer, curator, and writer. In doing so, I feel I have a very well-rounded view of the industry and what can be accomplished by those willing to put in the blood, sweat, and tears to make a career of their own. I know what it feels like and what can be done from either side, so I am sympathetic to those just starting out with presenting their work and opening themselves up to scrutiny and judgment. I've also forged many relationships with industry professionals of all types, so I pride myself on helping others make connections and receive opportunities. Networking is a large part of my time and efforts and has paid off quite well, so passing on these traits and ideas to others is at the forefront of what I can provide.

K

1. What do you look forward to most and least about portfolio-review events?

As far as I'm concerned, there are only positive aspects to attending a portfolio review. Being there allows me to connect with like-minded individuals in a much more profound manner. You see and experience the work in person and have meaningful and lasting conversations and professional relationships that will continue for years if properly handled. Sometimes it's a chance to meet people you've only met via social media or email before, so the bond becomes stronger.

If you are heading to a review with the idea that there is something you are not looking forward to, then you are doing it wrong.

2. Why do you attend portfolio-review events, and do you have any specific goals in attending?

The idea is to support the photographic community, and portfolio-review events are a large part of that. The goals are to find and highlight the talent and photographs created by this community. I have multiple projects that require recording or writing about who is at the forefront of making thought-provoking and intentional art. They also provide a means to strengthen your associations with colleagues to hammer out ideas and possible collaborations.

3. When you attend portfolio-review events, what kind of strain does this cause on your work schedule?

Thankfully, I have a completely freelance career, so the scheduling is at my discretion. That said, when things are busy (which is often), choices have to be made as to what is most important at that time. Much of what I can work on can also be done while on the road.

4. If you receive the reviewee list from the organization prior to the portfolio review, do you look at their work online in preparation for the review, or do you like to look at it fresh? Why or why not?

For myself, it comes down to how much time I have at that moment. It will often depend on mood as well. While I often like to get some information ahead of time, there is nothing like the impact of seeing something extraordinary—in that moment—for the first time.

5. What objectives do you recommend reviewees bring to the table?

A well-rehearsed idea of what their goals and aspirations are for the work they are presenting. It can be as simple as an elevator pitch or as long as a career-spanning dissertation. It really depends on what they are looking for from me—feedback, critique, opportunities, et cetera.

6. Do you ask at the start of your session what the reviewee wants?

One of the things I will often say is, "What brings you to see me today?" Some have ideas of what they might hope for or expect from me, and others do not. The answer to this question usually tells me immediately how much they intended to see me specifically and how prepared they are for the session.

7. What advice do you have for first-time reviewees?

Relax, and don't let your nerves get the best of you. We are all equal and all human, so don't put anyone on a pedestal and let it derail your thoughts and intentions for the meeting.

8. Who should lead the review—reviewer or reviewee? Why?

I don't know that there is a right or wrong answer to this. It really depends on the reviewee's comfort level. It usually just happens organically. If the reviewee doesn't have anything much to say, I always have questions. If they know the material well and have a pitch for it, then by all means, tell me, and we'll go from there.

9. What advice do you have for reviewees on how to manage the allotted time during the session?

Take several minutes to tell me about you and the work you've brought. Don't wax nostalgic over specific images and give me a story for every one. That's a waste of time. Ask questions and allow me to ask them as well. Don't be overly concerned with the time, though, as work that is received well will stick in my mind, and we will continue the discussion at another time, anyway. Always remember that this is the first step in what might be a longer conversation. It's relationship-building with you and those who can help you accomplish your goals.

10. How do you feel about a reviewee recording your session?

I have no issue with it whatsoever. In fact, it should be common practice for all of them. The time goes by quickly and the information received can easily be forgotten, especially when going from review to review. It's just a good way to take notes for review later.

11. How many different projects do you think are ideal for discussion in an individual review session?

Since I prefer to stick with the (fairly) standard time of twenty minutes for a review, I would say one project is preferred, but two can occasionally be discussed. Sometimes it's a good idea to go into the review with one project but have a second one on hand in case the first is not received well, or there is a little time left to at least introduce a second body of work to the reviewer.

12. How important is it for reviewees to have their idea completely fleshed out regarding their project?

If they are presenting a finished, or nearly finished, body of work or project, then it's very important. Most of the time, however, they are looking for feedback or additional ideas or direction with the work. Honesty and transparency are appreciated when the work is discussed. Personally, I love batting around ideas or potential ways to expand an idea and help an individual find clarity with their project.

13. Can a project be presented, in your opinion, as underdeveloped or overdeveloped?

Underdeveloped projects occur all of the time. But that's where we get to help with critique, ideas, and open discussion. If you sit down at the table and present the project as a work in progress, then that's perfectly fine. That's one of the reasons you should be there. Allow others to give you feedback and contribute to its development.

Overdeveloped projects are far more rare. There are times, especially with presentation, that a project is just "too much." What I mean to say is that during a review, you don't necessarily have to pull out all the stops and show every single idea or put on a whole dog-and-pony show. Oversized prints, crazy portfolio boxes, massive leave-behinds, and doing all the talking can easily work against you. And the reviewers will often warn the others when this happens to them. I've seen it many times.

14. How important is the technical quality of physical objects (for example, prints) being presented at the review session? How do you feel about work being presented on a tablet or computer?

Finished prints of the highest quality are always preferred. The tactile nature of them leaves a lasting impression every time. And yes, bring only the best prints you can. That said, seeing work on a tablet or laptop can work, but it leaves that special component out of the equation.

15. How do you feel about virtual portfolio reviews versus in-person portfolio-review events (pros and cons)? Is your ideal review session length twenty, twenty-five, or thirty minutes?

Virtual reviews are wonderful for those who cannot afford the travel expenses that come with out-of-town, in-person reviews. They help level the playing field and allow me to see work I may not necessarily have had the opportunity to see otherwise. The downside is not seeing the work in person. Handling final prints or art is an experience that benefits from the tactile nature of that experience. Sometimes it really doesn't matter, but for me it heightens the session and makes it more memorable.

Ideal session length is twenty minutes. If you can't get your ideas across in that time, you need to know your own work better. More time doesn't necessarily equate to a better review. If something clicks, the conversation will continue after the review is over, at another time. I always let people know when I want to continue the discussion.

Michael Kirchoff

16. Have you ever offered a commission, a show, a press feature, or representation during a review? Can you share a success story or stories with us that came from a productive meeting at a review session?

Press features and interviews happen on the spot fairly frequently. Usually, though, some time is needed to think things over after the meeting. Reviewees often (and should) take notes, and so do I. There have been many success stories like this, plus a few referrals to other reviewers that have helped lead to print purchases, representation, or book publishing. Reviewers discuss work behind the scenes all of the time, so a good (or bad) reviewee is often brought up to others who may be able to provide an opportunity of some sort.

17. Have you ever purchased artwork from a reviewee? If so, what do you base the price on, and is it signed by the artist?

I've purchased a few prints and many books during a review. The price was based upon what the artist set, and what I'm willing to pay is dependent on what my budget for such is at that moment. And yes, always signed.

K

18. How often do you connect or recommend a photographer who may not be right for you but a good match for a colleague?

Quite often. There are a few other reviewers I work closely and confer with, even if they are not at the same review event as me. We have similar aesthetics for the type of work we love most and trust each other's instincts. I find this to be quite common among other reviewers as well.

19. Can you share the best review you have been a part of, and why it was? (No names should be mentioned.)

Hmmm . . . hard to say what a best review would entail, but there is an artist I met over a year ago whom I am continuing to collaborate with on a long-form interview. I discovered their work during a formal in-person review at the early stages of a project that I found fascinating and unique. We had been keeping in touch for several months. Then we decided to document the project's growth over time, especially as it progressed and changed, in the form of questions and answers to address how the changes and decisions for the project are being made. There is no current end date for the interview, as there is no need to hurry the project along. We are letting it move along at a pace that works for it and not us. Time stamps are added to both questions and answers to document how the project shapes up. It's been interesting being "in" on the details as they change, and it should provide some insight into how a project is developed and creativity applied.

20. Are you open to looking at work outside of scheduled reviews or not so much? If so, how do you prefer a photographer approach you about the possibility?

Absolutely—time permitting. I'm all for seeing additional work from an artist or even someone who wasn't able to get me as a reviewer because they missed out due to the process of choosing reviewers from the event producers. That said, I often have limited time to do this formally. I usually have all my spare time planned out or committed to before the events start. Your next question about socializing often provides opportunities to see something more casually, though. And, honestly, that is often the better way.

21. How do you feel about reviewees and reviewers socializing away from the table? If you are comfortable sharing, what advice do you have for reviewees?

Always approach with a whiskey in hand to thank me for the vast knowledge I've bestowed upon you, and be prepared to pick up my tab at the end of the night. Okay, just kidding. I have no problem socializing with anyone at a review event—reviewers or reviewees. I do want to like any artist as a person, as well as for their talents. Who wouldn't? For me, it's all about collaboration, so why not work with people you can hang with? Nothing preconceived or expected, just easygoing people you can have a fruitful conversation with.

22. How do you prefer that the individuals you meet with follow up with you and how often?

If I like the work, I will actually ask them to add me to their newsletter list if they have one. Other than that, an occasional email, maybe three or four times a year, max. I'll also ask if they have a PDF presentation or document that contains images and contact info. I keep a digital archive of potential artists on my computer desktop.

23. In your opinion, what is the best "leave-behind"?

Something small, like a simple postcard with all of the appropriate contact info. Sometimes something handmade or more personal gets more attention. The best of these are often displayed on my office walls. Reviewers always return home with a plethora of leave-behinds, so please make it easy on us to carry and store them if needed.

24. What are the biggest "no-no's" for reviewees?

Sitting down at the table and immediately asking what I can do for them. Any presumption is an instant turn-off—no matter how much I might like the work after hearing something like that. Confidence is great, but arrogance will work against you every time. Let me make any determination of collaboration, and please allow me the time to make an informed decision, if any.

25. What one piece of advice would you impart to reviewees?

Define and build your goals for the work and for your career so they can help sustain each other individually.

K

Pradip Malde

Pradip Malde

Sewanee University

I was born in Arusha, Tanzania, in 1957. My parents were the children of Indians who emigrated to East Africa and, after having established a privileged life in Tanzania, became refugees from the turmoil that spread through the region in the 1970s. I have remained concerned about loss and belonging since then.

Out of this culturally rich and traumatic childhood, I have come to think of photographs as artifacts, and of all artifacts as membranes—where what may be explicit and immutable begins to lead us into the fluid realms of meaning and memory. I believe this has come from moving from Tanzania to India, then Spain, England, Norway, Scotland, and, now, the USA. Through my photographic work, technical research, and teaching, I have strived to learn how to embrace the passage rather than the port.

I studied photography at what is now the Arts University of Bournemouth, England, and completed an MA at the Glasgow School of Art in Scotland in 1979. It was around this time that I first saw platinum prints in person—photographs by Edward Weston and Paul Strand, but more enduringly, those of Gertrude Käsebier and of Frederick H. Evans's cathedral interiors. I felt a coming together of sound (Eric Satie and Peter Maxwell Davis), landscape (the Scottish Highlands and the Orkney Islands), and imagination-as-artifact (William Blake, the platinum print). I moved to Orkney soon after graduating in 1980. It was here that I began to research and learn how to make platinum/palladium prints.

I work thematically and often function on a parallel track with my teaching, which ranges from working with barely literate children to graduate-level scholars and artists. I strive to use photography as a catalyst for regeneration: recovery from experiences of loss and trauma, recognizing and breaking cycles of violence, and using the magnetic experience of the beautiful to help us consider and find solutions to our lesser aspects.

I am a photographer and a teacher.

1. What do you look forward to most and least about portfolio-review events?

A portfolio review offers an opportunity to look at and talk about photographs. It lets a community of like-minded people absorb and respond to ideas arising from making, processing, and thinking. The reviewee and reviewer often meet, show or see, and talk about the work for the first time. Hence, the conversation around a portfolio may seem spontaneous and improvised.

However, as with jazz or some of the oldest music traditions, improvisation takes preparation and practice; it requires skill. As I am sure many improvisatory

M

musicians, speakers, and actors feel, spontaneous expression from deep skill is mana—something new and singular, momentary, and precious because it offers insight into the here-and-now while reminding us of the past and the future. Improvisation subverts time. It is, I believe, what Aristotle called poiesis. Being asked to look closely and, at the same time, translate that experience into words is an exhilarating kind of improvisation. Add to this the conversation between the reviewee and the reviewer and the verbal adjustments each one makes as they regard the portfolio.

I have a limited attention span and a finite capacity to absorb images. However, sitting face-to-face with the author of a body of work sharpens my sensibilities. It forces me to muster all I know and understand about life, being humane, and, in this situation, photography. I love that moment of acuity, of trying to respond meaningfully to work that I may have never seen before and to link that response to an empathetic reading of the person before me—the artist who made the work.

The dreaded flip side of improvisation is, well, the abyss of an inappropriate review: a misreading of the work and the person, the limitations of the review format, or my biases preventing me from providing a meaningful review. I also feel uncomfortable in situations where reviewees and reviewers are trying to market themselves and their work, with the accompanying hustle. This is an unfortunate and inevitable aspect of some reviews. I touch on this in my response to questions 16 and 17.

2. Why do you attend portfolio-review events, and do you have any specific goals in attending?

Artists understand that our work is the sum of object-making and experience. We specialize in translating feelings and thought into the material world. This is a complicated kind of work, furrowed with technical frustrations and emotional challenges. It requires us to be (to extend Jerome Rothenberg's inspiring coinage) not only a technician of the sacred but also a scientist, a humanist, an artist, and a person enraptured. No wonder that an artist often feels isolated and vulnerable. Portfolio reviews can be a gathering of like-minded people on this same path but at different points along the journey. I cherish the opportunity to provide and receive (yes, reviewers learn) guidance, to see clearly when the other does not, and, vice versa, to bring specific individuals and institutions together, to suggest approaches to what may be insurmountable, and to remind and be reminded of our obligations to community.

Pradip Malde

3. When you attend portfolio-review events, what kind of strain does this cause on your work schedule?

I am fully both an artist and a teacher. As such, I am incredibly fortunate to have the support of an institution that values my participation in events (that is, portfolio reviews, workshops, exhibitions, civic and community engagement) that align with its mission: broadly, to foster healthy ecosystems.

4. If you receive the reviewee list from the organization prior to the portfolio review, do you look at their work online in preparation for the review, or do you like to look at it fresh? Why?

I prefer not to look at work ahead of the review. This approach lets me respond spontaneously and simultaneously to both the work and the person. I address the importance of spontaneity in question 1.

5. What objectives do you recommend reviewees bring to the table?

Be clear about your long- and short-term aspirations. Generally, think of the long-term as objectives and the short-term or task-specific as goals. However, being clear about how and what you do should not lock you down. Objectives and goals should be fluid, but bring these to a gel state in the period leading up to the review. Be able to answer questions about the portfolio, such as:

M

- Is this a complete body of work?
- What do you understand about the portfolio, and how can that define your objectives for it?
- What is preventing you from completing the work?
- What obstacles can this specific reviewer help you resolve? Research your reviewer's work and interests, and form some goals and questions (about your work) shaped by this.

6. Do you ask at the start of your session what the reviewee wants?

Yes.

7. What advice do you have for first-time reviewees?

I am specifically interested in understanding the difference between what the reviewee thinks the work is about, and what they feel when they look at the portfolio as if they did not produce it. It takes time and discipline to discern this difference. Think about it ahead of the session.

Be prepared to receive comments about your work from numerous points of view that sometimes seem contradictory. Reviews are rarely about what is right or wrong, or true or false, about your work, but they often present conflicting responses. It will help if you are prepared to leave a review ready to reflect and discern what is most appropriate for the work.

8. Who should lead the review—reviewer or reviewee? Why?

While it is hard to level out the power imbalance between reviewer and reviewee, the best reviews are when there is no lead, just fully engaged conversation, like a tango. It can go either way and should be intuitive. However, I often start by inviting the reviewee to say what they wish while I take a first look at the portfolio.

9. What advice do you have for reviewees on how to manage the allotted time during the session?

Reviewees should refrain from spending energy and time talking about other reviews, reviewees, or reviewers. Avoid going into technical details unless asked, but if asked, then be specific. While process is one integral part of what is expressed, the review should deal with the sum effect of all the parts. Focus on the portfolio. The reviewer does not need to know why they have been selected for the review or be engaged in casual conversation or coddled in any other way.

Similarly, reviewers should focus on your portfolio, not trivia (a reviewer once spent more time talking about their newly purchased watch than my portfolio). Be sure that the portfolio is easy to unpack and pack and that its presentation is not finicky yet still does full justice to the materiality of the image. Think about the sequence of the portfolio. Be clear about the wording of any questions you may have for each reviewer.

10. How do you feel about a reviewee recording your session?

I encourage reviewees to audio record the review because it lets both parties focus on the conversation. The reviewee should take short bullet-point written notes at the very least; be sure to have a notebook with you. When recording, mention titles when comments are being made about specific works so you can refer to images when needed. After the review, go over the recording and transcribe key points from it onto your written notes as soon as possible.

Pradip Malde

11. How many different projects do you think are ideal for discussion in an individual review session?

One. If it is not a single project, then it is okay to show a multitude of ideas that seem connected to the reviewee but are being presented to clarify a single project-in-progress.

12. How important is it for reviewees to have their idea completely fleshed out regarding their project?

It is important to have a body of work that may end up being clearly shaped by some ideas, but it is not important to have a completely formed idea. Here, too, having a sense of the overall objective matters. This question is related to question

13. Can a project be presented, in your opinion, as underdeveloped or overdeveloped?

Yes. The reviewer and reviewee should be open to exploring this during the review, but with sensitivity.

M

14. How important is the technical quality of physical objects (for example, prints) being presented at the review session? How do you feel about work being presented on a tablet or computer?

The print is an integral part of the project. It not only conveys the image but also expresses ideas and triggers responses shaped by the print's materiality. If the work is to be projected in its final, or primary, mode, then the reviewee should try to simulate this in the review; likewise, if the primary form is on-screen. The portfolio should be as closely aligned to the final form of presentation as possible.

15. How do you feel about virtual portfolio reviews versus in-person portfolio-review events (pros and cons)? Is your ideal review session length twenty, twenty-five, or thirty minutes?

Remote reviews are necessary sometimes, but they require extra time to explore, virtually, the primary form of the final work. Both reviewer and reviewee should understand how the materiality of a work shapes the full expression and how remote sessions compromise materiality. Remote review sessions need at least thirty minutes and, ideally, should go on for about fifty minutes. The ideal minimum in-person review length is twenty-five minutes.

16. Have you ever offered a commission, a show, a press feature, or representation during a review? Can you share a success story or stories with us that came from a productive meeting at a review session?

No. I strongly feel that reviews are opportunities for deep and focused conversations about the work on hand. The expectation of concrete "offers" changes that conversation—it is better to call sessions where these expectations are on the fore by their name: marketing sessions. Taking that approach encourages all parties to talk to each other with honesty and to place the experience of disappointment or success in the proper context. A review needs to focus on matters such as those described in my responses to the first two questions, which are soft-edged and suggestive. A marketing session lets people focus on promoting the work, with more specific goals and objectives.

17. Have you ever purchased artwork from a reviewee? If so, what do you base the price on, and is it signed by the artist?

No. For the same reasons as my response to question 16.

18. How often do you connect or recommend a photographer who may not be right for you but a good match for a colleague?

Occasionally, but here, too, what may not feel right usually indicates that I must work harder to give meaningful feedback.

19. Can you share the best review you have been a part of, and why it was? (No names should be mentioned.)

No. I have a terrible capacity to recall things, but I have a general memory of having had many wonderful reviews. These vaguely remembered goldies keep bringing me back to do more reviews.

20. Are you open to looking at work outside of scheduled reviews or not so much? If so, how do you prefer a photographer approach you about the possibility?

Yes, I look forward to reviews outside of the formal setting. It takes sensitivity from both sides to approach and arrange these because the entire portfolio-review event is exhausting, socially dense, and stressful.

Pradip Malde

21. How do you feel about reviewees and reviewers socializing away from the table? If you are comfortable sharing, what advice do you have for reviewees?

Reviewees and reviewers should be considerate, fully aware of the power dynamics, and avoid losing control of themselves and the situation. While I love a good drink and enjoy socializing, this is a professional occasion and always calls for respectful behavior.

22. How do you prefer that the individuals you meet with follow up with you and how often?

I always give reviewees my email and invite them to stay in touch about new developments in their work, with the caveat that I am often slow in responding.

23. In your opinion, what is the best "leave-behind"?

"Leave-behinds" are generous investments of time and thoughtfulness. They are always appreciated in any form. However, the best leave-behind is the resonance of a fully engaged conversation and the chance to see work that comes from a sincere and impassioned person. I encourage reviewees not to invest too much money, time, and energy in creating these gifts. Instead, focus on preparing your portfolio, then write a thank-you note that indicates some specific insight the reviewer helped you achieve.

24. What are the biggest "no-no's" for reviewees?

Avoid/set aside being arrogant. By the time you have been accepted for a review, you should not feel like you need to go out of your way to impress others, prove your worth, or manifest your insecurities in this way. Do not be dismissive of your work, be negatively critical of other reviewers or reviewees, or be disorganized or overly fussy. Keep your portfolio clean, organized, and easily accessible, and keep your demeanor focused on and ready to engage in conversation around the work. Do not present as stressed, anxious, defensive, or angry: Do some yoga or meditation—anything that will help you create a calm and focused atmosphere for you and those around you. Remember that everyone is there because of some shared concerns.

25. What one piece of advice would you impart to reviewees and reviewers?

Focus on and cherish (your fellow) reviewees, and put your ego aside.

Bayley Mizelle

Bayley Mizelle
Photographic Arts Council Los Angeles

I have served as the director of the Photographic Arts Council Los Angeles (PAC LA) for over three years. In addition to my work in contemporary art and arts education—in the fields of curation, writing, arts pedagogy, and consulting—I have been closely involved with the Los Angeles arts community, working with art spaces, galleries, and artists and producing and cocurating events and exhibitions. In previous years, I've worked on installations and portfolio reviews with The Lucie Foundation for Month of Photography LA, Frieze LA, Photo NOLA, Medium Festival of Photography, and others. While working in education, I was a grantee of the Citizen Artist AmeriCorps (CAA) Teaching Fellow Grant & Excellence in Education Award, through which I taught and developed arts educational programing in photography and creative writing for underserved inner-city youth programs in Los Angeles. I received a Bachelor of Fine Arts in Photography and Media, with a minor in Critical Studies for Creative Writing, from the California Institute of the Arts (CalArts).

As a reviewer, I am interested in subjects, photographers, and image-makers that challenge or celebrate the device of the image—the gesture of imaging or composing a photograph and all forms of interrogating objectivity. I work on projects and with artists or organizations that are aligned with my passion for experimental or archetypal image-based and archival practices and are dedicated to the subjects of aestheticism, photo ethics, narrative, the archive, history, and compositional play. I continue to work with artists and within the fields of photography as an independent curator and consultant, hoping to further the practice of building spaces for collective learning and cogeneration.

M

1. What do you look forward to most and least about portfolio-review events?

I mostly appreciate the ecosystem of collective learning that portfolio reviews generate—providing a space that supports both practice and industry; that is, established and emerging creatives coming together to learn more. It's that will to meet and share that I enjoy endlessly.

Conversely, there is an insufficiency of support systems to service artists of color through scholarships and funding that facilitate access to portfolio reviews and the benefits (that is, the immediate community of resources) that these events are essential at offering.

2. Why do you attend portfolio-review events, and do you have any specific goals in attending?

When I am invited to be a portfolio reviewer, I value the opportunities to build on the host's initiative for their event or program. I participate in reviews that have a vision/mission that I want to support; most often, those that uplift the practice of creative thinking and creative thinkers.

3. When you attend portfolio-review events, what kind of strain does this cause on your work schedule?

When attending events that are multiple full days of scheduled reviews, reserving that time away from my work schedule is required. During the time that I am not participating in any part of the review event (that is, back in my room or in between my scheduled reviews), I prepare time for work check-ins as needed. My role as a reviewer is a part of my role working in the field.

4. If you receive the reviewee list from the organization prior to the portfolio review, do you look at their work online in preparation for the review, or do you like to look at it fresh? Why or why not?

Yes, absolutely. It is inspiring to get an overview of the reviewee's work/practice/projects to prepare for a thoughtful conversation. I find that with such a brief amount of time for introduction and full discussion, it helps us both to connect in a space that can often be vulnerable for us both.

Visiting the work in advance also helps to place me in their practice or process—being able to note specific projects/works or recurring parts that might denote a prominent subject or interest that we can work from/toward in the allotted time together.

5. What objectives do you recommend reviewees bring to the table?

I believe objectives are a primary part of the review process and, often, subjectively a part of the creating and editing process. I also believe a reviewee's objectives for the outcome or engagement of the review do not have to be predetermined, and sometimes they cannot be. It is important for a reviewee to consider if where they are in their current process/practice, or what they plan to present, needs those objectives. Often, clarity on developing objectives—or the freedom to stray from previous ones—can come from the review process. An objective for a review could even be to discuss or further engage creative intention and outcomes of process for their work and for them as an artist.

Bayley Mizelle

6. Do you ask at the start of your session what the reviewee wants?

Opening a session, if a reviewee asks for support starting the conversation about their work or in a specific way that would best benefit their intentions for the review, I ask for those points directly. If I sense that either of us has hesitation with engaging what is presented or having a concentrated conversation, I will prompt them with questions about their overall process: if there are any difficulties they are facing that they'd like to use our time to work through or successful outcomes and inspiration that we can revisit together.

7. What advice do you have for first-time reviewees?

You don't need to know anything more than you already do to learn more! Holding space to engage the subject of what you do with others builds your understanding of support systems and the impact of how you think about what you do. Be fully present in your review. It is okay to cut it short. Don't let yourself get overwhelmed by deciding what to bring with you and what to leave in the studio or unprinted. Focus on what it is you are wanting to use the time to think about and on works/processes where the perspective of another person could be most useful; that will help you determine what to share in your portfolio.

M

8. Who should lead the review—reviewer or reviewee? Why?

This cannot be a fixed exchange. I find it important to avoid establishing hierarchies of perspective and knowledge as it can be highly demeaning to the overall encounter and opportunity of the portfolio review. Conversation, showing, and looking are the same occasion.

9. What advice do you have for reviewees on how to manage the allotted time during the session?

Oddly, start by considering what would be least helpful to what you'd like to use the time for, and if you had to leave something out of the conversation, what could not be left out? The intention is to help with prioritizing your time as a reviewee and understanding your needs for the review. It is okay to ask your reviewer for their support in guiding you through the allotted time and for feedback on how they can suggest helpful ways for you to prioritize what you need from a review.

10. How do you feel about a reviewee recording your session?

I require that my permission is requested and that I am informed of the recording taking place and/or if the recording is published. Reciprocally, I'll ask my reviewee to make an accompanying voice recording in response to the points that are covered in the recording of our conversation or of any inspiration from it. I adore this practice because it serves as a continuation of concept and/or being present in the creative and review process.

11. How many different projects do you think are ideal for discussion in an individual review session?

If the projects have a causal or common subject, a reviewee could share up to three projects for discussion; otherwise, keeping it to one or two is often most productive.

12. How important is it for reviewees to have their idea completely fleshed out regarding their project?

I don't find it necessarily important to have a fully determined concept or idea to have a productive or informative review. In fact, it can be limiting to the review process. On more than one occasion, I've had reviewees who worked with me as a reviewer because they needed help undoing an overly determined concept or way of thinking about their practice or particular body of work that had them feeling stagnant or uninspired. The purpose for having a review is the opportunity to build on where you currently are at any given point of your process or practice.

13. Can a project be presented, in your opinion, as underdeveloped or overdeveloped?

Of course, and portfolio reviews can be significant in identifying and nurturing that process of progress and presentation.

14. How important is the technical quality of physical objects (for example, prints) being presented at the review session? How do you feel about work being presented on a tablet or computer?

This idea continues to be a challenge for reviewees when they are thinking about the final object—how to present a concept as a tested process/material—and when they are faced with having to value a work or what they do. I think it's a challenge that reviewees should welcome, and as a reviewer, I like to reinterpret the idea and ask the reviewee how important the object/concept/intention is to them now, in its current state—its material, exchangeability, value—to their overall understanding of their relationship to it, and then how they imagine its relationship to others. If they work with prints or installations in physical spaces, having physical works present during the review can be most helpful. Works being presented digitally for review are fully acceptable as well.

15. How do you feel about virtual portfolio reviews versus in-person portfolio-review events (pros and cons)? Is your ideal review session length twenty, twenty-five, or thirty minutes?

In-Person Review Pros
• Physical quality of viewing and handling material and prints.
• Overall community impact cultivated by the event, often annually and/or in partnership with a larger arts festival and community public spaces.

In-Person Review Cons
• Portfolio reviews are often heavily attended social events and closely laid out within the space, making it difficult to have a concentrated and timely conversation.
• It can also be more challenging to keep the conversation strictly to the allotted time per review.

Virtual Review Pros
• Having a more structured and concentrated conversation feels more natural to the online platform.
• Viewing high-resolution scans and digital files of images can feel more direct to the editing or review process, removing the "distractions" of being in a physical space, as well as having the dynamic ability to hold the review in the space of the reviewee's choice (that is, their studio or workspace, with more equipment and process to reference, or a space that an upcoming exhibition or body of work will be exhibited or fabricated in).

Virtual Review Cons
• The sense of community vital to portfolio-review events becomes somewhat displaced on an online platform, since the event takes place within multiple individual and private spaces.
• The loss of physical material and what can be viewed limits overall participation to makers who have the equipment, expertise, and ability to digitize their work and archive to share on a digital platform.

M

16. Have you ever offered a commission, a show, a press feature, or a representation during a review? Can you share a success story or stories with us that came from a productive meeting at a review session?

I have not offered those directly during a review. A number of past reviewees have sent me letters with a specific idea or quote that came from our conversation, sometimes with years of time having passed, noting how much our review is still impacting how they've learned to think about their practice or particular body of work. Most recently, two past reviewees of color that I nominated to receive recognition were awarded emerging-artist and critical-impact awards by the organization that hosted the citywide photography festival and portfolio-review event. In addition to the honor, they were granted scholarships by the organization.

17. Have you ever purchased artwork from a reviewee? If so, what do you base the price on, and is it signed by the artist?

Though in the end I did not choose to collect the piece, I have inquired about purchasing a piece from one of my past reviewees. The price was determined based on the extent of the work of producing and printing the series that it was a part of and the uniqueness of the printing process, the paper and material used to produce the print, its archival quality and current condition, and its scale. It was signed verso and included small notations from exposure times for the light abstraction process they were using and development process. Each print process was individual and each print an edition of one (which was really a fun and key trait to understanding the artist's underlying curiosity of the photographic medium and image-making).

18. How often do you connect or recommend a photographer who may not be right for you but a good match for a colleague?

Often: being "right for me" is not my focus when I have a duty to be a resource as well. I think we are fortunate when we can redistribute power and wealth with our own. Being connected to a network of collectors, curators, educators, and artists in my role as the director of the Photographic Arts Council Los Angeles and as an artist consultant supports me in being able to facilitate those connections.

Bayley Mizelle

19. Can you share the best review you have been a part of, and why it was? (No names should be mentioned.)

The photography nonprofit that hosted the city-based festival and portfolio-review event had established an initiative that provided scholarships to Black photographers, offering grantees free admission to the festival and portfolio reviews. This initiative and scholarship directly impacted the diversity and accessibility of attendance for the entirety of the festival and portfolio reviews that year; some of the grantees were my reviewees and had expressed being overwhelmed by the opportunity to engage and share their work in this way for the first time. The reviewers and guest speakers/lecturers represented a diverse collective of both established and emerging prominent thinkers. The grantees were also given the opportunity to present individual artists talks in order to further broaden the reach of their work.

20. Are you open to looking at work outside of scheduled reviews or not so much? If so, how do you prefer a photographer approach you about the possibility?

I have and do accept requests for additional reviews and/or further consultations. Artists will usually contact me directly by email to send a proposal/inquiry or make arrangements for a consultation to prepare a more long-term plan for working together. I will also reach out to artists or provide my information if I would like to work with them or if I can see how additional sessions together can benefit their practice/body of work/project/space.

M

21. How do you feel about reviewees and reviewers socializing away from the table? If you are comfortable sharing, what advice do you have for reviewees?

Be as present as possible for your portfolio reviews/reviewers, and it is okay to let your reviewer know if they are not respecting your time, work, or the review process at any point.

22. How do you prefer that the individuals you meet with follow up with you and how often?

Reaching out directly by email is a great way for reviewees to keep in touch. I really appreciate a letter or note from a past reviewee with a brief continuation of thoughts or processes they might still be thinking of from our conversation, or updates from current project/series/ongoings. Event invitations and recent press links to share are nice, too.

23. In your opinion, what is the best "leave-behind"?

A postcard! Or ephemera—zine/mock-up/blueprint/test strip. It is important to have updated contact information and ways to access/share your work further.

24. What are the biggest "no-no's" for reviewees?

Don't be afraid to present new or unseen work/projects/plans/ideas. Don't let your tools or current knowledge and understanding limit your review (or process). Don't let the reviewer's opinion be your final criticism or perspective. Don't think you have nothing left to bring to your own process/practice when you feel stuck or unsatisfied post-review or conversation. Don't arrive unprepared to engage your work and/or reviewer. Don't forget: showing and seeing are the same occasion; reviewers are learning from you, too.

25. What one piece of advice would you impart to reviewees?

Always have questions—and sometimes answers—about your work.

Bayley Mizelle

Ibarionex Perello

Photographer, Writer, Educator, and Host of The Candid Frame Photography Podcast

Ibarionex Perello is a photographer, writer, and educator. Since 2006, he has also served as the host/producer of *The Candid Frame* photography podcast. With more than 600 episodes, the show has featured conversations with the best established and emerging photographers. Ibarionex has authored half a dozen books on photography, including *Chasing the Light: Improving Your Photography with Available Light* and *Making Photographs: Developing a Personal Visual Workflow.* He currently serves as a special-projects photographer for the Huntington Library, Museum, and Botanical Gardens (San Marino, California).

He is a recipient of the 2022 Chuck Westfall Technical Education Award from the Lucie Foundation. In 2023, the International Photographic Council honored him with an International Photography Hall of Fame award. He lives in Los Angeles with his wife, Cynthia, and their dog, Zoey.

1. What do you look forward to most and least about portfolio-review events?

I look forward to being surprised by a photographer who is producing unique, unexpected, and engaging work. I want to see something I've never seen or experienced before, or a subject matter, theme, and idea that's approached from a different perspective. The thing I least look forward to is uninspired work that makes the technique more important than the content.

2. Why do you attend portfolio-review events, and do you have any specific goals in attending?

I love seeing and discovering new work and talent. I enjoy it. I sometimes invite photographers as guests to my podcast.

3. When you attend portfolio-review events, what kind of strain does this cause on your work schedule?

My weekly schedule is often full. So, I need to schedule my availability around my nine-to-five work schedule and the time I dedicate to hosting and producing the podcast, writing, and family time.

P

4. If you receive the reviewee list from the organization prior to the portfolio review, do you look at their work online in preparation for the review, or do you like to look at it fresh? Why or why not?

Yes. I want to learn much about the photographer and their work before meeting them. It better prepares me to provide the best feedback I am capable of. It can often lead to a discussion based on more than what is presented to me on that day.

5. What objectives do you recommend reviewees bring to the table?

I recommend knowing exactly what you want from the review sessions. Be prepared with questions that will help you determine what your next steps will be with your work.

6. Do you ask at the start of your session what the reviewee wants?

It varies. Sometimes I ask at the beginning or wait until I have seen and discussed the work.

7. What advice do you have for first-time reviewees?

Produce a portfolio that has a clear focus, theme, or idea. Don't come with a collection of what you think are your "best" photographs. Be prepared to discuss why the work exists and why it was vital for you to create it.

8. Who should lead the review—reviewer or reviewee? And why?

It should be the reviewee. They are the only one who knows their work and what they want from the review session. I appreciate a photographer who clearly understands their work, where they want to go with it, and what kind of advice or insight they'd like to gain from the review.

9. What advice do you have for reviewees on how to manage the allotted time during the session?

Less is more. Don't show too much work. Create different variations of your portfolio and share them with people whose opinions you trust to help you refine the edit and presentation. Please pay attention to the quality of your prints and how they are presented. Let them showcase the pride and value you have in your work.

Ibarionex Perello

10. How do you feel about a reviewee recording your session?

I encourage them to do this. It is a great resource that allows you to process what various reviewers tell you.

11. How many different projects do you think are ideal for discussion in an individual review session?

I suggest focusing on just one. Preparing an excellent presentation on a body of work takes time and effort. Sharing more than one diminishes the time and attention that can be focused on each project.

12. How important is it for reviewees to have their ideas wholly fleshed out regarding their projects?

I think it's important, but they also need to be open to different ways to consider and discuss the themes and ideas of the work.

13. Can a project be presented, in your opinion, as underdeveloped or overdeveloped?

Yes. I consider a project underdeveloped when not enough photographs have been made. There are initial ideas and some images, but the project has yet to be allowed to gestate and develop. It's too early to solicit feedback from others. It's just time to put in the work. I think a body of work that is overdeveloped is usually because the photographer is not practicing a good editing process.

P

14. How important is the technical quality of physical objects (for example, prints) being presented at the review session? How do you feel about work being presented on a tablet or computer?

I think prints reflect a photographer's commitment to a body of work. It demonstrates that they have put consideration into their selects and their presentation. Unless the images can only be appreciated and understood by seeing them electronically, I strongly recommend quality prints.

15. How do you feel about virtual portfolio reviews versus in-person portfolio-review events (pros and cons)? Is your ideal review session length twenty, twenty-five, or thirty minutes?

I prefer having an in-person review session. However, I understand that virtual reviews have their advantages. It allows people who might not otherwise be able to connect to do so. Photographers and reviewers from all over the country and the world have an opportunity to meet and discuss work. Twenty to twenty-five minutes is an ideal duration for such sessions, especially for reviewers who must conduct multiple sessions during the day.

16. Have you ever offered a commission, a show, a press feature, or representation during a review? Can you share a success story or stories with us that came from a productive meeting at a review session?

I have had a couple of photographers who are guests on the show. I encourage people whose work I appreciate to stay in touch and keep me updated with their progress, especially should they have an exhibit or publish a book.

17. Have you ever purchased artwork from a reviewee? If so, what do you base the price on, and is it signed by the artist?

No.

18. How often do you connect or recommend a photographer who may not be right for you but a good match for a colleague?

I frequently recommend other people for photographers to reach out to or consider.

19. Can you share the best review you have been a part of, and why it was? (No names should be mentioned.)

The best sessions combine great work with a clear and passionate expression of why the work was created. Such creators believe in the value and importance of the work. They are eager to share what they have made and are looking for far more than just kind words and flattery.

Ibarionex Perello

20. Are you open to looking at work outside of scheduled reviews or not so much? If so, how do you prefer a photographer approach you about the possibility?

No, not so much. I like to keep the focus narrow. If a photographer wants to schedule time to evaluate other work, I may be available for a paid session over Zoom. However, I do those sparingly because of time constraints.

21. How do you feel about reviewees and reviewers socializing away from the table? If you are comfortable sharing, what advice do you have for reviewees?

This can be necessary networking time when they can get to know each other as people rather than a continuation of the review.

22. How do you prefer that the individuals you meet with follow up with you, and how often?

People periodically send me emails as things progress with their work or projects, especially with information on exhibits, publications, or book releases.

23. In your opinion, what is the best "leave-behind"?

A promotional card that contains an image presented in the portfolio, along with their contact information, including website, email, and Instagram account.

24. What are the biggest "no-no's" for reviewees?

Don't come unprepared, which includes a poorly edited selection of images. Do not arrive at the table without an idea of what you want from the session.

25. What one piece of advice would you impart to reviewees?

Work and complete short-term and long-term projects and, when appropriate, bring them to review sessions.

P

Mary Anne Redding

Mary Anne Redding

Turchin Museum

As well as an enthusiastic portfolio reviewer, I am a visual arts curator and writer. Currently I am the senior curator of the Turchin Center for the Visual Arts at Appalachian State University in the mountains of western North Carolina. I hold a BA in English literature from Ohio University, an MA in arts administration from the School of the Art Institute of Chicago, an MLS from the University of Illinois, Urbana-Champaign, and an advanced certificate in museum studies from Arizona State University.

I have written and published numerous essays on photography and contemporary art. Past positions include working as the curator for the Sioux City Art Center, the curator of the Marion Center for Photographic Arts, the chair of the photography department at Santa Fe University of Art & Design, and the curator of photography for the Palace of the Governors at New Mexico History Museum. Unbelievably, I have more than forty years' experience working as a curator, archivist, librarian, educator, and arts administrator.

My photographic publications include *A Country No More: Rediscovering the Landscapes of John James Audubon*, with photographer Krista Elrick (2021); *Gila: Radical Visions/The Enduring Silence*, with photographer Michael Berman (2012); the introduction for *Light in the Desert: Photographs from the Monastery of Christ in the Desert*, with photographs by Tony O'Brien and an essay by Christopher Merrill (2011); *Through the Lens: Creating Santa Fe* (Museum of New Mexico Press, 2009); and *Grasslands/Separating Species*, an exhibition catalog for 516 ARTS in Albuquerque, New Mexico; and an essay in *Land/Art New Mexico*, published by Radius Press in 2010. I currently serve on the advisory boards for CENTER and 516 ARTS in New Mexico.

R

1. What do you look forward to most and least about portfolio-review events?

I look forward to visiting a new city or revisiting a beloved city. I look forward to meeting new people and seeing new artwork. I enjoy seeing colleagues and friends. I love the conversations and connecting/reconnecting. The presentations by photographers and invited speakers are an added attraction. I always want to be listening and learning. Portfolio reviews provide a concentrated dose of intellectual stimulation.

2. Why do you attend portfolio-review events, and do you have any specific goals in attending?

As a portfolio reviewer and a curator, I attend portfolio reviews to discover something I haven't seen before or something I've thought about presented in a refreshing way. I want to see the intersections of lens-based media with the larger art world. What I am looking for is artwork that addresses critical issues facing our nation and the world today. Have you taken your personal interests and made them universally interesting? I want to see competent, creative responses to local, regional, and global climate change and the impact that the decline of natural resources and civility have on all life on the planet. You must have something important to say in an innovative and creative way. Does your artwork offer a new perspective or new insight into your chosen topic? Surprise me with your innovation, tug at my emotions, show me something I haven't seen before, or at least show it to me in a new way! I also attend portfolio reviews to connect with friends, colleagues, and artists in the extended photography community. Relationship-building is central to my curatorial practice.

3. When you attend portfolio-review events, what kind of strain does this cause on your work schedule?

Interesting question. I hadn't thought about it in just this way before because I think of attending portfolio reviews as being energizing; they reinvigorate my interest in my curatorial practice—making the mountains of administrative work worth the extra hours. I take time at the beginning and the end of reviews to visit local museums, art centers, and galleries. To reference Julia Cameron from *The Artist's Way*, I think of portfolio reviews as extended "Artist Dates."

4. If you receive the reviewee list from the organization prior to the portfolio review, do you look at their work online in preparation for the review, or do you like to look at it fresh? Why or why not?

I don't look up reviewees' work before coming to the table. If I don't know the artist, I don't want to be influenced by published reviews, other work on their website, or what ridiculous things might be out there on social media. Rather, I want a fresh encounter. Even if I know the artist and their creative work, I want to address the person sitting across from me, either in person or virtually, as I would meeting anyone for the first time—open, curious, and interested in the pending conversation. I'll follow up on Instagram and poke around on your website and other social-media feeds later if I am still curious.

Mary Anne Redding

5. What objectives do you recommend reviewees bring to the table?

Reviewees should be realistically objective. Expectations of both reviewee and reviewer can be overblown. The reviewer might be looking for something they haven't seen before—I always am, but I try to remain open to whatever is presented and bring my authentic response to the artwork. The photographer might expect to emerge with an exhibition opportunity, the promise of a magazine or an online assignment, a book deal, or a job offer or contract of some kind. While these opportunities are not outside the realm of possibility, the odds are that if a reviewer and reviewee are meeting for the first time, the outcome of the conversation will be, shall we say, more restrained. The purpose of a portfolio review should be to start, or perhaps to renew, a relationship so that both reviewer and reviewee come away with a positive impression of each other and look forward to their further conversations.

6. Do you ask at the start of your session what the reviewee wants?

Yes, I've learned to do this over the years. I can't promise I'll meet all your expectations, but listening is key to a mutually beneficial review. By asking you what you hope to get out of the review, I have a better idea of where to direct the conversation or how best to answer specific questions.

7. What advice do you have for first-time reviewees?

When you are signing up for your reviews, it's important to list your top reviewer choices first. Book publishers and curators are in high demand, and many are only able to do one day of reviews; if you really want to see someone, list them first on your selection roster. However, if you are matched with someone who was not one of your picks and/or has an aesthetic focus that differs from your work, this doesn't mean your review session is not going to be valuable. If you approach all your reviews with an open mind and the goal of learning something—with solid questions to ask—an unexpected reviewer could offer valuable insights that you wouldn't necessarily get from other sources. Prepare several general questions that you want to ask each reviewer and genuinely want to know the answer to. Have these in your notebook and refer to them.

Be prepared with a goal or purpose for each review, and let your reviewer know what you would like to get out of your conversation. It bears repeating: Write down in your notebook the questions that you want to ask each reviewer, to remind you if you should forget in the heat of the review.

Start showing your images right away, while giving your elevator speech and goals for your conversation. Do not *ever* make excuses about your work. If you are making excuses about your images, why are you at the review? Don't pepper your reviewers with negativity of any sort! You are there to listen and to learn. Be patient; do not ask if reviewers are going to give you a show or purchase your work. Reviews are a building process, and, generally, it takes time for things to evolve . . . shows, purchases, et cetera. In a few *rare* instances, they happen immediately; most times it is down the road. Asking, "Well . . . are you going to give me a show?" is annoying and unrealistic. In that case, the answer is probably *no*! Conversely, in the rare instance a reviewer says or does something inappropriate (rare, but it happens), let the host organization know immediately after your review, and be specific. Why? Host organizations want to ensure both brave and safe spaces for everyone in attendance.

8. Who should lead the review—reviewer or reviewee? Why?

Think of the review as the beginning of an extended, mutually enriching conversation. There should be an organic ebb and flow that isn't forced or dominated by either the reviewer or the reviewee. How else are you going to get to know one another? I want the dialogue to be mutual—equal parts listening, asking, responding, sharing.

9. What advice do you have for reviewees on how to manage the allotted time during the session?

Practice your presentation before the reviews begin. Write an outline and stick to it. It's amazing how quickly twenty or thirty minutes can pass and you're only halfway through what you want to say. Know specifically what it is you want to communicate about your project, and time yourself to make sure you can get through the essentials, knowing there will be questions and dialogue with your reviewer.

10. How do you feel about a reviewee recording your session?

Even if you are recording a session, have a notebook ready to take notes on feedback, comments, or ideas. You might think of something that you don't say because it would interrupt the flow of the conversation, or the idea isn't fully formed but you want to remember it—that thought won't be recorded. You can try to convince yourself that you'll remember everything everyone said, but you won't. By the end of a long day of reviews, the conversations can start to blur together.

Make a separate page for notes for each reviewer before you meet with them. Put the reviewer's name at the top of a page. One page per reviewer. Remember that you only have twenty to thirty minutes to be with each reviewer.

Mary Anne Redding

You will want to follow up on the notes you've made. *If* you are going to record the session, *ask first;* some reviewers don't want to be recorded. Respect their wishes.

11. How many different projects do you think are ideal for discussion in an individual review session?

It depends on what stages the projects are in. It also depends on what stage you are at in your career; student portfolio reviews are vastly different than those for emerging and professional artists—that's another entire conversation. In general, ideally, no more than two. Present the project that you feel is at the stage where it is ready for presentation in whatever form you envision. Have a second project ready to share in case there is additional time or the reviewer is extremely interested and asks to see more work.

12. How important is it for reviewees to have their ideas completely fleshed out regarding their projects?

I think it's important that you are articulate, know what you are doing and why you are doing it, and know why you have chosen this particular medium in which to express yourself. As a curator, I am not going to show your work if you can't write or speak your artist's statement. This is your life's work; be passionate! However, that said, attending reviews is two-fold—to get your work in front of industry professionals in the hopes of establishing a long-term relationship that leads to an exhibition, a book, an assignment. But reviewees should also be there to listen and learn. Most reviewers have a lot of experience working with artists; they are good at their chosen professions, and they might share something you have not thought about or offer a suggestion for presentation that changes your project for the better.

R

13. Can a project be presented, in your opinion, as underdeveloped or overdeveloped?

Yes, both, but it's difficult to answer this question. If the reviews are juried, an underdeveloped project won't be juried into the reviews. Don't think that not getting accepted is a complete rejection; think of it as a challenge to keep working on your project. Take seriously the feedback you are given, apply it if it sounds reasonable, and submit your portfolio again. If the reviews are open to anyone, sure, underdeveloped projects are presented. Again, listen to what the reviewer has to say: our job during a review is to help you strengthen your project—edit, discuss presentation, and so forth. If a project is overdeveloped, I think we have the same responsibilities and hope a constructive critique opens new ways of thinking about your creative work.

14. How important is the technical quality of physical objects (for example, prints) being presented at the review session? How do you feel about work being presented on a tablet or computer?

For an in-person review, the quality and presentation of the artwork is critical. Make museum-quality review prints, and don't put your photographs behind plastic; there is already glare in most review rooms. Of course, it's important that you make sure your prints are exhibition quality. And don't worry about the white gloves: They are too precious, and they are not archival or protection for your prints. Sweat seeps right through the cotton—ask a conservator. Your reviewers know how to handle fine-art prints, or they wouldn't be there. Yes, your work will get a little dog-eared, especially if there is a walk-through component to the reviews, but . . . the cost of review prints needs to be factored into your budget for attending reviews.

Obviously, for virtual reviews, the work is going to be presented digitally; that's fine. It's also fine to present work on a laptop or tablet in person—they are ideal if the reviewer wants to see more of a certain series or more projects. Do create a digital presentation, and don't just show off your website. I can look at your website later. Remember that the room you are in for in-person reviews may not be ideal for iPads or laptops, so don't be afraid to get up and move around. When you do, make sure your reviewer is okay with sharing personal space, especially as we learn to navigate the "new normal." Different people will have different ideas of what constitutes personal space—respect it. Also, make sure your iPad is clear of fingerprints, and bring lens-cleaning solution to wipe down the screen after each review!

15. How do you feel about virtual portfolio reviews versus in-person portfolio-review events (pros and cons)? Is your ideal review session length twenty, twenty-five, or thirty minutes?

I prefer in-person reviews; body language and attitude tell you so much about a person that is lost on the screen. I have done and will continue to do both. As far as timing, I think that decision is up to the hosting organization—I can work with any of the pleasures and challenges of those time periods.

16. Have you ever offered a commission, a show, a press feature, or representation during a review? Can you share a success story or stories with us that came from a productive meeting at a review session?

Once in a blue moon, I'll offer an artist the opportunity for an exhibition during a review, but it's rare—deliberately so. I prefer to establish an ongoing relationship. Most museums and gallery exhibitions are scheduled a year or two in advance, if not longer, so there's time to get to know one another. Occasionally something will happen and there will be an opening to fill quickly. However, no curator works in a vacuum: I want to get to know you, understand your working style, find out if you are organized and reliable, and know you will work well with the rest of the staff in my organization. Also, I have six galleries to fill; I'm looking for work that meets the mission of my art center.

17. Have you ever purchased artwork from a reviewee? If so, what do you base the price on, and is it signed by the artist?

Nope, not during the reviews. I don't want to show any sort of favoritism or establish that expectation in a review environment. Also, professionally, if I am going to work with an artist on an exhibition, I am establishing a long-term relationship; there are professional codes of ethics instituted by the American Alliance of Museums, the Association of Academic Museums and Galleries, and other professional arts organizations that I believe every curator should adhere to. I may purchase work well after the reviews, certainly after any professional relationship that may develop. When I do/if I do, I think it's important to pay artists for the full value of the work. Nobody in the industry should take advantage of their position to get a deal. We all want to be paid fairly for what do, don't we?

18. How often do you connect or recommend a photographer who may not be right for you but a good match for a colleague?

I love being a matchmaker!

19. Can you share the best review you have been a part of, and why it was? (No names should be mentioned.)

I've been doing reviews and studio visits with photographers and other artists for a long time. There have been a lot of great reviews over the years. There are different "bests" in different scenarios. (Nice side-step, don't you think?)

R

20. Are you open to looking at work outside of scheduled reviews or not so much? If so, how do you prefer a photographer approach you about the possibility?

I am open to looking at artwork outside of the scheduled reviews if I have time and feel like I can give you my full attention. If I have time and energy, I'll say so; if I don't, I'll let you know that, too. Don't take it personally—there is only so much time in the day! Reviews are as intense for the reviewers as they are for the reviewees. I don't want to meet with you if I am depleted and can't give you undivided attention.

21. How do you feel about reviewees and reviewers socializing away from the table? If you are comfortable sharing, what advice do you have for reviewees?

Sure, why not? The photo community is tightknit. I am all about relationship- and community-building. Some folks do not share this opinion. Inquire before you presume.

22. How do you prefer that the individuals you meet with follow up with you and how often?

Send your reviewer(s) a handwritten thank-you note or an email. Be sure to include an example of something you talked about during your review and how you might be implementing their suggestions into your practice. Don't expect a reply. Keep in mind that the reviewer's responsibility toward you is completed at the end of the review itself. They will contact you if they are interested in your work.

The most common first step, whether your review was in person or online, remains sending a thank-you note by regular mail. Make sure to ask the reviewer for their mailing address in addition to their business card. While corresponding by mail might seem outmoded in our hyper-digital era, the tactile nature of snail mail is more likely to get noticed and appreciated than the brief subject line of an unsolicited message in someone's overloaded inbox. A handwritten note is twice as important if your reviews were virtual! Send a small print, something tangible. As a curator, I won't do an exhibition without, at some point, seeing the actual photographs—the finished print, matted and framed or otherwise ready for installation. If our first encounter is digital, at some point it will be in person before I offer you an exhibition.

Mary Anne Redding

23. In your opinion, what is the best "leave-behind"?

Reviewers get a lot of leave-behinds to take home. The best will be distinctive *and* easy to carry. A leave-behind is an object that you give to your reviewer at the end of your review. Be sure to have enough leave-behinds for each event. This shouldn't be a last-minute postcard or something haphazardly thrown together; rather, it should be a well-designed promo piece that serves as an interesting reminder of your vision as a photographer. Invest in a graphic designer to help you create something that looks professional. Just because you know Photoshop doesn't mean you are a designer.

24. What are the biggest "no-no's" for reviewees?

There is nothing worse for a reviewee than waiting for a reviewer at a table where the person before you is slow to wrap things up—don't be that slow person! The virtual-review corollary is to be aware of the time limit because it will end automatically!

If you feel there is more to be discussed, ask for an appointment to meet afterward: If the interest is there, an additional meeting will happen. If the reviewer declines, don't be offended. Reviewers meet with a lot of reviewees and are also networking with their colleagues during the reviews. And, really, after a long day of talking, your reviewers might just need quiet time to recharge so they can bring their best self to the next review.

One note: Reviewers will remember who you are if you follow them into the bathroom or lunchroom to show them your work—and not fondly. It's happened. Don't do this. Really, don't do this. Everyone at the reviews is on a time schedule. Be respectful.

25. What one piece of advice would you impart to reviewees?

Before you submit your artwork to a portfolio review, be honest with yourself about whether you are ready for a conversation about the ideas and the technical presentation of your work. Ask yourself: *Is* this work polished enough to show to a curator, an art director, a photo editor, a book publisher—anyone in the photo industry? There is only one chance to make a great first impression. Before you put yourself and your creative work out there for a professional review, ask people you trust (not necessarily your best friend, unless they are excruciatingly honest and you can forgive them for it) for their honest evaluation. After all, you are investing your time and your money. You are looking for constructively critical feedback.

J. Sybylla Smith

J. Sybylla Smith

Independent Curator, Educator, and Consultant

I bring a concept-development lens to my work as a curator, teacher, and consultant. As an independent curator, my solo and group exhibitions feature 115+ international photographers in 30+ exhibitions. Locations include museum, gallery, university, and festival formats in the US, Mexico, Columbia, and Japan.

I teach my applicable framework of concept development, Concept Aware®, in lecture and workshop formats. On my podcast, *Concept Aware®: How You See & Why It Matters,* I host contemporary photographers, curators, and artists. My archive of over eighty episodes is an educational force—a veritable master class of concept development rooted in the contemporary photobook-making process. I share resources, challenges, and ideas with a global audience of image-makers. Currently, my podcast has over 14,000 listeners in 74 countries.

As an adjunct professor, guest lecturer, and thesis advisor, I have worked with the School of Visual Arts NYC, Harvard University, Wellesley University, Emerson College, the School of the Museum of Fine Arts at Tufts University, and Emmanuel College.

I consult with international photographers to refine ideas, develop portfolios, hone projects, and create exhibitions and/or photobook proposals. I jury for an array of global photography awards and juried exhibitions.

Visual images are powerful tools that possess the ability to communicate messages and meaning across cultures. I believe that photographs can serve as agents of awareness and creativity. They empower individual artists, and photography can be a catalyst for collective positive change.

As a portfolio reviewer, my focus is to support artists in their creative processes. I enjoy the collaboration and provide feedback, offer targeted connections, and share resources. I aim to make reviewees aware of how they see and why it matters. A goal is to place their work in context within the larger visual culture conversation.

S

1. What do you look forward to most and least about portfolio-review events?

Portfolio reviews never cease to amaze me. I am most impressed with the courage it takes to share one's work and to be vulnerable and seek reflection and critique. Sharing one's creative process is an intimate exchange. I feel privileged to be invited to share in this process, one based on establishing a relationship of trust. My favorite aspect of reviews is being introduced to new work. I am consistently delighted and surprised by the breadth and depth of work I encounter. Engaging with the passion that artists bring to their creative process is equally satisfying. Our conversations allow me to accompany the reviewee's choice-making as they develop an idea into a tangible object. I enjoy exploring how they see and understanding how this relates to their decision-making. I strive to facilitate their connectivity with their own creative process. My role is to facilitate their ownership of this dynamic conversation. In my opinion, this is an essential tool—maintaining focus on the process to allow the product to refine and evolve. My hope is the reviewee comes away from a review with the ability to identify impactful components of their unique visual voice.

The aspect I find least appealing is the inherent power differential between the reviewer and the reviewee. I acknowledge that my vantage point and those of fellow reviewers are unique and can impact the articulation (and, potentially, the amplification) of the work presented. However, in my opinion, too much credence is given to the opinions of the reviewers. The reviewees need to discern what rings most true from the variety of feedback they receive.

I had an incident where a reviewee cried in response to my feedback and said, "You know my work better than I do." I gently responded I did not — my outside vantage point brings a modicum of clarity and detachment from the effort and the emotion of the person making the image.

2. Why do you attend portfolio-review events, and do you have any specific goals in attending?

My goals in reviewing are three-fold. As a curator, I am interested in discovering and amplifying fully realized work. Perhaps the work I encounter is a perfect adjunct to a solo or group exhibition I am creating. Or I see a correlation between a particular subject, theme, or genre presented and the mission of another gallerist or art or educational institution. I enjoy providing introductions to facilitate these mutually beneficial connections.

As an educator, I utilize portfolio reviews as an opportunity to introduce aspects of my Concept Aware® framework. Portfolio reviews give me a window into new ways of seeing. I am able to frame the ways the reviewee sees and provide language for this process. This practice furthers clarification on ways to teach and write about my creative structure. On occasion, as a result of this introduction, a reviewee will seek out a Concept Aware® workshop to further learn about my applicable concept-development toolkit.

As a consultant, I can introduce how I work with creators to expand their creative process and to provide practical tools to engage in its dynamics. My role as a collaborator is a unique one, and by experiencing it, a reviewee knows more about what I bring to the table. My role in a metaphoric sense is that of a visual midwife—bringing their ideas to fruition with clarity and impact.

A side benefit of reviewing is observing the growth of individual artists. Experiencing the evolution of work on the part of the artist's development, as

J. Sybylla Smith

well as witnessing the amplification of their work in exhibition and/or book form, is a thrill. Reviews also afford an opportunity to be made aware of trends in subject matter and presentation innovation.

3. When you attend portfolio-review events, what kind of strain does this cause on your work schedule?

Being completely attentive to each reviewee necessitates that I clear my calendar for the event. I temporarily suspend my everyday workflow. Because I believe one goal of reviews is to establish relationships, I am proactive in establishing a connection with my reviewees.

I anticipate an increase in workflow when given reviewee contact. I write an email to establish a reciprocal relationship. Any time I have been given the reviewee's contact beforehand and have reached out to them ahead of the review, they express their gratitude. I state I wish to connect on social-media platforms and that I hope to share a credited image with a hyperlink to their website or social-media platform. I believe this exchange addresses the power balance I mentioned above; I establish us as collaborators.

Following each review experience, I create a small portfolio gallery made available on my website that features a chosen image from each reviewee with a hyperlink to their website. The portfolio galleries allow me to amplify each artist's work while providing a visual memory for me to revisit.

My online galleries address the reciprocal relationships I wish to foster between artists by providing a platform of inspiration to those who visit my website. I make a point of sharing and tagging all the artists I review when I post on social media.

4. If you receive the reviewee list from the organization prior to the portfolio review, do you look at their work online in preparation for the review, or do you like to look at it fresh? Why or why not?

Other than an introductory email as I stated in question 3, I like to start fresh. I believe sharing my initial responses to their work is an important part of the educational process. I am very specific in my reactions and try to make clear what I see as impactful imagery and to explain why. My being able to think out loud as I encounter their work imparts pertinent information. They see me make meaning and try to articulate their intentionality.

On occasion, if given contact information, I will read the "About" sections of the individual reviewees to gain an insight into where they are in their careers.

5. What objectives do you recommend reviewees bring to the table?

I always begin by asking what they wish to gain in the session and ask how I can be most helpful. I believe that reviewees should give pre-thought to identify a few specific goals. It is useful to get a sense of where they are in their creative journeys. Do they want to identify impactful images? Would editing and sequencing be useful? Are they looking for ways to get their work out there?

I believe reviewees need to choose which reviewers are a good match. Given my resume, I am someone who will hone in on their conceptual development and be able to offer contextualization.

6. Do you ask at the start of your session what the reviewee wants?

It is how I open each session. This gives us an idea of what their objectives are so that I can help them meet their goals. If they are unable to be specific, I will lead with the line of questioning mentioned in question 5.

7. What advice do you have for first-time reviewees?

I think it's a bold move to share your work with people and to be open to feedback. My advice is that you fully understand how each reviewer has particular likes, dislikes, experiences, and agendas. Each has specific areas of expertise. Take with you what resonates from each review and leave the rest. You're not going to please every reviewer; besides, this is not the point. You can count on the possibility of getting conflicting responses and even wholehearted disagreement among reviewers. A variety of feedback is helpful, and each offers food for thought. It's most important to suss out what is most pertinent to your work and to recognize what resonates with you from all the feedback received.

Always ask if you can record the session so you can be free of notetaking as well as have the potential to review the session. It is a dense, resource-filled time, and holding on to the salient issues can be a challenge.

8. Who should lead the review and why?

I believe that the review process is one of "give and take." I ask my reviewees to frame what their particular needs are in regard to their work. If someone is unsure as to how to proceed, I will engage with questions. I think it works best as an open conversation. Given the time constraints, I also check in to make sure we are addressing their priorities within our session.

J. Sybylla Smith

9. What advice do you have for reviewees on how to manage the allotted time during the session?

Being prepared with a few objectives and sharing them in order of priority is a key factor in having a successful review. Culling one's work so as to create a representative sampling is time efficient. The exchange of information can progress at a manageable pace while also allowing for further exploration as needed.

Bringing supplemental material on an iPad to share a larger project is acceptable when accompanied by providing select print samples. Installation views, if applicable, are welcome and convey a good amount of information in a short period of time.

If showing work in a large format, I recommend one to three examples at scale and the rest in a size that can be seen and handled on a review table.

10. How do you feel about a reviewee recording your session?

I welcome reviewees recording our session. This affords a focus on building our relationship. I find that recording allows the reviewee to relax and be fully present. In addition, they can circle back to listen again and pull specific helpful quotes and/or reflections.

11. How many different projects do you think are ideal for discussion in an individual review session?

The number of projects to present and discuss are decided on an individual basis, dependent on the reviewee's priorities. If different projects show an evolution, or if there is a question about their connectivity, then bringing more than one project makes sense. In my experience, most people come to reviews with one or two separate bodies of work.

I think for an in-depth reflection, around twenty images seems like a fair amount to review. This allows us to consider specifics on printing, to discuss individual content, and to brainstorm potential output/finishing options.

Often when I am shown multiple projects, I am able to see a correlation between them, and I find it useful to show the reviewee a cohesive grouping consisting of some images from each project. As a curator, I create a story and/or narrative when making an exhibition. The parameters of what makes each a separate project are more flexible, or fluid, from an outside point of view.

One of the most difficult tasks is for a photographer to edit and sequence their work. Their relationship to each image comes with many other attachments. This outside view of the work can offer valuable reflection and feedback.

S

12. How important is it for reviewees to have their ideas completely fleshed out regarding their projects?

It is not important for reviewees to have their ideas completely fleshed out regarding their projects. I think fleshing out is one purpose of reviews. Ideas are evolutionary, and each reviewee is at a different place on the continuum of understanding their own work. Articulating the layers of concept development is an essential aspect of fleshing out. This requires skill and practice. Being able to put one's work in a larger context is also a learned event. It is the outsider perspective that often illuminates aspects that have eluded the creator. Or, at least, it can facilitate the prioritization of the creator's ideas.

13. Can a project be presented, in your opinion, as underdeveloped or overdeveloped?

There is less issue with underdevelopment. I have been presented with projects in very raw form. My role is to meet the maker where they currently are. I do not have expectations of a level of completion to be able to engage with the work. All points on the evolution of a project have value.

I have also been presented with work that is developed with a specific target for either a book or an exhibition. I would caution a photographer who believes they can successfully develop their work as a solo endeavor. The caliber of the work will define what stage of development it is in. I also believe work in either a book or exhibit form is greatly enhanced by the input of other experts in collaboration with the creator. It is the book designer's and curator's role to animate and activate the creator's intentions. A book designer is skilled at offering options for layering the conceptual basis of the work with the use of typography, layout, and other design techniques. A curator excels at seeing cohesiveness from disparate parts and creating a compelling visual story. A curator provides ways to enter the work that may not be as obvious to the image-maker.

14. How important is the technical quality of physical objects (for example, prints) being presented at the review session? How do you feel about work being presented on a tablet or computer?

I believe that the technical quality of the physical object is very important. The caliber of the printing, paper choice, and decisions on sizing and finishing options are communicated through the physical object. Different work calls for different decisions based on the concept and ideas behind the work. Discerning which options will work requires a process of experimentation and refinement. It is very helpful when the image-maker shares the specifics of this aspect of their creative process. This affords the vantage point from which to consider which decisions strengthen the overall impact of the work. In essence, it outlines the parameters as the idea moves forward.

As noted above, bringing along work on a tablet or computer is welcome in addition to the actual object of a print. Sharing online galleries can augment the size of the project or provide another way of sharing the work—via a grid, video, or installation.

15. How do you feel about virtual portfolio reviews versus in-person portfolio-review events (pros and cons)? Is your ideal review session length twenty, twenty-five, or thirty minutes?

I find virtual reviews are quite effective. In some cases, I have found the reviewee is more relaxed and able to concentrate, free of outside distractions. However, I appreciate the in-person portfolio reviews for their more fluid social engagement. The ability to develop a one-on-one relationship is strengthened by in-person reviews.

I believe the ideal time for a review session is twenty-five minutes. I appreciate having a five-minute warning. The time limit focuses the discussion and keeps both parties moving through content without becoming tangential.

16. Have you ever offered a commission, a show, a press feature, or a representation during a review? Can you share a success story or stories with us that came from a productive meeting at a review session?

Yes, there have been instances during reviews where I have reflected that I believe the work is very realized and has potential for inclusion in an exhibition or the possibility of a press feature. If I see compatibility with a particular gallery as a source for potential representation, I will make an introduction.

I had a passing encounter with a photographer at a large in-person review while at the concierge desk of the hosting hotel. We exchanged cards after a brief conversation. As a result, this person sought me out as a reviewer during a subsequent virtual review. Following this encounter, she explored further consultation to work on a large body of work (6,000+ images). We entered into a mentor relationship as we collaborated on editing the imagery and conceptualizing the context for this very personal documentary project. Halfway through our process, she was given an exhibition opportunity at a large urban art center. I went on to curate this exhibition. We decided on the edit, sequencing, and all finishing decisions. We discussed installation and video options to layer the viewer experience. All our correspondence was virtual, including the layout for each wall. The multi-media exhibition was met with great success. A newspaper of significance in the host city interviewed me for an article on this unique and timely exhibition. Another international publication shared this story online, which received over 100,000 views.

During our collaboration, I also encouraged submission to other juried outlets. As a result, a selection of stand-alone images from this project were included in more than one group exhibition. I advised on a smaller edit of ten images for a globally juried submission; it was selected in the top tier of chosen portfolios. Our last collaboration was the completion of a traveling exhibition proposal, complete with layered educational and community resources to engage the larger community on this concerning issue.

17. Have you ever purchased artwork from a reviewee? If so, what do you base the price on, and is it signed by the artist?

I have not purchased artwork directly from a reviewee. I have purchased books made available through reviewees' websites and for their featured price.

18. How often do you connect or recommend a photographer who may not be right for you but a good match for a colleague?

I consistently make such connections. I often see a similar interest or an alignment of ideas or concepts between a photographer and a colleague. Making these mutually beneficial connections is an essential part of my involvement in portfolio reviews. Matching individual needs to the right person in an organization is a natural activity in my role as an advocate for visual creatives and fulfills my mission of amplifying important visual narratives.

19. Can you share the best review you have been a part of and why it was? (No names should be mentioned.)

One of my most exciting experiences in reviewing was seeing a master's student's work at an SPE conference several years ago. I was beyond impressed with how fully realized the concept development was on this engaging project. I knew this artist possessed exceptional concept-development skills. Throughout the next several years, I have relished watching the evolution of their artistic expression. They have taken the singular subject matter and explored its expression in multimedia fashion. They have gone on to develop a curriculum for the educational possibilities on this particular subject matter. It has been wonderful to watch the project expand in its specificity and universal application simultaneously. I am exploring avenues to further the geographic reach of this work in collaboration with a university gallery.

J. Sybylla Smith

20. Are you open to looking at work outside of scheduled reviews or not so much? If so, how do you prefer a photographer approach you about the possibility?

On more than one occasion, I have been approached to look at work outside the scheduled review time. I am open to this, and if my schedule can accommodate it, I welcome the opportunity. I am especially pleased when the introduction is made via a photographer who has had a successful review with me.

21. How do you feel about reviewees and reviewers socializing away from the table? If you are comfortable sharing, what advice do you have for reviewees?

I feel comfortable socializing with reviewees away from the table. I encourage authentic and organic relationship-building through the variety of activities available during an in-person review session.

22. How do you prefer that the individuals you meet with follow up with you and how often?

I appreciate a unique "leave-behind." These assist me in connecting the artist with their work. I appreciate a follow-up email within a week or two of the review to learn what aspect of our review was useful. As noted above, I am often proactive in establishing an exchange of contact information. I appreciate connecting on social-media platforms. And I am open to being contacted with updates on the work as it grows.

23. In your opinion, what is the best "leave-behind"?

I love a creative leave-behind that is conceptually layered and reflective of that particular person's idea formation. A good leave-behind is visually arresting and knowingly conveys the ideas around the work with confidence. I collect my strongest leave-behinds and use them as teaching tools.

S

24. What are the biggest "no-no's" for reviewees?

It's rare that I have a particular "no-no" for reviewees. It is helpful to come to the reviews with receptive curiosity. I do not want a reviewee to feel defensive of their choices. The point is to explore them.

25. What's one piece of advice would you impart to reviewees?

I congratulate the reviewees for their bold exploration of work and for allowing me to participate in their creative process. I advise the reviewee to sit with all the information and reactions they received. It is important to discern what resonates with them. I encourage them to give some time to sifting through and isolating the most pertinent nuggets of feedback or advice. And if a positive connection is made, circle back and inform the person who made the introduction of the outcome.

J. Sybylla Smith

Susan Spiritus

Spiritus Gallery

Founded in 1976, as one of the first commercial venues devoted exclusively to contemporary fine-art photography, the Susan Spiritus Gallery (susanspiritusgallery.com) remains focused on its commitment to feature and support the works of midcareer and emerging photographic artists.

During its first twenty years (1976–1996), the gallery mounted monthly one-person exhibitions and summer thematic group shows featuring many artists who were given their first public exposure. In addition, the gallery published several portfolios, including WESTCOASTNOW, CIRCUS, and DIORAMAS and sponsored a photographic symposium, "My Teacher/Myself," featuring work by Henry Holmes Smith and the students he taught who went on to become notable in the field, including Jerry N. Uelsmann, Betty Hahn, and Robert Fichter.

In 1996, the gallery moved and began to function as a private dealer and consultant. Since then, Susan Spiritus has focused her efforts on working closely with collectors, large multinational corporations, hospitals, legal firms, and universities to assist them in creating a special environment that enhances their interior space.

More changes occurred as the years progressed, and an online presence was developed for the gallery, which continues today. While I still have a physical gallery location, it is open by appointment only.

The answers below are the opinions of Susan Spiritus, owner of Susan Spiritus Gallery, responding to the questions asked about serving as a reviewer for portfolio-review sessions that I have experienced over the years.

1. What do you look forward to most and least about portfolio-review events?

Of course, I look forward to seeing and reviewing new work when I agree to be a reviewer. Oftentimes, I am told that my name on the review list fills up quickly because so many know of my name and gallery. I, on the other hand, do not know them and look forward to meeting new people in the field.

2. Why do you attend portfolio-review events, and do you have any specific goals in attending?

My goals in being a reviewer are to see new work and to figure out if there is a fit with the work in my gallery.

S

3. When you attend portfolio-review events, what kind of strain does this cause on your work schedule?

There is no strain on my work schedule because once I agree to being a reviewer, I schedule it on my calendar.

4. If you receive the reviewee list from the organization prior to the portfolio review, do you look at their work online in preparation for the review, or do you like to look at it fresh? Why or why not?

If time permits, I will scan the reviewee's works—not in any detail, but only to learn of the person's background and quickly look at the works submitted.

5. What objectives do you recommend reviewees bring to the table?

I would hope that the reviewee would have done sufficient research regarding the interests of the gallery and would be able to show me why they feel their work would be a satisfactory fit for Susan Spiritus Gallery.

6. Do you ask at the start of your session what the reviewee wants?

I always ask the reviewee why they signed up for the portfolio reviews and specifically what they want to achieve from being reviewed by my gallery.

7. What advice do you have for first-time reviewees?

It is so important for the reviewee to be organized, as time is short. If they are looking for advice on prices, sizes, and editions, I'm happy to assist and give my recommendations. If this is something that they have established, then we discuss and I advise.

8. Who should lead the review—reviewer or reviewee? And why?

I always let the reviewee start the session, as I want to hear from them.

9. What advice do you have for reviewees on how to manage the allotted time during the session?

The time slot of twenty minutes is theirs to use as they see fit. If they have multiple bodies of work and time permits, I'm happy to see what they have.

10. How do you feel about a reviewee recording your session?

I always allow the reviewee to record what I have to say, and I always stress that it is my opinion. They may ask another gallerist the same question and get a different answer.

11. How many different projects do you think are ideal for discussion in an individual review session?

As far as how many projects are ideal for discussion during a review period, I leave that to the time allotted. Sometimes, if time permits, we can get through two.

12. How important is it for reviewees to have their ideas completely fleshed out regarding their projects?

Projects do not need to be "completed"; often I have added comments and new suggestions that have greatly helped in a project's completion. Fresh eyes!

13. Can a project be presented, in your opinion, as underdeveloped or overdeveloped?

Yes, projects are often overdeveloped because the biggest challenge for an artist is to sufficiently *edit* the work, and, often, the artist will have too many (weak) pieces. Underdevelopment is just fine at this point …

14. How important is the technical quality of physical objects (for example, prints) being presented at the review session? How do you feel about work being presented on a tablet or computer?

Technically, having the physical print available to be seen during the session is a plus! However, when reviews were "in person," it was possible. Today, with the reviews being on zoom, that question is moot.

S

15. How do you feel about virtual portfolio reviews versus in-person portfolio-review events (pros and cons)? Is your ideal review session length twenty, twenty-five, or thirty minutes?

I much prefer in-person reviews for the reason stated in question 14, but today most are on Zoom. A twenty-minute session is just perfect.

16. Have you ever offered a commission, a show, a press feature, or representation during a review? Can you share a success story or stories with us that came from a productive meeting at a review session?

There have been several times when I knew that the work being presented was a perfect fit for my gallery and have expressed exactly that to the reviewee. I have indicated that I would like to represent the artist.

During a review a few years back, one of my reviewees did not show up, and I was left with an empty time slot. Someone quickly learned of this vacancy and asked if she could show me her work and said that she would leave if my original reviewee showed up. He did not. I looked at the work and knew immediately that it would fit with SSG and told her on the spot. We are still working together today.

17. Have you ever purchased artwork from a reviewee? If so, what do you base the price on, and is it signed by the artist?

I have never purchased work from a reviewee.

18. How often do you connect or recommend a photographer who may not be right for you but a good match for a colleague?

I have not connected reviewees with other galleries because I feel it is their responsibility to do the research to see if they are a fit.

19. Can you share the best review you have been a part of, and why it was? (No names should be mentioned.)

Best reviews . . . I reviewed a very strong body of work that I knew was not right for my gallery, but it was so powerful and presented a story that was so compelling and beautiful, I did give the artist several potential recommendations for her to pursue.

20. Are you open to looking at work outside of scheduled reviews or not so much? If so, how do you prefer a photographer approach you about the possibility?

If I have reviewed work previously and was particularly interested in the work, I certainly would look at it further outside of the review period. This should be set up in advance and not an on-the-spot request.

Susan Spiritus

21. How do you feel about reviewees and reviewers socializing away from the table? If you are comfortable sharing, what advice do you have for reviewees?

I have no problems with reviewees and reviewers socializing away from the table. The atmosphere is much more relaxed, and maybe other ideas will come forth.

22. How do you prefer that the individuals you meet with follow up with you and how often?

Of course, follow-ups are lovely to receive. It certainly can be of their own choice, but using an image that was reviewed is a quick way to remember the work/session.

23. In your opinion, what is the best "leave-behind"?

As far as a leave-behind item is concerned, that's only possible with an in-person review session and doesn't apply to Zoom meetings. With Zoom meetings, an email follow-up is lovely to receive.

24. What are the biggest "no-no's" for reviewees?

No-no's . . . persistent email messages following the reviews.

25. What one piece of advice would you impart to reviewees?

Organize and edit (if you can) beforehand. I understand that it's very difficult to edit your work, but often a body of work will be stronger if edited and sequenced properly. Know the sizes and editions for your work, along with your thoughts on prices. I'm always happy to advise on these issues, but it's best for you to have given this some thought beforehand.

S

Gordon Stettinius

Gordon Stettinius

Candela Gallery & Candela Books

Candela was founded in 2010, its mission being to elevate the discourse around contemporary photography—through exhibitions and programming and as an independent photobook publisher—for an already excellent arts community in Richmond, Virginia. The gallery produces eight to nine feature exhibitions a year; one or two book-related exhibitions; and one unbridled, free-for-all group exhibition each summer—"Unbound!," which, through the purchase of works from the exhibition, has built a collection of over 100 artworks and artists' books to date. We have promised, ultimately, to donate this work to a permanent collection.

As a reviewer, my background is fairly diverse. I have worked as a fine-art photographer and as a commercial photographer. I have managed a stock-photography agency, founded a publishing imprint, worked as an educator, taught workshops, published articles on photography, and represented as well as consulted on photographers' estates.

When I attend a review, I hope to see well-developed fine-art projects ready for exhibition and/or to be published, but I feel I can offer insights and career advice in response to a broad variety of working styles. Personally, I am not as interested in commercial or fashion work.

Candela Gallery has a community-minded philosophy, often presenting political, environmental, and/or subversive work, *but* our emphasis will always be upon the quality of the objects and their craft.

1. What do you look forward to most and least about portfolio-review events?

As a photo nerd, I am generally happy talking with photographers at any stage of their careers. *But* what I am looking for, on behalf of Candela Gallery, are photographers who have spent some years on their projects and which they are passionate about, have thought deeply about, and are ready to share, either as an exhibition or as a photography book.

2. Why do you attend portfolio-review events, and do you have any specific goals in attending?

Developing a career in photography is a long game. Beyond creativity, the career path is part social, part strategic, part chance, and part delusion.

S

I am always interested in hearing about other gallerists' or curators' projects because I might be able to suggest a photographer or two if their work aligns with the projects I am learning about. And I am trying to identify new talent who might present opportunities for our gallery. We have several ideas on our white board at any time, and we are always looking to add a new name that might bolster an idea in development.

Reviews have been pretty fruitful for me . . . If I meet twenty to twenty-five artists in a long weekend, there are different ways in which I might engage with several different people, and then, hopefully, I might manage as well to offer up a few useful ideas along the way. Ideas, large and small . . . group-show invitations, possible variations for the work in front of me, feature exhibitions, inclusion within a book project, maybe an introduction to another gallery or curator or collector . . . I am always hopeful I might make one or two amazing connections at any given event, but really, there are so many different types of possibilities at play in each review that they have generally been worthwhile for me to attend.

Beyond this, I also enjoy dinners and drinks and offsite gatherings at reviews because I spend most of my time, year-round, advocating for photography, running my mouth about this or that project or artist—basically, trying to make something happen for artists. It is great to be around a lot of people who are ready to share their lives in photography with me. It's like drinking from the original source.

3. When you attend portfolio-review events, what kind of strain does this cause on your work schedule?

Attending reviews as a reviewer is not a moneymaker. So, from that perspective, a four- or five-day, expenses-paid junket can be enjoyable, but it is still a distraction from other projects. However, gathering with like-minded people can be rewarding, and plugging into the larger network feels pretty essential to me still.

4. If you receive the reviewee list from the organization prior to the portfolio review, do you look at their work online in preparation for the review, or do you like to look at it fresh? Why or why not?

This depends upon how organized the specific reviews are, to be honest. When I receive a list of reviewees *and* a preview of the projects I am going to review, well in advance, this is the best case. Then I can do my homework, make some notes, and possibly dig a bit deeper into certain artists with whom I see potential engagement. But when I receive just a list of names, maybe a day or two ahead of time, as I'm trying to get out of town, then I will, out of curiosity, cruise their respective websites briefly. I won't spend too much time on websites, as they are often out of date and sometimes bloated.

Gordon Stettinius

5. What objectives do you recommend reviewees bring to the table?

For first-time reviewees, there is some value to bringing your work out into the open, receiving a variety of feedback, and, essentially, seeing if the work you are doing might find a little traction in the outside world. There may be a sense, at the end of it, that the critiques went off in every direction, making it difficult to consolidate all the conflicting impressions. But you may actually find a few key people who "get" you and your work and might wish to start an ongoing conversation. Concrete opportunities are few and further between. So, it is important to keep an open mind.

For experienced reviewees and midcareer types, I feel it is valuable to set the table for a reviewer. An artist might be looking for editing ideas, or networking ideas, or gallery representation, or help with budgeting, or concepting for books, or funding streams . . . I realize everyone is sort of looking for all of the above, but when an artist articulates their expectations and needs, we are able to learn a little bit about how they handle their affairs, how collaborative they might be, and how aspirational they are. As a gallerist, I view my artists' relationships as very collaborative. I like to know that the people I'm working with are out in the world making noise on their own behalf. This helps our PR and messaging go a bit further.

6. Do you ask at the start of your session what the reviewee wants?

I do. I feel capable of eating up twenty minutes just prattling on about my impressions of any given portfolio, *but* I will likely fare better if you set up a couple of goals for the conversation.

7. What advice do you have for first-time reviewees?

Start with twenty to twenty-five prints. Put a best face on your best project. A tight edit is useful, even with a huge project. Having more of the project in reserve can definitely be useful in case it is requested.

Any portfolio will be held back by its worst images. So, make sure there are only great images. A clear thread or distinct style within the work is usually best. This would be a good time to show that you are capable of making beautiful prints.

Some reviewers might move quickly through work. Some are going to want to consider your intentions and talk deliberately through the work, measure the impact of your sequencing, measure your interpretation of the image qualitatively (that is, consider the control you have over the printed work) . . . Different reviewers have different agendas.

S

8. Who should lead the review—reviewer or reviewee? And why?

I have never considered this a lead-and-follow situation. I think it is more of a call-and-response engagement. Listening is a skill that for many—myself included—needs a little further development.

9. What advice do you have for reviewees on how to manage the allotted time during the session?

Personally, I like to burn two to three minutes on where an artist is from, what they do for work, and so forth. Simple background info might reveal a regional connection or a strategy related to marketing a body of work. Knowing someone is a professor or a student or a dentist or a full-time artist allows for some insight about budget and business practices and studio access and so on.

Then, I am looking for a (hopefully) concise statement about the work. Then I like to run through the work quickly without forming any broad thoughts until I have run through it once. Next, I'll ask questions, make suggestions, ask about other solutions or avenues an artist has explored.

The time runs out quickly, and I might be pretty forward about following up with specific items or information. But I am generally receptive to receiving news and updates.

10. How do you feel about a reviewee recording your session?

I am fine with being recorded.

11. How many different projects do you think are ideal for discussion in an individual review session?

I think twenty minutes is not a lot of time for even one project. But I think having a second project in your pocket for the last few minutes, or if it feels a reviewer is not really responding to the first body of work, is a good idea. If you have two or three projects that are equally well resolved, giving the reviewer a choice of which way to go might be smart.

12. How important is it for reviewees to have their ideas completely fleshed out regarding their projects?

For me, well-considered projects are very important if you are looking for an actual opportunity from me. I enjoy in-progress projects, but my ideas have a different character. I am thinking it becomes more of an educator posture when a reviewer suspects they might influence a body of work.

Gordon Stettinius

13. Can a project be presented, in your opinion, as underdeveloped or overdeveloped?

Underdeveloped, yes. Overdeveloped . . . sounds like a good thing?

14. How important is the technical quality of physical objects (for example, prints) being presented at the review session? How do you feel about work being presented on a tablet or computer?

While it can be useful to offer supplemental information on a screen, for me, as a gallery owner and someone who deals in the sales and acquisitions of photographic objects, I feel viewing works on a screen isn't really enough. For the same reason, I am very resistant to looking at work on Instagram. I have no problem with an intuitive collection of work that might be a bit eclectic . . . but I have seen a trend in the world of image-makers that when the online presence is their primary distribution method, I may have no idea if they have developed any skills in the interpretation of their work into printed work—actual objects. I enjoy ideas, but I deal in objects. So, not presenting prints to a gallerist feels like a missed opportunity.

15. How do you feel about virtual portfolio reviews versus in-person portfolio-review events (pros and cons)? Is your ideal review session length twenty, twenty-five, or thirty minutes?

I much prefer in-person portfolio reviews. But I understand that travel and costs of participation can present a challenge, so the virtual portfolios can still be worthwhile.

16. Have you ever offered a commission, a show, a press feature, or representation during a review? Can you share a success story or stories with us that came from a productive meeting at a review session?

Many times. In twelve years, I have mounted several group and feature exhibitions showcasing people I have met, either formally or informally, at reviews. I have a feature exhibition coming up in the fall for an artist I met probably five years ago, when they showed me a different project. They stayed in touch. I was impressed initially, and because they kept showing me interesting work, I eventually put them on the calendar.

We also have an annual exhibition, which I happily endorse and to which I generally encourage people to submit. While this doesn't represent a huge opportunity, it is free to submit, so I don't feel there is much of a downside. That is a small overture I make often.

17. Have you ever purchased artwork from a reviewee? If so, what do you base the price on, and is it signed by the artist?

Yes. Many times. I attended several reviews as a photographer before ever standing as a reviewer. And on the couple of occasions when someone directly purchased my work, it was such a tremendous boost to my psyche and my budget that I haven't forgotten that feeling. I recognize these reviews, when all travel and accommodations are considered, are expensive. To sell a print in that context can go a long way toward recouping those expenses. I don't buy work every time I venture out as a reviewer, but I do enjoy supporting the work when I really enjoy it.

18. How often do you connect or recommend a photographer who may not be right for you but a good match for a colleague?

I will introduce people any time I can, because I view those connections as a win. If done well, both people might be better for it.

19. Can you share the best review you have been a part of, and why it was? (No names should be mentioned.)

Over time, this landscape has changed a bit. Most of the host venues I have attended have been excellent in terms of accommodations, food, and location. But I have been paying attention to how the reviews themselves have been evolving, and which venues are evaluating the populations they intend to serve. The costs of these reviews, plus additional expenses, can be prohibitive, and so I appreciate when an organization is working to promote diversity through grants, scholarships, student rates, and other such programs.

I cannot accept every invitation I receive, so I tend to support those organizations that are trying to broaden their reach and are examining their own role in a world that often feels dominated by privilege.

20. Are you open to looking at work outside of scheduled reviews or not so much? If so, how do you prefer a photographer approach you about the possibility?

I will say that a few rogue reviews will happen. Sometimes it is because another reviewer has stressed that I need to see some particular body of work or said the same to a photographer—that they should try to pull me aside if they can. But without that added extra juice of a referral from a colleague, I would suggest that the extra reviews can feel kind of intrusive. You might try to get someone's attention at a portfolio walk if that is at offer. Or, and this is a down-low strategy, just try to start up a conversation at dinner or over coffee in the morning. It truly is a long game. Follow up with an email that says, "I had really hoped to meet you . . ."

21. How do you feel about reviewees and reviewers socializing away from the table? If you are comfortable sharing, what advice do you have for reviewees?

There are some reviews that are set up nicely for mingling. And some that feel like they have partitioned the event. I enjoy meeting photographers as well as other arts professionals. I prefer the more casual atmosphere. But in a photo-intensive atmosphere, sometimes it is a relief to step out into the world and meet a dog on the street.

22. How do you prefer that the individuals you meet with follow up with you and how often?

A thank-you is a courtesy, I would say. Mentioning something memorable from our conversation might suggest that we had a meaningful exchange . . . Periodic follow-ups are encouraged. But more in the fashion of an update; that is, "Here is how my project has evolved in the last few months. I appreciated your thoughts about x and y." Or, perhaps, an update as to where the work is showing in the coming months.

When I feel as though I've been added to a monthly newsletter, I tend to tune those out.

On the awkward end of the scale, I have had photographers who continue to come at me with specific questions about which galleries I feel they should approach. Or what I think of this new edit or this new series. I am always—*always*—behind in my correspondence. So, when I feel like our conversation is more of an unpaid consultation, it can become a bit too much.

S

23. In your opinion, what is the best "leave-behind"?

All of the swag that I receive, or pick up myself, during a review often weighs as much as a yak's head. So, I will edit the leave-behinds down. And I will share the collection with the staff at the gallery along with my impressions. Our creative decisions are collaborative, and we each have a few ideas we are drawing up. Then one or two cards might make it onto the fridge, or the curious keepsake might sit on a desk or shelf for a while. But then the box gets tucked away.

There is a shelf life for leave-behinds, but I think they do get considered for a while. So, the goal for photographers is to make a positive impression, and then try to keep the conversation going without, if possible, overstepping.

24. What are the biggest "no-no's" for reviewees?

It doesn't happen often, but occasionally I meet someone in a review context who just appears incapable of listening. I am guilty, at times, of talking a bit too much myself and am prone to unproductive sidebar ideas and the like. And I do understand that some photographers who are further on in their careers may be looking for concrete, measurable opportunities. But I feel if there is ever a time to simply be an antenna, taking in all the signals, then sharing your work with a large number of professionals of different stripes may be that time.

I have varying relationships with many, many photographers. And sometimes, if I'm being honest, our relationships may feel a little transactional. Besides being a shared passion, photography is also a business. But I will say, often, how much I enjoy working with people I enjoy working with.

25. What is one piece of advice would you impart to reviewees?

My main advice for reviewees is that they should place a high value on the other photographers they meet. I remember when I was attending reviews as a photographer, I was very determined to meet a few specific curators. I placed these top curators' names at the top of my list every time but was seldom able to meet with them. And this sort of hyper-focused desire to meet with the key reviewers was, for me, a specific type of persistent mirage.

But when I considered the experience some years later, I realized most of my opportunities for exhibitions, for articles about my work, for print sales, for collaborations, came from other photographers I met along the way. Other artists in attendance would become fast friends and are incredibly valued colleagues today. These people I was hustling next to all day and sharing a beer with at night—so many of them went on to start their own galleries, or took museum jobs, or would become publishers or writers or collectors. The same is true for me … At the time, I didn't see how my own career would mutate and how most of my efforts today would revolve around advocating for and working on behalf of other photographers.

We have all met the photographer or artist who appears overly competitive, or self-absorbed, or fill in the blank … And it makes sense that there will be a variety of personalities in any given room full of photographers. For me, it boils down to kind of a goopy sentiment, but I do believe that helping other photographers will come back to you. So, remain open to the universe and its wonders, my sweet, gentle photo-minded friends.

Gordon Stettinius

Dana Stirling & Yoav Friedlander

Float Magazine

Dana Stirling is a fine-art photographer originally from Jerusalem, Israel, and now based in Queens, New York. She received her MFA in photography, video, and related media in 2016 from The School of Visual Arts and her BA in photographic communications in 2013 from Hadassah Academic College, Jerusalem. Her work, which examines the notions of family connections, memory, and mental health, has been showcased in group exhibitions at prominent venues and featured in various notable publications.

Yoav Friedlander is a miniature-scale-model fine artist and photographer whose worldview was influenced by the landscapes between Jerusalem and the Dead Sea. His work, reflecting his "Americanized Israeli" identity, blends scale-model creations with landscape photography, exploring the interplay of reality and its photographic representation. Friedlander studied photography at Hadassah Academic College, Jerusalem (BA) and at the School of Visual Arts in New York (MFA), examining how images shape and augment our understanding of the world.

Float Photo Magazine was founded in March 2014 by Stirling and Friedlander and was created with the goal to share and celebrate the work of a versatile roster of contemporary photographers from around the world. From young and emerging to established artists, *Float* features high-quality and creative work with the intention to inspire and push forward the photo community. In addition to its growing online and social platform, *Float* curates themed online magazine issues in which emerging and established artists share the pages to create a unique visual representation of the selected theme.

Float offers artists various opportunities and platforms for exposure: Instagram takeovers, book reviews, artist interviews, curated online magazine issues, online and physical exhibitions, and more. *Float* takes pride in collaborating with many other platforms to create a unique, open-minded, and welcoming space for photographers.

1. What do you look forward to most and least about portfolio-review events?

For me, meeting new people—both fellow reviewers and artists participating in the event—is the thing I look forward to the most. I will admit that the in-person events have been much more satisfying in that regard than the online reviews. In person, I got to really talk to people, even outside of the review time, got to know people, and even made friends, which I think is as important in this type of event.

The thing I look forward to the least is just how draining it can be mentally. Being so "on" the entire day and giving your best for each person can really drain your social battery, and it can be a pretty exhausting experience by the end of the day.

2. Why do you attend portfolio-review events, and do you have any specific goals in attending?

It can be for several reasons. Some reasons are selfish, in the sense that it helps push our platform forward and introduce it to artists who might not have known of us through other ways. It is a way for us to grow our community, platform, and our place within this art scene. In addition, when we meet artists whose work we love, we can help promote their work, and that is, of course, a benefit that both the artists and we enjoy—a win-win situation. I think it is also important to give back to the community you are a part of, and attending these events can definitely do that, too.

My goal is always to first try to give the artist what they are seeking as much as possible—I try to always ask the artist what they are looking to achieve from meeting with me. It can be advice, help, or even an honest request to be featured—but this allows me to guide my review in the direction that will help them the most. At the end of the day, the goal is to give something beneficial to the person sitting in front of you while being honest and helpful as much as possible.

3. When you attend portfolio-review events, what kind of strain does this cause on your work schedule?

It depends. Usually it happens on the weekends, so most of the time it is a loss of personal time on the weekend—which creates a streak of a really long week with no break. The benefit of the online reviews is that you don't need to travel, so the amount of hours and time commitment from you is much smaller and more manageable in a way. For us, we sometimes use these events as an "excuse" to see the city we are traveling to and even plan photo trips, so it makes it even better.

4. If you receive the reviewee list from the organization prior to the portfolio review, do you look at their work online in preparation for the review, or do you like to look at it fresh? Why or why not?

Sometimes yes, sometimes no. Honestly, it depends on how much time in advance I have to spend on it. I personally never found that seeing the website in advance had any real advantage, as artists usually want to explain and talk about the work regardless of whether you saw it. I think that with experience, you are able to

Dana Stirling & Yoav Friedlander

pretty quickly see the work for the first time and formulate an educated opinion on it and start talking about the issues, comments, or review of the work. For online reviews, I do sometimes have the website open, and I look at the images on the website while also in the Zoom review just because the quality of the images will always be better, and I want to form my opinion on their work in a fair way.

5. What objectives do you recommend reviewees bring to the table?

Realistic ones. I think one of the biggest "mistakes" I see is artists coming into these events with really grandiose feelings and expectations. I am not against being hopeful or reaching for the stars, but realistically, this is a very short time that you get to meet someone, and you need to maximize it in the best possible way. You should try to make a great first impression that will hopefully move you forward to future communications where you can work more on building that relationship and those opportunities you are looking for. Using the portfolio review time to really show your work and let us know who you are as an artist is the most important thing.

6. Do you ask at the start of your session what the reviewee wants?

Yes, absolutely. It is the most important question, in my opinion, because it can shape and shift the entire conversation, and it helps me focus on the things they are actually interested in instead of the things that I might think are important. For example, if someone really wants to focus on editing and image quality, why would I spend the time talking about conceptual notions? I would rather give them the time to share their concerns and help elevate their work in the way they see they need it the most.

7. What advice do you have for first-time reviewees?

I think the best advice I have for anyone doing reviews is to talk less. What I mean by that is that sometimes artists spend over half of their review time just talking about the work, explaining it and giving you all the backstory. It is always great and important to hear that info, but I think if you can make it cohesive and short and to the point, you can spend more time actually letting the reviewer talk—which is what is going to benefit you the most. You already know your work; this is your time and chance to allow someone else to see it and comment on it. Spend your time wisely—it is so short, and it goes by so fast. Spend it by listening and not talking.

8. Who should lead the review—reviewer or reviewee? Why?

I think it depends on the dynamics of the review; people interact differently, so it is hard to say, since it might be different with various people. I think usually the reviewer takes the lead: They will ask questions, give some comments, and advise. I think it is usually best for the reviewer to take the lead—they are more experienced, less nervous, and less emotionally invested because it is not their own work on display.

9. What advice do you have for reviewees on how to manage the allotted time during the session?

Practice a short "elevator pitch" of your work; allow maybe three to five minutes to talk about your work. Be specific about your intention with that specific reviewer in the beginning so that the time remaining is the most beneficial for you. If it is an online review, there is usually a timer at the top of the screen; just be mindful of it, and always look at it, even when your conversation is lively. For in-person reviews, time is much harder to keep—you could potentially ask to use a stopwatch if you feel like you need it. I think once you make your intro short, you will have plenty of time to talk with the reviewer. From my experience, people who struggle with time are always the people who spend too long talking about the work.

10. How do you feel about a reviewee recording your session?

I never have an issue with it. I think in that moment, sitting across from someone can be a little overwhelming, and we don't always listen all the way because we are anxious. I think it can be beneficial to listen to the recording later, so you can really soak in all the info that was given to you, and you can be more present in the moment and not worried you will forget it.

11. How many different projects do you think are ideal for discussion in an individual review session?

Personally, I think one project is best. Reviews are so short and so quick that going into too much just makes it so that what you talk about is on the surface level. I think with one project you can dive deeper into it and understand it more, and the time can be spent wisely. If a reviewer is interested in you and your overall sense as an artist, they could always potentially look at other projects in the future if or when you reach out to them to continue your communication.

Dana Stirling & Yoav Friedlander

12. How important is it for reviewees to have their ideas completely fleshed out regarding their projects?

In my opinion—not at all. Artists come in at various stages of their work to these events. Sometimes the work is complete and they are looking for promotion and for that "next step," and sometimes the work is still being thought out and they are there to get some feedback as they move forward with the work. I think both things are important, and this just means that the tone of the review will change with each approach.

13. Can a project be presented, in your opinion, as underdeveloped or overdeveloped?

Not really. When projects are completely done in the eye of the artist, if you, as a reviewer, are not interested in it for your platform, it just makes it harder to create a positive and productive conversation, since the artist has closed the door on you giving advice because they believe the work is complete and cannot be changed. So that might be a challenge, but it is really up to the artist; they just might not always get much from the review if they don't fit the review's esthetic or approach.

14. How important is the technical quality of physical objects (for example, prints) being presented at the review session? How do you feel about work being presented on a tablet or computer?

I personally think that seeing the prints in person is a great way to experience the work—if they are well made. I don't think it is a must, and I would personally never look down on a presentation on an iPad or a computer, as at the end of the day, if the work is strong and interesting, it will be great in any media chosen.

15. How do you feel about virtual portfolio reviews versus in-person portfolio-review events (pros and cons)? Is your ideal review session length twenty, twenty-five, or thirty minutes?

Virtual reviews have the benefit of a more relaxed financial burden on the artists. It allows people to come together regardless of their location or any other obstacles they might face in traditional reviews. Virtual reviews also allow the reviewers themselves to carry on with their regular work schedule without going out of town and giving up more of their personal time for the event—all while still being able to provide great feedback and help to the people they meet. Of course, the biggest con is not having the human connection in real life, and I think, more than anything else, losing the ability to meet people and chat outside of the scheduled reviews—both with the artists and with fellow reviewers. Not everyone feels as comfortable talking to a large group of virtual squares, so I think many people get lost in the grid.

16. Have you ever offered a commission, a show, a press feature, or representation during a review? Can you share a success story or stories with us that came from a productive meeting at a review session?

Yes, of course. I usually tell the artist at the end if we think their work is a good fit for our platform. We ask that they reach out via email, and we continue the communication with them. I have too many people whose work we've been able to showcase based on meeting them in reviews to name them all.

17. Have you ever purchased artwork from a reviewee? If so, what do you base the price on, and is it signed by the artist?

We have not.

18. How often do you connect or recommend a photographer who may not be right for you but a good match for a colleague?

Sometimes it really does depend on the situation, but I have tried to connect people to one another when I see a fit.

19. Can you share the best review you have been a part of, and why it was? (No names should be mentioned.)

They are all very different, and they all offered a different overall experience. We did have a great time in a review where we actually met a lot of people in the lobby of the hotel. The best time was actually *between* the scheduled reviews because we got to meet people in a casual and friendly way and talk about art and their own work with no restrictions, and in a very organic way. We met many people in person, and it created a very unique experience.

20. Are you open to looking at work outside of scheduled reviews or not so much? If so, how do you prefer a photographer approach you about the possibility?

Absolutely. I think as long as the interaction is honest and respectful, we are always happy to see and hear from artists outside of the schedule. We know that at these events it is hard to meet everyone on the list, so we try to be as accommodating as possible. I think if you approach the reviewers on their "off" time, you need to

Dana Stirling & Yoav Friedlander

336

find the right time, so, for example, maybe not while they are eating or having a conversation with others; always ask if this is a good time and if they are willing to. You should also always be prepared for a rejection if they are not able to do so, and don't take it personally.

21. How do you feel about reviewees and reviewers socializing away from the table? If you are comfortable sharing, what advice do you have for reviewees?

I think it is welcomed, and I have seen many friendly interactions between artists and reviewers. Again, it is something that will happen naturally and organically, and I think the best advice is to be brave and forward in approaching reviewers away from the table, but also gentle about it and understand that everyone is different, and interactions with different people will vary, and people's approach to their off time is different. You just need to navigate it strategically and gently and, again, be open to rejections and don't let it affect you personally.

22. How do you prefer that the individuals you meet with follow up with you and how often?

Email is the best way. I think the title of the email should be the name of the event so it allows the reviewer to remember the context of the interaction. I recommend reminding them in the email itself who you are, noting the work, and attaching the website or maybe some sort of PDF of the work to allow them to understand who they are talking to.

23. In your opinion, what is the best "leave-behind"?

Personally, I think physical leave-behinds can be hard on the reviewer. For the artists it is just one piece of paper, but when you meet with ten to twenty people, it starts to accumulate and can be a burden in some cases. I think the best leave-behind is a memorable review—we will remember you and your work regardless of any leave-behind you give us if it left a mark and we are interested in both you and the work. I don't think there is anything wrong with giving a leave-behind; I just don't think it is as important as putting the effort into the review itself, and maybe a good email afterward. Make a real connection with the person in front of you—that's the best thing you can do.

S

24. What are the biggest "no-no's" for reviewees?

Talking too much. Allow for the time to be beneficial by allowing the reviewer to take charge. Show the work and talk about it, of course, but it shouldn't be a lecture about your own thoughts and your personal connection to the work. Allow for a conversation, a back-and-forth between you and the reviewer.

25. What one piece of advice would you impart to reviewees?

When participating in a portfolio review, my key advice would be to emphasize your unique style and storytelling approach. Showcase a cohesive body of work that not only demonstrates technical skill but also reflects a consistent and distinct creative vision. This helps reviewers understand not just what you can do technically, but also who you are as an artist. Providing context or narratives behind your photos can enhance the overall impact of your portfolio, making it more memorable and engaging for those reviewing your work.

Dana Stirling & Yoav Friedlander

Douglas Stockdale

PhotoBook Journal

I am a visual artist, a book nerd, a science geek, and the senior editor/founder of *PhotoBook Journal*, with over 1,000 contemporary photobooks reviewed over the past fifteen years. As a contemporary book-review magazine, we are constantly evaluating recently published artist and photographic books to try to understand the implications of the author's art and photography in the context of their concept, book design, and production aesthetics.

I have been a portfolio reviewer for the last eight years, reviewing both in-person and virtually, with an expertise on storytelling and visual narratives that result from photographic editing and image sequencing. I am also a workshop leader for book-development workshops for three photographic organizations; during these workshops, a portfolio review is conducted for each participant as a group critique. Previously I was a portfolio reviewer for *LensCulture* and a book reviewer for photo-eye.

My personal artistic projects investigate aspects of family, passing of time, memory, science, and the collective impact on social realities. I use a variety of mediums, depending on my project concept, including expired 120 film, digital photography, and alternative photography (cyanotype printing), and I will incorporate the use of acrylics, watercolors, and Prismacolor pencils to further develop my visual narratives.

My projects have resulted in being published by Edizioni Punctum and self-publishing four artist books and two books on photographic techniques. My books and artwork are in permanent collections in the United States, Europe, and Asia. Likewise, I have curated both photographic and book exhibitions here in the US and in Europe that have been subsequently exhibited worldwide, and I am a frequent speaker and panelist on contemporary photography.

Websites: www.douglasstockdale.com; www.photobookjournal.com

S

1. What do you look forward to most and least about portfolio-review events?

For the in-person events, it is a wonderful time with other reviewers, reviewees, and others who might be attending. I enjoy spending time with acquaintances and friends who I might not have seen since the last review we participated in together, as well as appreciating the opportunity to create new relationships. The second thing I look forward to with in-person events is to look at and examine the physical artwork. For these in-person reviews, there is a lot of creative energy, with constant interactions and related discussions.

The downside is that it can become intense and at times overwhelming with back-to-back reviewees, and at the end of the day, the whole event can become a bit of a blur. One of the reasons I like the reviewee leave-behinds is that it allows me to quickly recall our discussions and provides something that I can jot a quick note on if there is a follow-up needed.

2. Why do you attend portfolio-review events, and do you have any specific goals in attending?

It is an opportunity to meet some new individuals, see some interesting artwork, and work on my own artistic network. It seems that I always gain a personal insight from discussing others' artistic concepts and reviewing their supporting artwork.

As to goals, that can vary based on who is attending, where the event is held, and what personal projects I have in process. For in-person events, there are many more opportunities for side conversations and meetings. I do try to keep my time open-ended and not have a jam-packed schedule, as I can never tell how an event like this might unwind. That's an aspect that seems to be missing for the virtual portfolio reviews, but I do see the upside of a virtual portfolio-review process with access to a broader audience, a more diverse slate of reviewers, and a corresponding reduction in expenses for everyone evolved.

3. When you attend portfolio-review events, what kind of strain does this cause on your work schedule?

A portfolio-review event is scheduled well enough in advance that it allows me to move my workload around it. Nevertheless, last-moment things can still happen that require some artistic juggling of schedule, such as when something happens for my day job that needs immediate attention, but that is the big exception rather than the rule. Most portfolio-review events occur at the end of the week and into the weekend, which can help with personal scheduling.

I have participated in so many of these events that I understand what I need to have finished just prior to the event, and I allow some schedule wiggle room for immediately afterward. One of the upsides of the virtual reviews is the reduction in travel time and the ability to micro-schedule my work with the reviews.

4. If you receive the reviewee list from the organization prior to the portfolio review, do you look at their work online in preparation for the review, or do you like to look at it fresh? Why or why not?

If I have time, I will do a quick check of their websites to help orient me to the concepts and quality of their work. For me, that's just part of my preparation, as

I might see something that really increases my curiosity and that I would like to learn more about. I just think it helps me to sustain a discussion with someone whom I may have never met before.

5. What objectives do you recommend reviewees bring to the table?

Everyone who attends should be making this investment in their time and money for a purpose, whether it is for a very specific project or for something broader in scope. Likewise, they have selected to spend time with me, hopefully for a specific purpose. I remember the first time I attended a portfolio review as a reviewee some twenty years ago, and honestly, I had no idea of what was going to happen. For that occasion, it was a learning opportunity about the review process, and my objective was to find out how I should prepare for the next review.

The interviewee really should determine what it is that they want to leave with at the end of the day after talking with me and others. Each person is on their individual artistic journey—whether they are just starting or somewhere midcareer—so each person's objectives will be different.

What is it that they need right now or over the next year? Technical or aesthetic feedback on their photographs? Or feedback on their concept and ideas for a project or series? Specific ideas on editing their project or how to sequence their work for publication? Make a pitch for publication, exhibition, or representation? Networking referrals that they need to follow up with afterward?

My personal strategy for portfolio reviews as a reviewer is to use the small honorarium from the organization to reinvest back into the organization to become a reviewee myself for the event. I think that creates a win-win for the organization as well as for me. There is always a small group of reviewers I do not know or am not as familiar with as I would like, and this provides me an opportunity to build on a relationship in conjunction with sharing one of my projects. Thus, I am usually on both sides of the table at these events, and I have very specific objectives for each person I am meeting with. To keep it simple, I always keep this to one objective for each person, since time is so fleeting during these reviews.

S

6. Do you ask at the start of your session what the reviewee wants?

Yes, always. I need to know what their personal objectives are to keep the limited time we have together focused on what they believe they need. Having that initial orientation at the start also allows me to think about how else I might be of assistance while we discuss their work.

That does not always mean we do not veer off in another direction, as it may become apparent during our discussion reviewing their artwork that they should consider a slight, or perhaps a huge, course correction. One of the underlying values of meeting with someone who has a lot of experience is to help provide a litmus test for artistic concepts and ideas.

7. What advice do you have for first-time reviewees?

First, realize that we, the reviewers, are here to try to help you. This event will probably not be a make-or-break career opportunity for you, so chill a little, because any underlying tension can affect the resulting discussion. You don't want to convey that you are desperate.

Have a really good idea of why you are attending and what you want to get out of each review with each reviewer. Depending on how you are matched up to requested reviewers, more than likely you will have a diverse audience. Try to make the most of it by having a game plan going in as to what you want at the end of the day.

Let us know up front what you want out of the review. It does not hurt to be candid that this is a first review. It may become apparent to us that you need more basic assistance in reaching your goals; for example, if you state you have thirty objectives—when you should have maybe just one prime objective and perhaps a couple of things related to it.

Really focus on just one portfolio for each reviewer in order to maximize your feedback. For some first reviewees, this may seem overwhelming if they have multiple projects going on. When you obtain your reviewer list, you can also customize a portfolio for each interviewer, depending on your objectives.

A rule of thumb is that a portfolio should not be more than fifteen images, and I think even that might be too much in the time allotted. Thus, when coaching first-time reviewees, I recommend just ten photographs; start out with the strongest, and end with an equally strong closing image. Having some additional back-up photographs would be prudent, but plan to focus on discussing ten photographs. This can become a lesson on critical editing, as frequently photographers may have 100 "best" images; so, which to select? You may want to consider having a trial review with friends beforehand to help make the final sorting.

Related to this is understanding that reviewers see lots and lots of photographs. We usually have a good idea about your work after reviewing the first three photographs. The remaining images help us to understand the depth and consistency of your work, as well as the quality of the narrative you are attempting to build.

Take what we say with a grain of salt because you will probably hear directly opposing ideas and recommendations. Yes, this will happen; I hear about this very frequently. Thus, this process may become confusing and overwhelming, so plan on some time to take notes after each session and time to destress, and plan to follow up if you have more questions or want some clarification.

As reviewers, we have our own experiences, ideas, and personalities, which sometimes makes it seem like our ideas are expressed rather bluntly. The short time we have together is of the essence, and we have found that it may be far better to be a little more direct in getting our point across. Just have patience and don't be offended. Remember the first point above: we are really here to try to help you.

8. Who should lead the review—reviewer or reviewee? Why?

Good question, and I am not sure if there is a hard rule about this for me. I am comfortable to have it proceed either way. After the introductions and the reviewee states their objectives, the review usually has a predictable progression.

Since the interviewee should have well-thought-out objectives for our discussion, it might be more of a benefit for them to lead. I have some strong ideas about how a review should proceed, and I don't mind taking the lead if the reviewee is reticent. When the reviewee takes the lead, I will continue to monitor our progress, and if I sense that we are drifting off track, I don't have an issue interrupting and redirecting the conversation.

9. What advice do you have for reviewees on how to manage the allotted time during the session?

I think the classic rule of thumb is a fifty–fifty split on time: In the first half are an introduction, project/photo concept overview, and looking at photographic prints or, when online, the images. The second half should be more about our discussion, including feedback on their project and body of work, as a give-and-take on ideas and concepts and how the artwork is working or if it is not squarely hitting the mark for me. In the first half, the reviewee should be doing more of the talking, and in the last half, they should be doing more listening.

10. How do you feel about a reviewee recording your session?

I don't have an issue if someone wants to record our conversation, just not video. Also, the recorded conversation is just for that person and this review, and it is not meant to be disseminated to go out on social media or other distribution.

With the amount of potential information, overload might be occurring— such as when they have already had four straight reviews—so having a recording might be very helpful. I find it helpful to jot some quick notes during a discussion, but if someone tries to write down every single word, I think the quality of listening and the resulting discussion suffers.

S

11. How many different projects do you think are ideal for discussion in an individual review session?

I recommend only one project per interviewer; while it is not an issue to have a back-up, plan to discuss only one portfolio. The short amount of time we have doesn't really allow us to expand on potential issues and ideas for more than one project.

When someone sits down with multiple boxes of prints, I immediately ask which of them is the most critical for us to spend our time on. Due to their investment in this entire process, I find that some individuals want to try to maximize their investment and show as much as they possibly can. The trouble is that they can go really fast to try to show everything, and then it becomes a chaotic blur of images and they miss the opportunity to obtain some meaningful feedback. You can't do both; it is a case of either/or. And it becomes frustrating for me to try to endure a constant barrage of images.

12. How important is it for reviewees to have their ideas completely fleshed out regarding their projects?

I am open to someone trying to figure out where they are going with a project and requesting feedback on ideas and concepts. It is best that they are upfront on this issue at the start of the review.

Due to my editorial position with PhotoBook Journal, I am frequently asked to review a book dummy, or a series of photographs that is intended to be published. I am frequently asked to provide feedback on the editing, design, layout, and sequencing of photographs and related artwork for publication.

Being able to have an opportunity to obtain feedback on a project that is still in process is one of the great benefits in attending a portfolio review. A person might have access to a more diverse and broadly experienced sounding board than what could be found in their local artistic community. Even if the various recommendations from the reviewers are at odds with each other, it is the synthesis of this feedback that might provide strategic insights on the direction that they are heading toward, even if it is as subtle as a slight course correction. The potential impact could be immense. The review process can provide the reviewee with a much broader perspective than they might otherwise obtain.

13. Can a project be presented, in your opinion, as underdeveloped or overdeveloped?

Yes, this is one of the many issues I have encountered during portfolio reviews. For those projects that are underdeveloped, it usually appears that the photographer is just grazing the surface of his subject. This can be a result of not thinking broadly

Douglas Stockdale

enough or self-imposing unnecessary limits on themselves. This can be visually manifested when the same idea for photographing a subject is repeated too many times; for example, a black-and-white waterfall composition is repeated numerous times for a multitude of waterfalls that they photographed. It appears like the same photograph with some slight variations.

For the overdeveloped project, this can result from an unclear definition of what their concept is or not understanding when they have completed their project. As we discuss a potential publication, it may be apparent to me that they have too much material and that they are overwhelmed—that this body of work needs some careful and tough editing. Even when the project appears overdeveloped, upon closer examination there still may be an issue in that they still have some missing links to create a cohesive story, which could be one reason that they do not feel the project is "completed."

14. How important is the technical quality of physical objects (for example, prints) being presented at the review session? How do you feel about work being presented on a tablet or computer?

If in person, I would prefer to look at actual prints, especially since photobooks are also physical objects. I believe that if a person is really serious about their work, they will strive to put their best foot forward with high-quality prints that fully express their artistic intent. Nothing worse to have someone keep apologizing and explaining why the printing is so bad and how it does not represent their best work.

With the recent virtual portfolio reviews since COVID, I think most reviewers are relatively comfortable with a virtual review. As a fine-art photographer and reviewer at portfolio reviews that are primarily for fine arts, we need to see physical prints. In my opinion, bringing a tablet to an in-person portfolio review is a missed opportunity. I suspect that if the portfolio-review event is oriented toward photojournalism, nonprofit/documentary, or advertising, there might be a different perspective on this issue, since the resulting photographs might be intended for different media venues.

15. How do you feel about virtual portfolio reviews versus in-person portfolio-review events (pros and cons)? Is your ideal review session length twenty, twenty-five, or thirty minutes?

I have provided both in-person and virtual portfolio reviews, and for my tastes, in-person seems better suited when the reviewee would like to discuss physical artwork, such as photographs, a book dummy, or a published book. This is especially true if their artwork has a tactical element to be evaluated, such as when many of the alternative photography prints and multimedia pieces have sewn, painted, or otherwise physically manipulated properties. I recently completed a project that was printed on metalized photo paper that had an inherent vibe that was difficult to virtually review.

From my experience, a virtual portfolio review seems to work better if we incorporate a process that allows us to move the images around, such as the Preview app on a Mac, a tool I use in my book workshops to complete portfolio critiques. This aspect is probably more important for those who chose to review with me, since there is usually feedback requested on editing, layout, and sequencing of photographs relevant to book publishing.

As to a portfolio-review length, sometimes twenty minutes seems too long, while for others, thirty minutes would not be enough. Nevertheless, for most reviews, the twenty minutes—what seems to be the norm—usually seem to fly by. A twenty-minute duration is a bit like speed dating; it provides an opportunity for an introduction and a brief discussion to get to know someone's concepts and artwork. The limited time does help to ensure everyone stays focused and on point, and if the chemistry is good, there is always a chance for a follow-up discussion at a later time. Thus, for me the twenty-minute norm seems to work just fine for these occasions.

16. Have you ever offered a commission, a show, a press feature, or representation during a review? Can you share a success story or stories with us that came from a productive meeting at a review session?

One of the reasons a reviewee might seek me out is that they have a recently published book that they would like to obtain some feedback on as well as pitch me for a book review on *PhotoBook Journal*. If the book is a good match for the *PhotoBook Journal* readership, and I suspect that one of my reviewers would be interested, then I will indicate our interest. The norm is to ask for a formal book submission, which I will then forward to the reviewer who I think would be the best match for the book. On occasion, a reviewee might leave a signed copy of the book with me to share with my book-review team.

There have been a number of success stories that led to the publication of a book review on *PhotoBook Journal*. This varies from books already published to those with a pending publication date, which the photographer subsequently follows up on with me when the book is in print. It is nice to have a chance to talk with an author to obtain some additional insights about them and why they are publishing their work

Douglas Stockdale

17. Have you ever purchased artwork from a reviewee? If so, what do you base the price on, and is it signed by the artist?

As a book artist, I have been involved in book trades; usually the books we trade are signed, and in my case, most of my artist books are in a signed and numbered edition. I do not attend portfolio reviews with the intent or purpose to acquire artwork for myself or others.

18. How often do you connect or recommend a photographer that may not be right for you but a good match for a colleague?

I do make recommendations to other colleagues, especially if someone is looking for a book publisher and it seems obvious to me who might be a good match. For *PhotoBook Journal,* we have editorial guidelines as to what we would consider reviewing and those subjects that we don't review, such as a technical how-to photographic book.

19. Can you share the best review you have been a part of, and why it was? (No names should be mentioned.)

The reviewee was seeking me out regarding a couple of her self-published artist books and was really concerned about how to move forward. Each of her artist books utilized some unique book materials that could not be duplicated, yet she wanted to create more than one artist book based on each book's concept. These artist books would be very similar due to the materials, but each would not be an exact copy. These were very personal and touching artist books, and I could understand why she wanted to produce more than one.

During our discussion, I explained how she could use either an edition series or variable edition. She was very excited about how she could move forward utilizing an edition series—with each book in the edition still being unique. We traded artist books so that I could review hers on *PhotoBook Journal,* then subsequently I obtained another of her artist books, which was also reviewed. I incorporate that same concept of a variable edition when creating the unique works based on the same source material for my cyanotype prints.

20. Are you open to looking at work outside of scheduled reviews or not so much? If so, how do you prefer a photographer approach you about the possibility?

That is a possibility, which has frequently occurred with someone after they have attended one of my book-development workshops. This can be initiated as an email inquiry and needs to be negotiated as a coaching session.

21. How do you feel about reviewees and reviewers socializing away from the table? If you are comfortable sharing, what advice do you have for reviewees?

I am open to this, as I think that this is an important part of the in-person portfolio reviews since this event is all about being a networking opportunity. Just be fair and understand that a reviewer might have a really tight schedule, such as preplanned meetings with others. Don't be offended if the answer to a request to meet either during the event or afterward is a pass.

Frequently there are social events planned during these events for networking or a portfolio walk, which is a great time to seek someone out.

22. How do you prefer that the individuals you meet with follow up with you and how often?

By email and not to become a pest. Also acceptable is to be placed on someone's mailing list in which there are quarterly updates sent out as to what they have accomplished and/or what they have in the works. Frequently, someone may follow up related to a new or pending book publication, and I am open to a submission inquiry for a potential book review by one of my *PhotoBook Journal* reviewers.

23. In your opinion, what is the best "leave-behind"?

I prefer something small and concise that would include a photo of one of their artworks and a quick bio or artist statement that includes a website and an email. This is also ideal for me to quickly jot some notes about the review, especially if I commit to providing something after the event.

24. What are the biggest "no-no's" for reviewees?

Bringing too much work and trying to jam it all into one session, whether that is having too many examples from a single project or expecting to be able to discuss multiple projects.

My patience does become short if someone tries to dominate the entire conversation and does not take the time to listen for feedback.

Turn off the cell phone, and, please, don't even think about taking a call during a review unless it really is a dire emergency. To add to that, I do not really want to see any of your cell-phone photos.

Douglas Stockdale

25. What one piece of advice would you impart to reviewees?

An artistic career is a long-term process and requires time to evolve organically: Focus on trying to learn one thing from each reviewer, while working on developing personal relationships with the various reviewers as well as with your fellow reviewees. Enjoy the process. An artistic career is a long and winding road.

S

Barbara Tannenbaum

Barbara Tannenbaum

Cleveland Art Museum

I was officially a specialist in modern and contemporary art when I became the chief curator at the Akron Art Museum, a post I held from 1985 to 2011. Soon after I arrived there, the museum's photography collection exerted a magnetic pull, and I began focusing my major curatorial efforts on that medium. I attribute that, in part, to the fact that my uncle was a serious amateur photographer who studied at the Institute of Design. I spent my childhood accompanying him to photo exhibitions and assisting him on shoots and in the darkroom. Since 2011, I have been the curator of photography at the Cleveland Museum of Art. During my four-decade career as a curator, I have organized over 120 exhibitions; lectured throughout the United States and in Canada, Brazil, and China; and authored numerous publications, including monographs on Ralph Eugene Meatyard and TR Ericsson and print-on-demand photobooks.

I love looking at photographs and talking with artists, which is exactly what happens in a review. Because of the masterpiece nature of the Cleveland Museum of Art, I am rarely able to offer emerging artists exhibitions or purchases. However, I believe that I can offer sage advice and guidance based on many years of experience in the field.

What don't I enjoy about reviewing? I am not a big fan of the blur. Sorry; that's just my personal taste. I prefer not to review photography that is primarily commercial, such as advertising photography. I am fine with nudity in photos if it is truly at the service of artistic expression. I delight in viewing a range of types of work and modes of expression, and I especially enjoy discussing exhibition and book projects that are still in the developmental phase.

1. What do you look forward to most and least about portfolio-review events?

For me, spending days in a row looking at art and talking with artists is a luxury and a delight. At the museum, much of my time is spent at my computer doing correspondence, research, and other screen-based tasks. I look forward to chatting with artists not just about their own art but also about other art they find interesting. Artists are often ahead of curators in sniffing out some of the ways in which photography is shifting and transforming. I learn a lot from them.

Portfolio reviews are unique to photography: No other field offers regular opportunities for curators, dealers, and publishers to meet face-to-face with artists in the presence of their artworks. I enjoy the challenge of having twenty minutes to look at work that is new to me, analyze it, listen to the artist, and figure out what I can say that will help that person improve their art or advance their career, depending on whether they are just starting out or they are seasoned professionals. Reviewing beginners sometimes forces me to go back to the beginning and define what makes a good work of art, which is a rewarding exercise.

The things I like least about portfolio reviews are logistical and petty. Evening events are important and useful, but then dinner often ends up being very late and not the healthiest of meals. I never get enough sleep at reviews. But that is because there is so much to see, do, and discuss.

2. Why do you attend portfolio-review events, and do you have any specific goals in attending?

In addition to the pleasure that I derive from looking at art and meeting with artists, I want to get a broad overview of what artists are making now. I also feel an obligation to give back to the field by making myself accessible to artists at a variety of career levels. I rarely attend reviews with any specific goals in mind, although sometimes I am looking for work on certain topics.

3. When you attend portfolio-review events, what kind of strain does this cause on your work schedule?

Attending a review event in person usually involves four days of reviews and two days of travel, which is a serious time commitment. Being away from the museum for a full week means that all my other work gets backed up. That is true despite the fact that I (and most other curators) usually put in at least one or two hours each evening at reviews to catch up with museum email. I end up putting in lots of overtime before I go away and upon my return, so attendance does involve some sacrifice on my part and on the part of my institution.

4. If you receive the reviewee list from the organization prior to the portfolio review, do you look at their work online in preparation for the review, or do you like to look at it fresh? Why or why not?

Whether I look at work online beforehand depends on how many people I will be reviewing. I tend to peruse online information more regularly for virtual than for in-person reviews. If the organization sends a folder with several images by each artist, it makes the process more efficient but gives a limited view of the artist's production. A list with websites allows me to gain a more complete picture, but then the looking takes longer. Either way, a look at someone's work before the review helps me focus the discussion and think ahead of time about places that might be interested in showing the work. Twenty minutes goes by so quickly.

Barbara Tannenbaum

5. What objectives do you recommend reviewees bring to the table?

My hope is that reviewees will regard review events as a chance to efficiently meet and introduce their art to a large number of curators, dealers, publishers, and collectors. No matter what else comes of the reviews, the artists will have a vastly broadened exposure of their work to leading professionals in the field. That is a rare opportunity and a great benefit.

Don't expect attending a review to make you an overnight art star. Don't expect to walk away from the table with an exhibition, purchase, or book deal. All curators have a backlog of artists they want to show—but they have limited opportunities to offer. For instance, I "only" do three to five shows a year, which is a lot.

Reviews are speed dating, not arranged marriages. Sometimes those twenty minutes are the start of a long-term relationship, but tangible benefits may not be reaped until years later. The photos I am being shown may not fit the priorities or mission of my institution. However, I often recommend photographers to editors, curators, or collectors for whom that work is more directly relevant.

6. Do you ask at the start of your session what the reviewee wants?

After introductions, I ask about the reviewee's goal for the body/bodies of work they are showing. Are they seeking advice on sequencing, editing, et cetera, or are they seeking leads toward an exhibition or publication?

7. What advice do you have for first-time reviewees?

Don't expect to show 80 or 100 pictures, or 4 to 5 bodies of work, in twenty or even thirty minutes. Sequence your work so it presents a cogent overview of your project. Begin and end with really strong images to make a good first, and a lasting final, impression. Take advantage of the breaks between your reviews to meet and see the work of the other photographers. Discussions with your peers are a great way to learn and broaden exposure for your own art.

8. Who should lead the review—reviewer or reviewee? Why?

The structure of our interchange depends on the individuals. Most reviewees have an "elevator speech" describing their project, which is helpful for the reviewer. But if someone is new to the review process or very reticent, then I will ask questions to draw out what they feel their work is about and what their goals are for it. If the reviewee has a lengthy monologue, that person should plan to allow the reviewer some time to speak at the end. Presumably you are here to get my input about your work.

9. What advice do you have for reviewees on how to manage the allotted time during the session?

Start showing your images as soon as you begin talking; they are the crux of the matter, and twenty minutes pass very quickly. If you have a spiel, don't make it too long. Ideally, there should be time for discussion, for the reviewer to sum up their suggestions, and for you to ask additional questions to clarify those comments.

10. How do you feel about a reviewee recording your session?

I am fine with being recorded on audio as long as that material does not subsequently appear on social media or in publication. To me, reviews are intimate exchanges—sessions between the reviewer and the artist should remain private.

11. How many different projects do you think are ideal for discussion in an individual review session?

It depends on the complexity of the projects and how succinctly the artist can summarize them. To my mind, one or two projects is enough for twenty minutes, although I have had productive reviews where we have covered three projects. Sometimes an artist's goal is to introduce a particular curator to the scope of their work rather than get advice or go into depth on individual projects. Those sessions are more of a show-and-tell and have a different purpose.

12. How important is it for reviewees to have their ideas completely fleshed out regarding their projects?

Some of the most interesting discussions I have are with artists whose projects are in their formative or middle stages. You do need to have enough images completed to convey the project's direction and aesthetic. If the project is already complete and ready for prime time, then I try to help the artist figure out which institutions they should approach for exhibition and publication.

13. Can a project be presented, in your opinion, as underdeveloped or overdeveloped?

The reviewee is not going to get as much out of a review if their project is totally unformed. Sometimes people bring a random assortment of photos to be reviewed. We can discuss the aesthetic merits of the individual images, but a crit with a professor or a group of peers might be more profitable than a review. I'm not sure what "overdeveloped" means. If the project is finished, then we discuss where to place it and how to approach curators, institutions, and publishers.

Barbara Tannenbaum

14. How important is the technical quality of physical objects (for example, prints) being presented at the review session? How do you feel about work being presented on a tablet or computer?

The old saying is, "You only get one chance to make a first impression." At least a couple of the prints you bring to a review should be examples of finished prints ready for exhibition. If your works are so large that you cannot transport a print of that scale, then at least bring a segment of an image printed at that scale so the reviewer can see what the print quality is. I'm not averse to looking at images on a computer, but I would never recommend an artist to someone else, show their work, or purchase a print unless I had seen actual finished prints to scale. Also, quite a lot of photographs do not show to their best advantage on a computer screen. If the work is video or interactive, then the use of a computer can be a necessity.

15. How do you feel about virtual portfolio reviews versus in-person portfolio-review events (pros and cons)? Is your ideal review session length twenty, twenty-five, or thirty minutes?

I prefer in-person portfolio reviews. Computer screens don't always show work to its best advantage, nor does one get a sense of the scale and physical presence of the prints through virtual images.

In-person events also have evening openings, lectures, and social events that allow for less formal but more in-depth contact, which can result in getting to know people better. I treasure and remember fondly many nights of talking photography and other topics with artists and fellow reviewers in the bars at various review-event hotels.

The pros of virtual reviews are that you get to review people from all over the world without either of you having to travel. It is also much more affordable for the reviewees.

I am very accustomed to the twenty-minute review length and find it appropriate for most reviews. FotoFest has occasionally run separate days of much longer reviews (one to two hours, perhaps) that were great for analyzing long-term projects or book layouts.

16. Have you ever offered a commission, a show, a press feature, or representation during a review? Can you share a success story or stories with us that came from a productive meeting at a review session?

I have never made such an offer during a review. The institutions for which I have worked are large enough that such decisions are made in consultation with the director and other staff. However, I have, in the longer run, exhibited and purchased work from people I met at reviews, and I have recommended more artists for fellowships, for grants, for residencies, and to other curators.

17. Have you ever purchased artwork from a reviewee? If so, what do you base the price on, and is it signed by the artist?

I have purchased a few works for myself (not for my institution) from reviewees. I always ask the artist what the price is and do not expect a special discount. I have also purchased work from reviewees for my institutions, but those purchases came one or more years after the review. Those artists had firmly established prices for their works, so the price was not in question.

18. How often do you connect or recommend a photographer who may not be right for you but a good match for a colleague?

At almost every in-person review event, I have recommended or connected one or more photographers to colleagues. I tend to review far fewer people at virtual events, so fewer recommendations come out of those experiences.

19. Can you share the best review you have been a part of, and why it was? (No names should be mentioned.)

I have had many engaging, stimulating, and exciting encounters at review tables over the years. It is impossible for me to single out one review. I've also never been a "favorites" kind of person. Sorry.

20. Are you open to looking at work outside of scheduled reviews or not so much? If so, how do you prefer a photographer approach you about the possibility?

I often do some extra reviews at in-person events in addition to those on my schedule. A photographer can just ask me (not during someone else's review, though—wait for a break), and if I have time, I will squeeze them in. Reviewers already have a long day (no breaks like the photographers sometimes get), so we do get tired. I can do an extra one or two reviews if the lunch break is long and an extra two at day's end. That is probably my limit. So, if you ask and I say no, please understand that it is because I am fatigued or need a break or I need to answer some urgent emails from work before the evening activities begin.

Barbara Tannenbaum

21. How do you feel about reviewees and reviewers socializing away from the table? If you are comfortable sharing, what advice do you have for reviewees?

I think the time to socialize and get to know artists better is a great benefit of in-person reviews. I have many friends who are photographers and have met some of them at reviews. Just realize that not everyone is a good match socially. Remember, reviews are speed dating, not arranged marriages. And remember that I may already have friends among the reviewers and reviewees with whom I want to spend time and whom I don't often get to see. Review events don't leave reviewers much free time, so that one meal or drink with an old friend may be precious to me.

22. How do you prefer that the individuals you meet with follow up with you and how often?

Now that very few people have physical "leave-behinds" and everyone has websites, it can be useful to get a thank-you email that includes the basic info on what we discussed and that gives me information on how to view your work. Be sure to include your email address, website URL, Instagram handle, gallerist, et cetera, so that I can reach you and also forward information about your work to colleagues and collectors. The snail-mail address also helps me know what region you are in, in case a curator is looking for a local photographer for a project. Once that initial correspondence is carried out, unless I encourage an ongoing correspondence, please contact me only when you complete and exhibit or publish your project or have new bodies of work or send out a regular update/ newsletter. If you publish a book and want to send me a copy, that is generous of you, but it would be wise to write me and ask first.

Be warned: I look at almost everything I receive, but I rarely have the time to write back with an analysis of work. Usually, my response is only to thank you for the update and let you know I got it.

23. In your opinion, what is the best "leave-behind"?

Leave-behinds seem to be out of favor these days, which is sad. It can be very helpful to have a physical object to share with others. The best leave-behind is a smallish pamphlet that shows off some of your best images, is printed well, explains your project, has your complete contact information (email, snail-mail address, phone, *and* website), yet is not too heavy or large. We all have limited room in our suitcases.

24. What are the biggest "no-no's" for reviewees?

Do not follow me into the bathroom and slip your portfolio under the stall door (yes, that has happened to me more than once).

Do not tell me that I am wrong about your work and do not understand it, then pack up in a huff. That may be true, but as my mother always said, you get more flies with honey than you do with vinegar. While the encounter may be personal and emotional for you, it is a professional situation. Try to take the long view. You may get different, and even opposing, opinions about your work over the course of the three or four days. Mine is just one of those opinions. I might be wrong. If most of the responses you get to your work are critical, then you may want to determine what they have in common and consider those ideas carefully.

Unless I specifically ask for them, do *not* send me actual artworks. That creates extra work for the museum's registrars and requires the museum to spend money to return the prints to you.

25. What one piece of advice would you impart to reviewees?

Remember that all of us in that hotel ballroom are there because we love photography.

Barbara Tannenbaum

Jane Yeomans

Bloomberg Businessweek

Jane Yeomans currently works at Bloomberg, where she commissions and licenses photography for *Bloomberg Businessweek*, Quicktakes, and a variety of online projects. Previously, she worked as a freelance photo editor and researcher for book projects, design firms, and publications, including *The New Yorker, New York Magazine, Vanity Fair,* ESPN, and many others. She has been commissioning and licensing photography for many years in New York City, where she currently resides. She has a deep love of photography over a long and varied career and believes in the power of photography to both illuminate and shape a story.

1. What do you look forward to most and least about portfolio-review events?

Meeting new photographers, seeing new work, meeting colleagues.

2. Why do you attend portfolio-review events, and do you have any specific goals in attending?

To meet photographers and see work to both license and assign. And to meet others in the photo industry.

3. When you attend portfolio-review events, what kind of strain does this cause on your work schedule?

I generally juggle reviews with my workload.

4. If you receive the reviewee list from the organization prior to the portfolio review, do you look at their work online in preparation for the review, or do you like to look at it fresh? Why or why not?

I do not look at websites; I would rather wait to have someone present their work, especially as I find websites can often be misleading. And I love to meet photographers in person so I can get a sense of who they are and what they are like and have them present their work to me.

5. What objectives do you recommend reviewees bring to the table?

Show the best work, know what you'd like to get hired to do.

Y

6. Do you ask at the start of your session what the reviewee wants?

Where they are from, what their work is about, and so on. I love to find out about a person to understand their work better.

7. What advice do you have for first-time reviewees?

Be organized, be thoughtful. Bring your best work; sometimes less is more, but if you have a second, or personal, project, have it ready.

8. Who should lead the review—reviewer or reviewee? Why?

I like the reviewee to lead; this can lead to a Q&A after and to discussions about the work they are showing.

9. What advice do you have for reviewees on how to manage the allotted time during the session?

Show the work first and save questions for after.

10. How do you feel about a reviewee recording your session?

I am fine as long it's personal and not published/shared without my permission.

11. How many different projects do you think are ideal for discussion in an individual review session?

Really depends on the size of the project; sometimes one is enough, and I am always happy to see projects that are in process or early stages.

12. How important is it for reviewees to have their ideas completely fleshed out regarding their projects?

I think it really depends on the project. Some projects benefit from feedback and other eyes on them.

13. Can a project be presented, in your opinion, as underdeveloped or overdeveloped?

Yes, I think—especially if the work is strong.

Jane Yeomans

14. How important is the technical quality of physical objects (for example, prints) being presented at the review session? How do you feel about work being presented on a tablet or computer?

I don't care if the prints are not "finished." I am happy to look at rough proofs, Xeroxes, anything as long as it is on paper. I look at a screen for work, so the last thing I want to do is look at work on a tablet or computer.

15. How do you feel about virtual portfolio reviews versus in-person portfolio-review events (pros and cons)? Is your ideal review session length twenty, twenty-five, or thirty minutes?

I prefer in person, although virtual has made reviews more democratic for people who cannot afford the travel. I think twenty minutes is often good, sometimes too short, so maybe twenty-five is best.

16. Have you ever offered a commission, a show, a press feature, or representation during a review? Can you share a success story or stories with us that came from a productive meeting at a review session?

Here are some; I can share PDFs if you need:

Kelda Van Patten, Photolucida, in person:
https://www.bloomberg.com/features/2022-cpi-inflation-indicators/?sref=JpB0s1yi

Stella Kalinina, Palm Springs:
https://www.bloomberg.com/news/features/2022–04–27/gentrification-battle-comes-to-los-angeles-neighborhood?sref=JpB0s1yi

Alex Gagne, SPD reviews:
https://www.bloomberg.com/news/articles/2019–07–26/great-white-shark-fever-sweeps-cape-cod?sref=JpB0s1yi; https://www.bloomberg.com/news/features/2021–10–11/mlb-rule-changes-atlantic-league-tests-tweaks-meant-to-save-baseball?sref=JpB0s1yi

Eric Kunsman, virtual:
https://www.bloomberg.com/news/features/2021–08–31/where-can-i-find-a-pay-phone-eric-kunsman-documents-america-s-last-phones?sref=JpB0s1yi

Rachel Boillot, PhotoNola:
https://www.bloomberg.com/news/features/2020–09–21/southern-bancorp-is-bringing-equality-to-banking-with-loans-for-the-underserved?sref=JpB0s1yi

Y

Kiliii Yuyan, PhotoNola:
https://www.bloomberg.com/news/features/2019–08–28/greenland-s-rare-earth-minerals-make-it-trump-s-treasure-island?sref=JpB0s1yi

Carrie May, PhotoNola:
https://www.bloomberg.com/news/features/2019–03–06/what-happens-to-mardi-gras-beads-after-festival-ends?sref=JpB0s1yi

Rachel Pick, SPD reviews:
https://www.bloomberg.com/news/features/2018–10–20/vancouver-is-drowning-in-chinese-money?sref=JpB0s1yi

Mark Parascandola (saw this project on Photolucida Critical Mass): https://www.bloomberg.com/news/photo-essays/2019–10–29/behind-the-scenes-of-china-s-multibillion-dollar-film-studios?sref=JpB0s1yi

17. Have you ever purchased artwork from a reviewee? If so, what do you base the price on, and is it signed by the artist?

No, I have not.

18. How often do you connect or recommend a photographer who may not be right for you but a good match for a colleague?

Often, as I keep the list from each review I attend and share with my team.

19. Can you share the best review you have been a part of, and why it was? (No names should be mentioned.)

PhotoNola. This was a great review, as most of the reviewers were galleries, museums, publishers—so most photographers had prints, printed books, and it was a treat to hold paper, not a screen. I ended up hiring at least four photographers. Also Medium Photo. One of my favorite reviews as most photographers have a very focused body of work.

20. Are you open to looking at work outside of scheduled reviews or not so much? If so, how do you prefer a photographer approach you about the possibility?

I do often meet when someone has to miss their slot, I have to cancel, et cetera. I am open to rescheduling, and email is the best way to get in touch.

Jane Yeomans

21. How do you feel about reviewees and reviewers socializing away from the table? If you are comfortable sharing, what advice do you have for reviewees?

I am totally comfortable, but when I am outside of review time, I don't want to be asked to review work; a conversation is great to have.

22. How do you prefer that the individuals you meet with follow up with you and how often?

Email is the best, and as often as every couple of months. As I say to photographers all the time, persistence pays off.

23. In your opinion, what is the best "leave-behind"?

A postcard. Choose an image you love from your portfolio. I keep the ones that remind me of the person's work. I love the little treats I have been given (especially if I am in a new city and someone local gives a local piece of candy, et cetera; nothing fancy).

24. What are the biggest "no-no's" for reviewees?

Don't be disorganized. Have your work ready to show, and make sure your presentation is easy to pack up so the next reviewee does not have to wait for you—respect your peers.

25. What one piece of advice would you impart to reviewees?

Keep your work easy and simple to show; don't make elaborate books and boxes that take time to assemble and disassemble. Reviewers want to see the work. I would rather see a box of color Xeroxes of a great photo project than have to watch someone construct a presentation. Time passes very quickly in a review; the best thing to do is show your best work in the simplest manner. The conversations will begin from looking at the work.

Y

EPILOGUE

Q & A with Debe Arlook and Eric T. Kunsman

Debe Arlook (b. 1962) is an award-winning Los Angeles–based artist crossing the boundaries of conceptual and documentary photography. Originally from New Jersey, she attended American University in Washington, DC, and graduated with degrees in film and media arts and psychology, which inform her photographic practice.

Inspired by her dedication to personal growth and spiritual practices, Arlook's projects express the porous boundaries between human and mystical experiences. She blends multiple photographic styles using landscape, conceptual, and documentary photography to communicate these observations.

Arlook is the recipient of the 2024 Working Assumptions Grant and the Klompching 2024 People's Choice Award. She is a FRESH 2024 Finalist; Critical Mass TOP 200 Finalist 2024, 2021; FOCUS Photo L.A. Finalist 2023, 2019; Critical Mass Top 50 Finalist 2022; CENTER Social Award Honorable Mention, 2022; and LensCulture Summer Open Finalist 2022. Her work is widely published and exhibited in museums and galleries in solo and group exhibitions in the US and Europe and in numerous private collections. Features include those in *LensCulture, Feature Shoot, All About Photo, Lenscratch, Fraction Magazine, Strange Fire, L'Oeil de la Photographie*, and *Frames Magazine*. Arlook is best known for her project *one, one thousand . . .* , an unconventional documentary revealing the impact lifelong dependency has on a mother and son, as well as *Witness and foreseeable cache*, both focusing on the experience of meditation seen through a study of America's sublime landscape. Books and catalogs include *Memory Orchards: Photographers and Their Families* (Candela Books), *california love—a visual mixtape* (Cali Editions), *Perceive Me* (Edition One Books), *HUQ: I Seek No Favor* (for the fiftieth anniversary of Roe v. Wade, fifty artists and thinkers respond to the decision overturn).

In 2016, she founded Arlook Printing Services, providing boutique assistance for fine-art photographers, including project development, portfolio preparation, and exhibition planning. Arlook is a mentor and consultant for emerging and established artists. In addition to leading lectures and presentations, she teaches teenagers and adults and conducts multigenerational workshops based on creating a personal visual language and trusting one's artistic journey. She has been on faculty at the Los Angeles Center of Photography since 2021. Arlook is a contributing editor for *PhotoBook Journal* (an international virtual magazine) and an advisor with Pasadena Photography Arts (PPA educates and promotes established and emerging photographers worldwide) and Open Show Pasadena (a global platform that offers photographers at all levels an opportunity to present their work online and in person in thirty-one cities and fifteen countries).

To learn more about her, visit www.debearlookphotography.com.

Q & A

As a photographer, why do I attend portfolio reviews?

Attending reviews is a great way to reach a broad audience while deepening relationships with colleagues on both sides of the table. Depending on my needs, I receive suggestions about the work, exhibiting, installation, and publishing, as well as contact recommendations. During in-person events, I see my colleagues' work and their presentation techniques. It also offers new and unexpected opportunities, like Eric and I partnering to create this book. We live on different coasts, and had we not met during reviews, this book would not exist. The short game is to have work seen by multiple reviewers working in various venues and fields that align with my intention. The long game is what comes from these meetings and events. I am passionate about my practice and cherish the relationships I make.

What have I learned from putting the book together?

I learned that reviewers are paid an honorarium for online reviews. For in-person events, they are paid for travel, accommodations, and some meals, but 95 percent of the time, they are not paid for review sessions. Reviewers who meet with photographers outside of sessions are a special breed.
I initially thought all reviewers knew how to review work, but I learned that some go into a session green. I believe it is the responsibility of an organization to vet reviewers and guide newbies on the best practices for holding review sessions. At the same time, it is each individual's responsibility to educate themselves and to know what they are doing. This is where our book can help.

Have I made mistakes/faux pas?

I wouldn't say I've made mistakes because it's all a learning experience. But if I had a better practice following up with reviewers (that is, perhaps more regularly via individual emails and/or newsletters), would I be further along in my career? Maybe. Maybe not.

Pet peeves

I was attending an in-person event when the reviewer showed up about ten minutes late to our session. She was kind and apologetic, but she was not helpful. She kept saying, "beautiful work" and "nice," while looking through my portfolio. She ended the session with, "Keep shooting." It was obvious she was not fully present. Artists pay for reviewers' time and attention.

After many years of in-person and online reviews, only one felt cold and awkward. This particular reviewer came with an ego. The session was curt, uninformative, dismissive, and concluded by the reviewer before the allotted time was up. It was as if I had done something wrong, which was not the case. That day I witnessed a similar experience with this reviewer and another photographer and, over time, heard multiple negative experiences involving this person. No one is above anyone else . . . on either side of the table. Please leave egos at home. Be courteous and considerate. If a reviewer feels a session is complete before the allotted time, please remember that they are working and the person across the table paid for the session. It is my opinion that the reviewer extend kindness and inquire if there is anything else the reviewee would like to address.

Numerous photographers have confided that they have received insensitive treatment from reviewers when showing deeply vulnerable, personal work. I implore reviewers to be neutral and kind when responding. Pause before reacting and focus on the fundamentals of the work.

Favorite and least favorite aspects of reviews

My favorite aspect involves deepening relationships with colleagues on both sides of the table. My least favorite is interacting with people who give off a superior, dismissive attitude. Fortunately, it doesn't happen often.

Most memorable review

One time, I did not show a single image during an online review with a reviewer I had not met before. It wasn't my intention, but we were connecting on a deep level, and the work felt less important than the conversation. At a certain point, I questioned myself on whether showing the work would be constructive, realizing I would have been rushed and not able to give the work the time it deserved. I expressed my thoughts to the reviewer, who concurred and suggested we schedule a time to meet outside of reviews. We did so for considerably more than twenty minutes, and a friendship developed.

The moral of this story is to go with your instincts and let go of the "what can you do for me" thought. I begin each session by genuinely connecting with reviewers about their work or connections we may have. I do this so the reviewer can get to know me (people gravitate to working with people they like) and to invite a personable exchange.

Advice for Reviewees

- Leave your ego at home and let go of expectations.
- Kindness goes a long way.
- Reviewers are people, too; they are there to advise, not do things for reviewees.
- Ask lots of questions *and* be aware of how much you speak versus listen.
- Research portfolio-review events/organizations. Choose reputable events that are best for you and your work.
- Research reviewers before you make selections. Select reputable reviewers whose work aesthetic aligns with yours.
- Talk to other artists and get their thoughts about events and reviewers.
- It's good practice to meet with reviewers you resonate with multiple times over the years. You'll strengthen your relationship, and they'll see the development of your projects.
- For online reviews, arrange sticky notes around the computer screen—you'll have easy access to key points while facing the camera as you speak.
- For in-person reviews, offer thin, small leave-behinds—something easy for the reviewer to bring home. Most likely, they are traveling. Size prints appropriately for each project. Use a portfolio that's easy to carry, pack, and unpack. If you believe the prints must be seen big, save on printing with one larger print or show the scale in a photograph or electronically.
- Be open to hearing what you may not have expected to hear, and take criticism with a grain of salt.
- Save money by attending in-person reviews close to home or online reviews. With numerous review events, reviewers you'd like to meet with might travel to events near you.
- Be patient after reviews are over. Some opportunities can happen quickly, and others can take years.
- After you've prepped, reviewed, posted on Instagram, and written follow-up letters/emails, you may experience a letdown. It's part of the process.
- Tone down false hopes; sometimes promises are empty.
- Ask yourself: Did the critique resonate with me? Can I look more deeply into what I heard and make new discoveries, or is it best if I dismiss what I heard and go with my instincts?
- Be kind and gentle with yourself. The emotional component of being critiqued can be vulnerable.
- Ask yourself what you want out of the event and individual sessions.

Advice for Reviewers

- Leave egos at home
- Be kind, constructive, and respectful.
- Give full sessions. This is a paid transaction. If you're done talking about the work, engage the reviewee in other ways.
- If a photographer picks up a last-minute review spot with a reviewer they don't really know, the session flow may be different than if had they "known" the reviewer. It's good practice for those on both sides of the table to be open to the conversation moving in different areas. A shift in mindset benefits both sides of the table.
- If being a reviewer is new for you, please ask the organization and your colleagues how to do it well before you dive in.

Questions to ask yourself about attending or not attending reviews

- Are you ready but not attending because of fear? Google "Bob Newhart Stop It" for support
- Is my work ready to show, or is it too soon? First impressions only happen once.
- Am I past my financial quota for photography this year?
- Do I need a break? It's more than okay to pause, reset, and make time to create—it's necessary.

Eric T. Kunsman (b. 1975) was born and raised in Bethlehem, Pennsylvania. While in high school, he was heavily influenced by the death of the steel industry and its place in American history. Exposure to the work of Walker Evans during this time hooked Eric into photography. Eric had the privilege of studying under Lou Draper, who became Eric's most formative mentor. He credits Lou with influencing his approach as an educator, photographer, and contributing human being.

Eric holds his MFA in book arts/printmaking from University of the Arts in Philadelphia and holds an MS in electronic publishing/graphic arts media, a BS in biomedical photography, and a BFA in fine art photography, all from Rochester Institute of Technology in Rochester, New York.

He is a photographer and book artist now based out of Rochester. Eric works at Rochester Institute of Technology (RIT) as an assistant professor in the Visual Communications Studies Department at the National Technical Institute for the Deaf (NTID) and is an adjunct professor for RIT's School of Photographic Arts and Sciences.

In addition to lectures, he provides workshops on topics including his artistic practice, digital printing, and digital workflow processes. He provided industry seminars for the highly regarded Printing Applications Lab at RIT. His photographs and books are exhibited internationally and are in several collections. He currently owns Booksmart Studio, which is a fine-art digital printing studio specializing in numerous techniques and services for photographers and book artists on a collaborative basis.

Kunsman is a 2024 JGS Fellowship for Photography Recipient from The New York Foundation for the Arts. His work has been exhibited in more than thirty-five solo exhibitions at such venues as Nicolaysen Art Museum, Casper, Wyoming; Hoyt Institute of Fine Art, New Castle, Pennsylvania; Los Angeles Center for Digital Art; and numerous university galleries. His work has also been a part of more than 150 group exhibitions over the past four years, including exhibitions at the Center for Photography, A. Smith Gallery, SPIVA, San Luis Obispo Museum of Art, Spartanburg Museum of Art, Atlanta Photography Group, CEPA Gallery, Site: Brooklyn, Colorado Photographic Arts Center, Philadelphia Photo Arts Center, and many more.

Eric was named one of ten B & W photographers to watch of 2018 by BWGallerist; was a winner of *Dodho Magazine's* B & W Best Photographers of the Year in 2019 and a finalist in 2022; won the Association of Photography (UK) Gold Award for Open Series in 2019; was a finalist in Top 200 Critical Mass 2019, 2020, 2021, 2022; was a finalist in Top 50 Critical Mass 2022; was a Top 15 Photographer for the Rust Belt Biennial; and was a *Lensculture* B & W Jurors' Pick 2021. His project Felicific Calculus was also awarded a Warhol Foundations Grant through CEPA Gallery in Buffalo, New York. Eric's work has also been published in magazines such as *Bloomberg Businessweek, LensWork, Dodho, B&W Photography, Analog Explorations, All About Photo, Black+White Photography* (UK), and *Dek Unu,* along with online articles by *Analog Forever Magazine, Catalyst: Interviews,* Texas Photo Society, and others.

There's no "given formula" for what demands Eric's focus as a photographer. Kunsman is as drawn to the landscapes and neglected towns of the American Southwest as he is to the tensions of struggling rustbelt cities in the US Northeast. Kunsman is attracted to objects left behind, especially those that hint at a unique human narrative, a story waiting to be told. His current work explores one of those relics: working payphones hidden in plain sight throughout the neighborhood near his studio in Rochester, New York. Associates suggested they signified a high-crime area. This project has shown him something very different.

To learn more about him, visit www.erickunsman.com.

Q & A

As a photographer, why do I attend portfolio reviews?

I attend portfolio reviews for a few reasons. The first is to build upon my community of photographers, including reviewers and reviewees, as much has come out of creating my photo community. The second reason is to share my work with people who may not be aware of it; we cannot count on social-media algorithms. For me, showing the work in print form brings another level of discussion and seriousness to my work.

What have I learned from the responses in this book?

No single approach works for everyone; you need to be true to yourself, as your personality will dictate whether someone wants to work with you and your work. Also, portfolio reviews are a long game; the review is just an introduction and the beginning of relationships—as long as one does not mess it up. Like juried exhibitions, not everyone will be a perfect fit for you and the work you are creating, but if you maintain that relationship, there's a possibility they will respond to your next body of work.

Have I made mistakes/faux pas?

One of the mistakes I made that still makes me red in the face when I talk about it occurred during my first time attending the Santa Fe Portfolio Reviews in 2017. It was also one of my first portfolio reviews outside of the Society for Photographic Education (SPE) portfolio reviews. I was showing my project "Thou Art . . . Will Give . . . ," which had been completed and had already received around fifteen solo exhibitions. I wanted to take the body of work further and thought the Santa Fe Portfolio Reviews would be the place to do so. However, the work being completed led me to talk too much about the series in each of my twenty-minute reviews, as I wasn't looking for feedback but pushing the work. My biggest mistake, however, was in my leave-behinds. I gave reviewers a full packet that contained my CV, postcards, artist statement, and two to three small exhibition-quality prints in an envelope. Looking back on it, I can guarantee you that 99 percent of those packets were thrown away because there was too much for a reviewer to take home with them.

Pet peeves

I once had a reviewer who couldn't get past the fact that I produce books at my company, Booksmart Studio. Instead of looking at my work, he kept saying, "Why are you showing me your work?" The reviewer couldn't get past his own ego to have a simple discussion and look at my work. Ironically, I picked up the review because another participant did not show up for that review, and perhaps my experience is why many people were skipping appointments with this reviewer. Another pet peeve is when people do not interact with other portfolio reviewees because they do not see the value in building a community.

Favorite and least favorite aspects of reviews

My favorite part of the reviews is getting feedback on work that is not completed because it can help steer you in directions that you hadn't previously thought about, and it can also help you solidify ideas that you will not be adding to your project.

My least favorite part of the portfolio reviews is the pressure of pushing beyond my introverted tendencies and talking with new individuals, which is one of my weaknesses. This also spills over to my reviews sometimes—when I am sharing my work with someone I have not met before, which is most of the time at reviews. I still get nervous before I walk into the room with my portfolio for each session, and then I forget who I am walking in to see and need to keep checking my list.

Most memorable review

My most memorable review was when we did not even look at a single photograph for the first five minutes. After that, we flipped through the photographs, but I did not use my elevator pitch or story behind the work. Instead, we just talked about the reason behind the work. The review turned into an incredible discussion rather than me pushing my work, which was much more meaningful to both me and the reviewer. Ironically, this led to that reviewer championing my work in a few different ways.

Advice for reviewees

My advice is to make sure that you make every connection you can during your time in the portfolio review. We are simply building communities that can pay dividends far beyond any single portfolio review. After all, look at how Debe and I decided to publish this book at a dinner at PhotoLucida in 2022. Do not push these relationships; they should come naturally. We're not building relationships to benefit ourselves but each other.

Print a small copy of your review schedule and keep it on you. Set up an alarm on your phone so that you do not miss a review, just in case you are having good conversations with fellow reviewees.

Advice for reviewers

Please remember, we are putting our hearts and souls on the line, and some of us are better at sharing our ideas and have more experience. Take the time to see the potential in what we are sharing with you, even if it is not a perfect fit for your organization. We are attending the review to gain advice from individuals with experience in all facets of photography because we all love photography.

Questions to ask about attending or not attending reviews

Are you ready to put the work out in public and willing to listen to ideas to help the project grow?

Are the reviewers a good fit for your plan to disseminate your work?

Is your body of work at a point where you can gain enough valuable information from reviewers and the community to outweigh the cost of attending the portfolio review?

What have I learned from putting the book together?

I learned that reviewers are trying to build relationships and discover work just as much as we are trying to have them discover our work. The reviewers talk a lot among each other and share notes about the individuals they are reviewing.

ACKNOWLEDGMENTS

This book is based on collaboration, camaraderie, mutual support, and shared experiences. Without the generosity and commitment of our contributors, you'd be doing something else right now. Forty-eight people took time away from their busy schedules to contemplate questions in order to assist and educate you, our photographic community. We are forever grateful to Paula Tognarelli, who is almost as busy in "retirement" as when she was the executive director of The Griffin Museum, for writing the foreword and to Laura Moya (the executive director of Photolucida, 2004–2022) for her unwavering support and advice from the very beginning. The commitment and passion our contributors have for the art of photography and their dedication to supporting our community is awe-inspiring. This process has been a labor of love.

We wish to acknowledge our friends and colleagues who are not included in this book. We thank you for your friendship, wisdom, practice, and support, as well as the mark you make in the world. If you think you are one of those people, you are.

Debe Arlook

I am grateful to Eric Kunsman for saying "yes" to a spontaneous idea thrown out to a group of exhilarated yet exhausted and hungry photographers for anyone to catch. We are copilots on a journey that would not have taken flight without him. Eric is an exceptionally talented artist, a passionate print and bookmaker, a dedicated educator, and a family man. I don't know how he does so much, so well. With his wealth of experience and support, he has been the yang to my ying during this process and the best collaborator I could have asked for. I thank my family for their encouragement and support over the years and countless others in the photo community who have been a part of my ever-evolving practice. As an individual practicing artist, I would not be at this stage of my career without the support, camaraderie, guidance, and generosity of my colleagues.

Eric T. Kunsman

First and foremost, I need to thank my family for always supporting my photographic journey and sometimes being tortured as they often wait in the car while I photograph. My wife's support has allowed me to attend many portfolio reviews, which has allowed me to build my community. Debe Arlook was the perfect partner with whom to go down this rabbit hole of a journey to create this book. Our ideas and processes often were one and the same, as our collaboration just gelled. The hardest part of creating this book was our busy schedules, because Debe is also overbooked with exhibitions, mentoring, and taking care of her family. However, we made sure we delegated tasks, and our strengths were the perfect balancing act for our collaboration. I would also like to acknowledge the organizations and photography community members I have engaged with over the years, as you all have helped push my practice farther than I could have imagined.

Colophon

Editor
Alexandra Hoff

Copy Editor
Anne Cook

Design
Eric T. Kunsman

Production
Marnie Soom

Printer
National Technical Institute for the Deaf at RIT, Visual Communications Studies
Department, Xerox Iridescent Press

Binding
Students from the Book Publishing Club, National Technical Institute for the
Deaf at RIT, Visual Communications Studies Department

Paper
Hammermill Tidal Copy Paper 20 lb.

Cover Paper
Swathmore Cambric, Midnight Black, 100# Cover